W9-BMJ-333

THE FATHERS
OF THE CHURCH

A NEW TRANSLATION

VOLUME 122

THE FATHERS
OF THE CHURCH

A NEW TRANSLATION

ST. BASIL
OF CAESAREA

AGAINST EUNOMIUS

Translated by

MARK DELCOGLIANO

and

ANDREW RADDE-GALLWITZ

THE CATHOLIC UNIVERSITY OF AMERICA PRESS
Washington, D.C.

The paper used in this publication meets the minimum
requirements of the American National Standards for Information
Science—Permanence of Paper for Printed Library Materials,
ANSI z39.48-1984.
∞

LIBRARY OF CONGRESS CATALOGING-IN-PUBLICATION DATA
Basil, Saint, Bishop of Caesarea, ca. 329–379.
[Contra Eunomium. English]
Against Eunomius / St. Basil of Caesarea ; translated by Mark DelCogliano
and Andrew Radde-Gallwitz.
p. cm. — (The fathers of the church ; v. 122)
Includes bibliographical references and index.
ISBN 978-0-8132-0122-1 (cloth : alk. paper)
1. Eunomius, Bp. of Cyzicus, ca. 335-ca. 394.   I. DelCogliano, Mark.
II. Radde-Gallwitz, Andrew.   III. Title.   IV. Series.
BR65.B34C6613 2011
273'.4—dc22
2010035483

To Amy and Kristen

CONTENTS

ACKNOWLEDGMENTS

The successful completion of any translation requires more than dogged effort. Out of sheer generosity other scholars have encouraged and supported us in our endeavor and offered critical feedback on our work. Their suggestions have helped us clarify our ideas, improved the quality of our translation, and saved us from howlers and other infelicities contrary to good English prose. First of all we would like to thank our mutual dissertation advisor Lewis Ayres, who put us into contact with the editor of the Fathers of the Church series and advised us at every step along the way. His own work on the fourth-century Trinitarian controversies has shaped our thinking about the era in general and Basil of Caesarea in particular in ways that we will probably never fully comprehend. We would also like to thank our teacher Steven Strange, whose seminars on ancient philosophy have been fundamental to our contextualizing of Basil within philosophical traditions and whose weekly Greek reading groups have been vital to our facility in Greek. We consulted him on many philosophical points in the course of our project, and the eagerness with which he shared his extensive knowledge with us is nothing less than a model of what scholarly collaboration ought to be.

At the Annual Meeting of the North American Patristics Society in May 2008, we chaired a session entitled "Translating Basil of Caesarea's *Contra Eunomium*." Its subject was a discussion of a draft version of our translation of *Against Eunomius* 1.6–7, 2.4, and 2.28–29. We would like to thank our respondents, Lewis Ayres, John Behr, and Stephen Hildebrand, for agreeing to take part in the session and for their insightful comments. Our thanks as well to those who participated in the session, particularly Robert Wilken and Kelley Spoerl; our translation is better because of their remarks. We would also like to thank Christopher Beeley and Timothy McConnell, both of whom read through our entire translation and generously offered extensive feedback on it. We have incorporated many of their suggestions into our final version. Our thanks as well to Amy Levad, who copy-edited our introduction and a substantial portion of our translation before its final submission. Our editor, Carole Monica Burnett, has made the entire process pleasurable: thank you. It goes without saying that any errors and bungled prose remain ours.

Finally, we would like to thank our wives, Amy Levad and Kristen Radde-Gallwitz, for their support and care. We spent an inordinate amount of time together translating Basil, and our wives were extraordinarily patient with us as we pursued our mutual obsession with Basil and other fourth-century concerns. We dedicate this translation to them.

MARK DELCOGLIANO
ANDREW RADDE-GALLWITZ

January 2, 2009
The Feast of St. Basil the Great

ABBREVIATIONS

General

Gr.   Greek.
LXX   Septuagint.

Periodicals and Series

FOTC   Fathers of the Church. Washington, DC: The Catholic University of America Press, 1947–.

GCS   Die griechischen christlichen Schriftsteller (der ersten drei Jahrhunderte). Leipzig: J. C. Hinrichs, 1897–1949; Berlin: Akademie-Verlag, 1953–.

GNO   Gregorii Nysseni Opera. Leiden: Brill, 1958–.

JTS   *Journal of Theological Studies.*

PG   Patrologia Cursus Completus: Series Graeca. Ed. J.-P. Migne. Paris, 1857–1886.

SC   Sources Chrétiennes. Paris: Cerf, 1941–.

Critical Editions and Translations

Courtonne   Y. Courtonne. *Saint Basile: Lettres.* 3 vols. Paris: Société d'édition 'Les Belles Lettres,' 1957–1966.

EW   R. P. Vaggione. *Eunomius: The Extant Works.* Oxford: Clarendon Press, 1987.

Strange   S. K. Strange. *Porphyry: On Aristotle's Categories.* London: Duckworth, 1992.

Urk.   H.-G. Opitz. *Urkunden zur Geschichte des arianischen Streites 318–328.* Berlin and Leipzig: De Gruyter, 1934. Cited by document number.

Secondary Literature

Ayres   L. Ayres. *Nicaea and its Legacy.* Oxford: Oxford University Press, 2004.

Behr   J. Behr. *The Nicene Faith.* Crestwood, NY: St. Vladimir's Seminary Press, 2004.

Drecoll   V. H. Drecoll. *Die Entwicklung der Trinitätslehre des Basilius von Cäsarea: Sein Weg vom Homöusianer zum Neonizäner.* Göttingen: Vandenhoeck & Ruprecht, 1996.

Hanson   R. P. C. Hanson. *The Search for the Christian Doctrine of God: The Arian Controversy 318–381 AD.* Edinburgh: T & T Clark, 1988.

Hildebrand   S. M. Hildebrand. *The Trinitarian Theology of Basil of Caesarea: A*

Synthesis of Greek Thought and Biblical Truth. Washington, DC: The Catholic University of America Press, 2007.

Kopecek   T. A. Kopecek. *A History of Neo-Arianism*. 2 vols. Cambridge, MA: The Philadelphia Patristic Foundation, 1979.

Rousseau   P. Rousseau. *Basil of Caesarea*. Berkeley: University of California Press, 1994.

Vaggione   R. P. Vaggione. *Eunomius of Cyzicus and the Nicene Revolution*. Oxford: Oxford University Press, 2000.

The Works of Basil of Caesarea

Ep., Epp.	*Epistle, Epistles.*
Eun.	*Against Eunomius.*
Fid.	*On Faith.*
Hex.	*Homilies on the Hexaemeron.*
Hom.	*Homilies.*
Ps.	*Homilies on the Psalms.*
Spir.	*On the Holy Spirit.*

The Work of Eunomius of Cyzicus

Apol.	*Apology.*

Other Patristic Works

Apol. c. Ar.	Athanasius of Alexandria, *Apology against the Arians.*
Ar.	Athanasius of Alexandria, *Orations against the Arians.*
Cels.	Origen, *Against Celsus.*
Decr.	Athanasius of Alexandria, *On the Decrees of Nicaea.*
E. th.	Eusebius of Caesarea, *Ecclesiastical Theology.*
Ep. Serap.	Athanasius of Alexandria, *Letters to Serapion.*
Eun.	Gregory of Nyssa, *Against Eunomius.*
Jo.	Origen, *Commentary on the Gospel of John.*
Or.	Gregory of Nazianzus, *Orations.*
Pan.	Epiphanius of Salamis, *Panarion.*
Princ.	Origen, *On First Principles.*
Spir.	Didymus, *On the Holy Spirit.*
Syn.	Athanasius of Alexandria, *On the Synods.*
Synt.	Aetius, *Syntagmation.*

Philosophical Works

Comm. not.	Plutarch, *On Common Notions against the Stoics.*
Disc.	Epictetus, *Discourses.*
Enn.	Plotinus, *Enneads.*
Ep. Her.	Epicurus, *Epistle to Herodotus.*
Ep. Men.	Epicurus, *Epistle to Menoeceus.*

Abbreviations of classical and patristic texts not listed above follow H. G. Liddell, R. Scott, and H. S. Jones, eds., *A Greek-English Lexicon* (Oxford, 1940), and G. W. H. Lampe, ed., *A Patristic Greek Lexicon* (Oxford, 1961).

SELECT BIBLIOGRAPHY

Editions of the Works of Basil of Caesarea and Eunomius of Cyzicus

Courtonne, Y., ed. *Saint Basile: Lettres.* 3 vols. Paris: Société d'édition 'Les Belles Lettres,' 1957–1966.

Garnier, J. *S. P. N. Basilii, Caesareae Cappadociae archiepiscopi, Opera omnia. De fide.* PG 31.676–92.

———. *S. P. N. Basilii, Caesareae Cappadociae archiepiscopi, Opera omnia. Homiliae in Psalmos.* PG 29.209–494; 31.103–15.

———. *S. P. N. Basilii, Caesareae Cappadociae archiepiscopi, Opera omnia. Homiliae et Sermones.* PG 31.163–483, 490–563, 590–617, 1438–75, 1487–98.

Giet, S., ed. *Basile de Césarée. Homélies sur l'hexaéméron.* 2d ed. SC 26. Paris: Cerf, 1968.

Mendieta, E. A. de, and S. Y. Rudberg. *Basilius von Caesarea. Homilien zum Hexaemeron.* GCS n.f. 2. Berlin: Akademie Verlag, 1997.

Pruche, B. *Basile de Césarée, Sur le Saint-Esprit.* 2d ed. rev. et aug. SC 17bis. Paris: Cerf, 2002.

Sesboüé, B., G.-M. de Durand, and L. Doutreleau, eds. *Basile de Césarée, Contre Eunome suivi de Eunome Apologie.* 2 vols. SC 299 and 305. Paris: Cerf, 1982–1983.

Vaggione, R. P., ed. *Eunomius. The Extant Works.* Oxford Early Christian Texts. Oxford: Clarendon Press, 1987.

General

Anastos, M. V. "Basil's Κατὰ Εὐνομίου, A Critical Analysis." Pages 67–136 in P. J. Fedwick, ed. *Basil of Caesarea: Christian, Humanist, Ascetic. A Sixteenth-Hundredth Anniversary Symposium.* 2 vols. Toronto: The Pontifical Institute of Mediaeval Studies, 1981.

Ayres, L. *Nicaea and its Legacy. An Approach to Fourth-Century Trinitarian Theology.* Oxford: Oxford University Press, 2004.

Behr, J. *The Nicene Faith.* The Formation of Christian Theology, vol. 2. Crestwood, NY: St. Vladimir's Seminary Press, 2004.

Bernardi, J. *La prédication des pères cappadociens.* Paris: Presses universitaires de France, 1968.

Cavalcanti, E. *Studi Eunomiani*. Orientalia Christiana Analecta 202. Rome: Pontificium Institutum Orientalium Studiorum, 1976.

Clarke, W. K. L. *St Basil the Great: A Study in Monasticism*. Cambridge: Cambridge University Press, 1913.

Courtonne, Y. *Un témoin du IVe siècle oriental: Saint Basile et son temps d'après sa correspondance*. Paris: Les Belles Lettres, 1973.

DelCogliano, M. "Basil of Caesarea on Proverbs 8.22 and the Sources of Pro-Nicene Theology." *JTS* n.s. 59 (2008): 183–90.

———. *Basil of Caesarea's Anti-Eunomian Theory of Names: Christian Theology and Late-Antique Philosophy in the Fourth-Century Trinitarian Controversy*. Supplements to Vigiliae Christianae 103. Leiden: Brill, 2010.

Drecoll, V. H. *Die Entwicklung der Trinitätslehre des Basilius von Cäsarea: Sein Weg vom Homöusianer zum Neonizäner*. Göttingen: Vandenhoeck & Ruprecht, 1996.

Durand, G.-M. de. "Un passage du IIIe livre contre Eunome de S. Basile dans la tradition manuscrite." *Irénikon* 54 (1981): 36–52.

Elm, S. *Virgins of God: The Making of Asceticism in Late Antiquity*. Oxford: Clarendon Press, 1994.

Fedwick, P. J. *The Church and the Charisma of Leadership in Basil of Caesarea*. Studies and Texts 45. Toronto: The Pontifical Institute of Mediaeval Studies, 1979.

———. ed. *Basil of Caesarea: Christian, Humanist, Ascetic. A Sixteenth-Hundredth Anniversary Symposium*. 2 vols. Toronto: The Pontifical Institute of Mediaeval Studies, 1981.

Giet, S. *Les idées et l'action sociales de s. Basile*. Paris: Gabalda, 1941.

Hanson, R. P. C. *The Search for the Christian Doctrine of God: The Arian Controversy 318–381 AD*. Edinburgh: T & T Clark, 1988.

Hildebrand, S. M. *The Trinitarian Theology of Basil of Caesarea: A Synthesis of Greek Thought and Biblical Truth*. Washington, DC: The Catholic University of America Press, 2007.

Holman, S. R. *The Hungry are Dying. Beggars and Bishops in Roman Cappadocia*. Oxford: Oxford University Press, 2001.

Holmes, A. *A Life Pleasing to God: The Spirituality of the Rules of St Basil*. Cistercian Studies Series 189. Kalamazoo: Cistercian Publications, 2000.

Hübner, R. "Gregor von Nyssa als Vorfasser der Sog. Ep. 38 des Basilius: Zum unterschiedlichen Verständnis der οὐσία bei den kappadozischen Brüdern." Pages 463–90 in J. Fontaine and C. Kannengiesser, eds. *Epektasis: Mélanges patristiques offertes au Cardinal Jean Daniélou*. Paris: Beauschesne, 1972.

Kalligas, P. "Basil of Caesarea on the Semantics of Proper Names." Pages 31–48 in Katerina Ierodiakonou, ed. *Byzantine Philosophy and its Ancient Sources*. Oxford: Clarendon Press, 2002.

Kopecek, T. A. *A History of Neo-Arianism*. 2 vols. Patristic Monograph Series, No. 8. Cambridge, MA: The Philadelphia Patristic Foundation, Ltd., 1979.

Koschorke, K. *Spuren der alten Liebe: Studien zum Kirchenbegriff des Basilius von Caesarea*. Freiburg: Universitätsverlag, 1991.

Lienhard, J.T. "*Ousia* and *Hypostasis:* The Cappadocian Settlement and the Theology of 'One Hypostasis.'" Pages 99–121 in S.T.Davis, D.Kendall, and G.O'Collins, eds. *The Trinity: An Interdisciplinary Symposium on the Doctrine of the Trinity.* Oxford and New York: Oxford University Press, 2000.

Meredith, A. *The Cappadocians.* London: Chapman, 1995.

Parys, M. van. "Quelques remarques à propos d'un texte controversé de saint Basile au Concile de Florence." *Irénikon* 40 (1967): 6–14.

Prestige, G.L. *St. Basil the Great and Apollinaris.* London: SPCK, 1956.

Radde-Gallwitz, A. *Basil of Caesarea, Gregory of Nyssa, and the Transformation of Divine Simplicity.* Oxford Early Christian Studies. Oxford: Oxford University Press, 2009.

Riedmatten, H. de. "La correspondance entre Basile de Césareé et Apollinaire de Laodicée," *JTS* n.s. 7 (1956): 199–210; 8 (1957): 53–70.

Robertson, D.G. "Stoic and Aristotelian Notions of Substance in Basil of Caesarea." *Vigiliae Christianae* 52 (1998): 393–417.

————. "Relatives in Basil of Caesarea." *Studia Patristica* 37 (2001): 277–87.

————. "A Patristic Theory of Proper Names." *Archiv für Geschichte der Philosophie* 84 (2002): 1–19.

Rousseau, P. *Basil of Caesarea.* Berkeley: University of California Press, 1994.

Sesboüé, B. *Saint Basile et la Trinité: Un acte théologique au IVe siècle.* Paris: Descleé, 1998.

———— and B.Meunier. *Dieu peut-il avoir un fils? Le debat trinitaire du IVe siècle.* Paris: Cerf, 1993.

Silvas, A.M. *The Asketikon of St Basil the Great.* Oxford: Oxford University Press, 2005.

————. *Gregory of Nyssa: The Letters.* Leiden: Brill, 2007.

Steenson, J.N. "Basil of Ancyra and the Course of Nicene Orthodoxy." D.Phil. diss., Oxford University, 1983.

Sterk, A. *Renouncing the World yet Leading the Church: The Monk-Bishop in Late Antiquity.* Cambridge: Harvard University Press, 2004.

Strange, S.K. *Porphyry. On Aristotle's Categories.* Ancient Commentators on Aristotle. London: Duckworth, 1992.

Tieck, W.A. "Basil of Caesarea and the Bible." Ph.D. diss., Columbia University, 1953.

Vaggione, R.P. *Eunomius of Cyzicus and the Nicene Revolution.* Oxford: Oxford University Press, 2000.

Van Dam, R. *Kingdom of Snow: Roman Rule and Greek Culture in Cappadocia.* Philadelphia: University of Pennsylvania Press, 2002.

————. *Becoming Christian: The Conversion of Roman Cappadocia.* Philadelphia: University of Pennsylvania Press, 2003.

————. *Friends and Families in Late Roman Cappadocia.* Philadelphia: University of Pennsylvania Press, 2003.

Wickham, L.R. "The *Syntagmation* of Aetius the Anomean." *JTS* n.s. 19 (1968): 532–69.

INTRODUCTION

INTRODUCTION

I. THE SIGNIFICANCE OF THE WORK
AGAINST EUNOMIUS AND OF THIS TRANSLATION

Basil of Caesarea's treatise *Against Eunomius,* which is published in English translation for the first time here, will be of interest to a range of readers. Students of early Christianity and of Christian theology more generally will find here a set of theologically profound and historically influential reflections upon the mystery of the Trinity and the nature of theological knowledge. Basil finished the three books *Against Eunomius* in 364 or 365 CE, and this work reflects the intense controversy raging at that time among Christians across the Mediterranean world over the question of who the God whom Christians worship is. In this treatise, Basil for the first time in his corpus attempts to articulate at length a theology both of God's unitary essence and of the distinctive features that characterize Father, Son, and Holy Spirit. This distinction of common essence or nature and individuating properties, which some (perhaps misleadingly) hail as the cornerstone of "Cappadocian" theology, has some fourth-century precedents. Yet it was Basil's arguments in *Against Eunomius* that provided the touchstone for debates that would continue to rage after his unexpected death in late 378. These debates between Basil's target, Eunomius, who wrote a response to Basil's work shortly before the bishop of Caesarea's death, and Basil's younger brother, Gregory of Nyssa, who defended his deceased brother in his own three books *Against Eunomius,* were indelibly marked with the imprint of Basil's *Against Eunomius.*

Despite the impact of *Against Eunomius,* Basil himself continued to revise his own account of the Trinity in subsequent works. This does not diminish the importance of *Against Euno-*

mius, however. On the contrary, it allows us to read it as a fascinating snapshot of a process of doctrinal development and definition. Older historical accounts of the fourth-century doctrinal controversies corralled participants into two competing camps: those in support of the Council of Nicaea and its term *homoousios,* and those opposed to it. Basil's *Against Eunomius,* however, would make no sense if this were the case. He uses the term *homoousios* only once in this text to describe the relation of Father and Son, and there, in the judgment of Lewis Ayres, "the term does not function as a point of departure for the argument."[1] Moreover, Basil's later distinction between "substance" (*ousia*) and "person" (*hypostasis*) is strikingly absent from *Against Eunomius.* The emphasis on formulae dilutes the richness of a text like *Against Eunomius* as a source for both historical and theological reflection.

Unfortunately, Basil's Trinitarian theology has not received sufficient attention in English-language scholarship.[2] Only recently have scholars working on the development of Christian doctrine turned their attention to Basil as a pivotal figure in the fourth-century controversies and as an interesting theologian in his own right.[3] Stephen Hildebrand's 2007 book is the first English monograph devoted to Basil's Trinitarian thought.[4] More recently, our own monographs have explored key issues in Basil's Trinitarian theology.[5] Nonetheless, many interpretive issues

---

1. Lewis Ayres, *Nicaea and Its Legacy. An Approach to Fourth-Century Trinitarian Theology* (Oxford: Oxford University Press, 2004), 195.

2. There were monographs in French and German in the 1990s: Bernard Sesboüé, *Saint Basile et La Trinité* (Paris: Desclée, 1998), and Volker Henning Drecoll, *Die Entwicklung der Trinitätslehre des Basilius von Cäsarea* (Göttingen: Vandenhoeck & Ruprecht, 1996).

3. Joseph T. Lienhard, "*Ousia* and *Hypostasis:* The Cappadocian Settlement and the Theology of 'One *Hypostasis,*'" in Stephen T. Davis, et al. (eds.), *The Trinity* (Oxford: Oxford University Press, 2000), 99–121; Ayres 187–229; Behr 263–324.

4. *The Trinitarian Theology of Basil of Caesarea* (Washington, DC: The Catholic University of America Press, 2007).

5. Mark DelCogliano, *Basil of Caesarea's Anti-Eunomian Theory of Names: Christian Theology and Late-Antique Philosophy in the Fourth-Century Trinitarian Controversy,* Supplements to Vigiliae Christianae 103 (Leiden: Brill, 2010); Andrew Radde-

remain unresolved regarding the development of Basil's Trinitarian theology from his early letters, through *Against Eunomius,* and into his late works such as *On the Holy Spirit.* We hope that this translation contributes to the emerging discussion of Basil's Trinitarian thought, not least with respect to *Against Eunomius* itself.

In *Against Eunomius,* we see the clash not simply of two dogmatic positions on the doctrine of the Trinity, but of two fundamentally opposed ways of doing theology. Basil's treatise is as much about how theology ought to be done and what human beings can and cannot know about God as it is about the exposition of Trinitarian doctrine. Basil rejects Eunomius's view that humans can know the essence of God. His response requires him to articulate how one can have meaningful knowledge of something that falls short of knowledge of that subject's essence. He insists that humans cannot comprehend what it is to be God, but that this in no way leaves theology with nothing to say. Rather, the theological endeavor directs the theologian ever more fully to what humans *do* know of God, especially through Scripture: God's goodness, justice, wisdom, and benevolent providence. It is these conceptions, which we learn from God's activities, that provide good theology with its subject-matter.

Basil's treatise is highly rhetorical and includes the kind of invective all too familiar to students of fourth-century Christian theology. Yet amidst this (sometimes hilarious) vitriol is a call to epistemological humility on the part of the theologian, a call to recognize the limitations of even the best theology. Basil himself refined his theology through the course of his career, making *Against Eunomius* a testament to the early development of a brilliant mind aware of the provisional—but not arbitrary—character of theological formulae. Basil's capacity for clarifying his views over time in fact enabled him to become one of the architects of the Trinitarian doctrine that eastern and western Christians to this day profess as "orthodox." We hope that this translation will help acquaint a wider readership with the theology of this understudied, yet profoundly important, Father of the Church.

Gallwitz, *Basil of Caesarea, Gregory of Nyssa, and the Transformation of Divine Simplicity,* Oxford Early Christian Studies (Oxford: Oxford University Press, 2009).

II. BASIL'S LIFE: AN OVERVIEW

Basil was a brilliant and complex man. Aristocrat, rhetor, theologian, polemicist, preacher, pastor, bishop, reformer, politician, ascetic, friend, and foe: his multifaceted character and his range of concerns makes summarizing his life difficult, and comprehensive biography perhaps even impossible.[6] Every biographical sketch of Basil must inevitably pick which aspects to highlight and which to mention only in passing. The survey of Basil's life presented here is meant to introduce the theological treatise *Against Eunomius*, and accordingly our focus will be the stages of Basil's intellectual and theological formation and his increasing engagement with the theological controversies raging in his day. We unfortunately give subjects such as his activities of social concern, his role as pastor, his reorganization of ecclesial structures, and his ascetic teaching only scant attention.[7]

Basil was born ca. 329/30 CE at Caesarea in the Roman province of Cappadocia. His wealthy, landowning family had been Christian since the pre-Constantinian period and was distinguished as much for its Christian piety as for its wealth and status.[8] The family estates were located in Annisa[9] in the province of Helenopontus on the Black Sea coast of northeastern Asia Minor. His mother, Emmelia, was a noblewoman from Cappadocia, probably descended from a high-ranked family of civil servants. The wealth and status of Basil's family were due largely to her. His father, also named Basil, a native of Pontus Ptolemoniacus, was a teacher of rhetoric in the provincial capital of Neo-

6. The necessary starting point for anyone interested in Basil is Philip Rousseau's biography: *Basil of Caesarea* (Berkeley: University of California Press, 1994).

7. Of particular worth here is Paul Jonathan Fedwick, ed., *Basil of Caesarea: Christian, Humanist, Ascetic*, 2 vols. (Toronto: The Pontifical Institute of Mediaeval Studies, 1981), which contains several excellent articles on these subjects.

8. For the basic chronology of Basil's life, with a critical discussion, see Paul J. Fedwick, "A Chronology of the Life and Works of Basil of Caesarea," in Fedwick, ed., *Basil of Caesarea: Christian, Humanist, Ascetic*, 1.3–19.

9. Also spelled "Annesi." Modern-day Uluköy in Turkey (it was called Sonnusa until 1958), about 8 km from the junction of the Yeçil Imrmak (Iris) and the Kelkit Çayi (Lycos). See Rousseau 62 n. 7.

caesarea[10] during Basil's youth. Basil the elder's family had been deprived of property during the persecution of Maximin Daia, and Emmelia's grandfather had died a martyr's death.[11] Basil's paternal grandmother, Macrina the Elder, had had contact with the circle around Gregory Thaumaturgus, the "apostle" of Pontus, who had once been a student of Origen. Macrina was instrumental in the religious education of Basil and his siblings.

Basil was the eldest son of ten children, nine of whom survived infancy. His sister Macrina the Younger (so-called to distinguish her from her grandmother) was around three years older than he, and his younger brothers Naucratius and Peter (later bishop of Sebasteia) were about five and ten years younger, respectively. Gregory (later bishop of Nyssa) was between five and ten years younger than Basil.[12] A second sister named Theosebia was probably slightly older than Gregory.[13] Basil also had three more sisters, whose names are unknown. The members of Basil's family exerted immense influence on his religious conversion and were deeply intertwined with his ecclesiastical career; more will be heard of them later.

Basil was first educated in grammar and rhetoric by his father in Neocaesarea. After his father's death ca. 345/46, he continued his education in Caesarea, probably with maternal uncles. During this period he met his lifelong friend Gregory, later bishop of Nazianzus.[14] In 348/49 he spent a year studying in Constantinople, for a while under the famous rhetor Libanius. About a year later, he and his friend Gregory traveled to Athens to continue their education in rhetoric and philosophy. Basil remained until 355/56, studying under the renowned rhetors Prohaeresius (who was a Christian) and Himerius, among oth-

---

10. Modern-day Niksar in Turkey. Neocaesarea was about 65 km, or a three-day journey, from the family estates in Annisa.

11. Gregory of Nyssa, *Life of Macrina* 20.10–14 (Pierre Maraval, *Grégoire de Nysse. Vie de saint Macrine*, SC 178, 206; cf. 144 n. 3).

12. The best summary of Gregory of Nyssa's life is Anna M. Silvas, *Gregory of Nyssa: The Letters* (Leiden: Brill, 2007), 1–57.

13. On Theosebia, see Silvas, *The Letters*, 98–100.

14. For a summary of Gregory of Nazianzus's life, see Christopher Beeley, *Gregory of Nazianzus on the Trinity and the Knowledge of God* (Oxford: Oxford University Press, 2008), 3–62.

ers. It is not known specifically with whom Basil studied philosophy in Athens at this time, but the culture of the intellectual life of the city shortly after his time there is preserved in Eunapius.[15] That Basil received a solid philosophical formation is evident in his writings, and we will have occasion below to discuss the deployment of his philosophical education in *Against Eunomius*. What we know of Basil's education and his later writings indicates that he was well-trained in rhetoric and philosophy at some of the best institutions of his day.[16]

In 355/56, disillusioned by student rowdiness and factionalism, Basil left Athens, against the wishes of his friend Gregory. He returned to Caesarea to teach rhetoric, and his younger brother Gregory became one of his students.[17] But after a short while, perhaps less than a year, he abandoned teaching. For a year or so during 356 and 357 Basil followed Eustathius "the philosopher" through Coele-Syria, Palestine, Mesopotamia, and Egypt, but apparently without ever catching up with him.[18] This Eustathius is probably to be identified with Eustathius, bishop of Sebasteia since 356. As a leading figure in both the theological conflicts and the ascetical movements of the era, he had attracted the young Basil's attention as a churchman worthy of emulation. Eustathius became something of a mentor to the young Basil both ascetically and theologically.[19] On this same tour Basil also visited monastic sites and thus was exposed to the burgeoning ascetic movements of his day and the manifold forms they took. No doubt the information gained on this trip critically shaped Basil's own development and informed his later ascetic writings. Inspired upon his return to Caesarea in 357 to emulate the greats among the ascetics he had encountered,

15. Eunapius studied in Athens from 362/63 to 367/68. See Wilmer Cave Wright, ed., *Eunapius: The Lives of the Sophists*, Loeb Classical Library (Cambridge: Harvard University Press, 1922). Prohaeresius and Himerius are included in Eunapius's account.

16. See Rosemary Radford Ruether, *Gregory of Nazianzus: Rhetor and Philosopher* (Oxford: Clarendon Press, 1969), 18–28, for a discussion of the curriculum of rhetorical and philosophical studies most likely followed by Basil and Gregory.

17. Gregory of Nyssa, *Ep.* 13.4.   18. *Epp.* 1 and 223.2.

19. See Rousseau 72–76; Silvas, *The Letters*, 56–60.

probably at this time he elected to be baptized by Dianius, the bishop of Caesarea.[20]

After his baptism Basil returned to his family estate in Annisa to join his mother, his sister Macrina, and others in their pursuit of an ascetic life. After Macrina had professed virginity as a teenager in the 340s, her mother and others joined her in the ensuing years in the practice of traditional household piety. Their practices multiplied and evolved so much that by the early 350s the household had effectively been transformed into a kind of ascetic community.[21] Yet Basil cannot be considered a "member" of this community since he formed another community and lived at a distance from his family on the far side of the Iris River. Perhaps he did so because he sought to pursue an ascetic life, or as he calls it, a "philosophical life," whose goals and ideals differed from those of his family. It is possible that his younger brother Gregory joined him in this endeavor.[22] Basil's vision of his "philosophical life" during this period is preserved for us in two letters he wrote to his friend Gregory trying to persuade him to join him in Annisa.[23] After further persuasive efforts that continued into 358, Gregory joined Basil and his small community. The friends immersed themselves in the study of scripture and Christian theology, and during this period they may have produced the *Philocalia,* an anthology of Origen's works, if they are really its compilers.[24] Though Gregory stayed with Basil only for a year or so, his departure was but the prelude to another pivotal change in Basil's life.

Basil next shows up at the Council of Constantinople in January 360. This council ratified a creed that enshrined Homoian

20. It is uncertain whether Basil was baptized before or after his monastic tour.

21. For a description of the household ascetic community, see Gregory of Nyssa, *Life of Macrina.* For a critical discussion, see Susanna Elm, *Virgins of God: The Making of Asceticism in Late Antiquity* (Oxford: Clarendon Press, 1994), Chap. 3.

22. See Silvas, *The Letters,* 9–10.

23. *Epp.* 14 and 2. For a discussion of the character of Basil's "philosophical life" during this period, see Rousseau, Chap. 3, and Elm, *Virgins,* 60–68.

24. The nature and function of the *Philocalia* continues to be debated; see Neil McLynn, "What was the *Philocalia* of Origen?" *Meddelanden från Collegium Patristicum Lundense* 19 (2004): 32–43, who argues that the staff of Eusebius of Caesarea's library produced the collection and that Gregory of Nazianzus purchased a copy during his stay in Palestinian Caesarea in 345/46.

theology, which, aiming at political compromise, limited its doctrinal affirmations to confessing that the Son was "like" the Father *according to the scriptures,* and nothing more. The Homoian
leaders also managed to orchestrate the depositions of the leaders of their opponents, the Homoiousians (who argued that the
Son was like the Father *in substance*), including Basil's mentor
Eustathius of Sebasteia. It is not clear what prompted Basil to
travel to the imperial capital. His learning and talent had not
gone unnoticed by Dianius of Caesarea, the bishop who had
baptized him. It was probably shortly before the council that
Dianius ordained him a reader.[25] If it was Dianius who brought
Basil to Constantinople, he most likely wanted to take advantage of both Basil's theological advice and his superior rhetorical power.[26] Basil was also probably drawn to the proceedings
because of his theological and ascetical sympathies with Eustathius of Sebasteia.[27] Whatever his reasons for going, he took
his brother Gregory along with him.[28]

Nevertheless, Basil played a negligible role at the council. It
is unlikely that he participated in the debates.[29] Once it became
clear to Basil that the Homoiousians had lost the contest and

25. It is possible that Dianius ordained Basil as a reader shortly *after* the
Council of Constantinople, not before. There is no scholarly consensus on the
matter, save that it was around the time of the January 360 council.

26. Basil's superior rhetorical power at the time of the council is noted by
Philostorgius, *h.e.* 4.12.

27. Kopecek 361; Rousseau 98–101.

28. Gregory of Nyssa, *Eun.* 1.82. See also Silvas, *The Letters,* 11–12 and Rousseau 98.

29. Gregory of Nyssa says that he and his brother "were present at the time of
the contest and did not mingle with the contestants" (*Eun.* 1.82). Basil's non-par-
ticipation is also noted by Philostorgius, who attributed it to timidity (*h.e.* 4.12).
It is often claimed that the young Basil was chosen as the spokesman for the Homoiousians at the council but when faced with debating the deacon Aetius (the
spokesman for the Heteroousians), he declined out of fear. See, for example,
Hildebrand 21 and 214; Kopecek 300–301 and 361–62; Behr 263; and Richard
Lim, *Public Disputation, Power, and Social Order in Late Antiquity* (Berkeley: University of California Press, 1995), 119–20. But this claim is based on a misinterpreta-
tion of Philostorgius, *h.e.* 4.12; the historian refers to Basil, the bishop of Ancyra,
as the representative of the Homoiousians. This interpretation is corroborated
by the fact that the Basil in question declined to debate with Aetius because it
was inappropriate for a bishop to dispute with a deacon. At most a reader, Basil
of Caesarea could not have lodged such a complaint. Thus the spokesman must

were doomed to deposition and banishment, he fled Constantinople and returned home.[30] Because of this Basil was later accused of cowardice; while Gregory defends his brother against the charge, he does not deny that Basil left the proceedings early.[31] The Council of Constantinople marks the beginning of Basil's life as a Cappadocian cleric and his entrée into the wider ecclesiastical world and its conflicts.

At this council, in order to replace one of the deposed bishops, the deacon Eunomius was made bishop of Cyzicus.[32] A few years older than Basil, Eunomius was also Cappadocian by birth, born in Oltiseris in the extreme northwest of Cappadocia near Galatia. He had studied in Constantinople, Antioch, and Alexandria, where ca. 346–348 he became a disciple of Aetius. Aetius and Eunomius returned to Antioch ca. 350 and became part of the circle around Eudoxius, who was made bishop of Antioch in 358 and soon thereafter ordained Eunomius as deacon. There is no record of Basil and Eunomius meeting at the Council of Constantinople, though Eunomius is our source for Basil's early departure from it. Basil never mentions any personal knowledge of his opponent. Soon after the council Eunomius published his *Apology*, which Basil would refute a few years afterward in his *Against Eunomius*.[33]

After the council, those bishops like Dianius who were not deposed returned to their sees. A few months after, during the summer of 360, Dianius, like so many eastern bishops, was coerced by imperial threats into subscribing to the council's Homoian creed.[34] This prompted Basil to leave Caesarea once

---

have been Basil of Ancyra. See also Raymond Van Dam, *Becoming Christian: The Conversion of Roman Cappadocia* (Philadelphia: University of Pennsylvania Press, 2003), 197 n. 22.

30. Gregory of Nyssa, *Eun.* 1.79. Here Gregory summarizes the account of Eunomius, who said that Basil was present when the bishops were debating and encouraged them, but does not mention Basil actually participating.

31. Gregory of Nyssa, *Eun.* 1.79–90.

32. On all aspects of Eunomius's life, see Vaggione, *passim,* and Van Dam, *Becoming Christian,* Chap. 1. On Eunomius's theology, see Vaggione, *passim,* Kopecek 306–46, and Michel R. Barnes, *The Power of God* (Washington, DC: The Catholic University of America Press, 2001), 173–219.

33. We discuss the dating of these two documents below at p. 33.

34. Dianius's theological leanings are hard to assess. He was one of the

again for Annisa, this time on account of, among other things, his suspicion of Dianius's orthodoxy.[35] He resumed his "philosophical life" for a period of about two years. In early 362 Gregory joined him again, distraught over his recent ordination as presbyter by his father, the bishop of Nazianzus. Their common retreat lasted only a few months since Gregory soon returned home and Basil was back in Caesarea by mid-362. There Basil reconciled with Dianius before the latter died. In later years, Basil had nothing but reverence for Dianius's memory.[36]

Eusebius succeeded Dianius as bishop of Caesarea and probably at this time ordained Basil as presbyter.[37] After about a year or so, Basil broke with his new bishop as a result of some mis-

---

recipients of the letter Julius of Rome had written to Eusebian bishops after holding a council at Rome in early 341, which found Athanasius innocent of misconduct and exonerated Marcellus's theology as orthodox (preserved in Athanasius, *Apol. c. Ar.* 21–35). Dianius attended the "Dedication Council" of Antioch held during the summer of 341 (Sozomen, *h.e* 3.5), which produced two creeds that reflect Eusebian theology. He reportedly brought along Asterius (*Synodicon Vetus* 42). Dianius was also present at the "eastern" council of Serdica in 343 and signed its decrees, along with, among others, Basil of Ancyra and Eudoxius, then bishop of Germanica, later of Antioch. Though Dianius appears to be allied with the Eusebians in the early 340s, there were numerous shifts in political and theological alliances during the ensuing period of nearly twenty years. For example, Basil of Ancyra and Eudoxius of Antioch had become enemies by the time of the Council of Constantinople. Hence, Dianius's position in 360 cannot be known for certain, given the scant evidence for his own views. See the next note for further comments on Dianius's theology.

35. In his denial of the charge that he had anathematized Dianius after his subscription to the Homoian creed, Basil reported that Dianius on his deathbed claimed to have subscribed to it only "in the simplicity of his heart" and never to have abandoned the Nicene faith (*Ep.* 51). While one suspects that here Basil is being more apologetic than factual, it does appear as if Dianius's many virtues did not include theological acumen, which may partly explain why he brought Basil to Constantinople in 360. Hence, any attempt to locate Dianius within a specific *theological* trajectory, as can be done for others of the period, may simply be begging the question, for his own theological views may not have been sufficiently refined to warrant labeling them as belonging to any particular group.

36. See *Ep.* 51.

37. Philostorgius (*h.e.* 4.12) states that Basil was a deacon at the Council of Constantinople, but he was at most a reader at this time. Socrates (*h.e.* 4.26) records that Meletius of Antioch ordained Basil a deacon. See Kopecek 300 n. 1 for a discussion.

understanding and returned to his ascetic retreat at Annisa for a third time. After Basil had spent eighteen months in Annisa, his friend Gregory mediated a reconciliation between him and Eusebius. Gregory may have been motivated by Eusebius's recent display of theological inadequacy when debating Homoian theologians during the emperor Valens's visit to Caesarea in 365. In several letters, Gregory appealed to Eusebius that he be reconciled with Basil and encouraged Basil to put his talents at the service of the wider church.[38] Therefore, Eusebius may have recalled Basil to Caesarea in large part for the purpose of engaging in theological debate. But in the following years Eusebius came to lean on Basil as much for his pastoral and administrative talents as for his theological expertise. This was most evident in Basil's coordination of relief efforts during the Cappadocian famine of 369. During this period Basil was the *de facto* chief pastor of Caesarea, preaching regularly and organizing social charity, the care of the sick, the distribution of surplus, and hospices.[39]

When Eusebius died in 370, Basil was regarded by some as his obvious successor, yet his election to the episcopate was not without opposition. Despite Basil's tremendous success as a pastor in Caesarea, some were resistant to him because of such issues as his family connections (and their wealth), the arrogance that some perceived as resulting from his elite education, his eagerness to incorporate asceticism into the church's life, and his abiding concern with ecclesial matters far beyond the boundaries of his own diocese. Gregory of Nazianzus's father, Gregory the Elder, the long-time bishop of Nazianzus, played a decisive role in securing Basil's election.[40] Nonetheless, his consecration as bishop was surrounded by controversy and factionalism within the Caesarean church, which thwarted his effectiveness as bishop, at least in the early years of his episcopacy.[41]

As bishop of Caesarea, Basil became more and more em-

---

38. Gregory of Nazianzus, *Epp.* 8, 16, 17, 18, and 19.
39. See Rousseau 136–44.
40. J. McGuckin, *Saint Gregory of Nazianzus: An Intellectual Biography* (Crestwood, NY: St. Vladimir's Seminary Press, 2001), 169–76.
41. See Rousseau 145–51.

broiled in the varied ecclesiastical matters and disputes of his day. Only a few of his most important episcopal activities and experiences can be mentioned here. During Basil's episcopacy, Cappadocia played a strategic role in Emperor Valens's campaigns against and diplomatic missions to the Persian emperor.[42] In order to achieve the administrative and fiscal efficiency necessary for these objectives, Valens decided to divide the province of Cappadocia into two smaller provinces, effective September 372. But when visiting Caesarea in January 372 in preparation for this, the emperor and his prefect Modestus were so impressed with Basil, despite their being doctrinally at odds with him, that Valens co-opted Basil in several ways that advanced Roman military and diplomatic strategies concerning the Persian empire. He entrusted Basil with oversight of the selection of bishops in Armenia, as a way of consolidating Roman interests in this crucial buffer-state.

Nonetheless, the division of Cappadocia proceeded as planned, seriously undermining Basil's position as the metropolitan bishop of the undivided Cappadocia. In order to secure his continuing influence after the division, Basil orchestrated the appointment of several of his allies to sees in the newly created province of Cappadocia Secunda. In 372 he appointed his friend Gregory (with the connivance of his father, Gregory the Elder) as bishop of Sasima and his brother Gregory as bishop of Nyssa. The next year Amphilochius, a cousin of Gregory of Nazianzus, was appointed bishop of Iconium. Gregory of Nazianzus resented the appointment to Sasima and probably never assumed his duties. He was indignant with Basil for using him as a pawn in his ecclesiastical schemes; Basil was irate with Gregory for not taking up his post. The incident led to a rift in the friendship between Gregory and Basil that was never fully repaired. Basil ousted Gregory from his circle of confidants and never again trusted him as an ally in his ecclesiastical agenda.[43] Despite the rift, the two men and their families remained cordial, though not intimate.

Basil also had a falling-out with his one-time mentor Eustathi-

---

42. Van Dam, *Kingdom of Snow*, 109–17.

43. Rousseau 234–39; McGuckin, *Saint Gregory of Nazianzus*, 189–203.

us of Sebasteia over the issue of the divinity of the Holy Spirit.[44] Sometime after 371, Eustathius's views on the Holy Spirit became suspect to some of Basil's Armenian allies. Over the next few years Basil had a series of meetings and exchanges with Eustathius aimed at gathering evidence of his orthodoxy. Mutual distrust slowly developed, and by 375 the two had devolved into attacking each other. Basil tagged Eustathius a "Pneumatomachian"—that is, a fighter against the Spirit—for denying the divinity of the Holy Spirit. Eustathius accused Basil of Sabellianism on account of his earlier association with Apollinarius of Laodicea, now known more for his Christological heresy. Sabellianism emphasized the unity of the triune God in a way that failed to recognize the real and permanent distinctions between Father, Son, and Holy Spirit. Eustathius connected Apollinarius with Sabellianism because of his promotion of the Nicene term *homoousios*, though modern scholars view the charge as unfounded. As a young man, Basil had probably corresponded with Apollinarius in the early 360s, inquiring about *homoousios*.[45] Since Eustathius exploited Basil's connections with Apollinarius in making his case against him, Basil had to distance himself from Apollinarius, even though the Laodicean bishop was a staunch adherent of the Nicene Creed. Eustathius died around 377, still at enmity with Basil.

As Basil's rupture with Eustathius had major significance in his own life, so the debate over the divinity of the Holy Spirit was increasingly significant in the life of the wider church.[46] The issue had only come to the fore in the late 350s and early 360s. The third book of Basil's *Against Eunomius,* as well as Athanasius's *Letters to Serapion* and Didymus the Blind's *On the Holy Spirit,* represents some of the earliest attempts to argue systematically for the full divinity of the Spirit.[47] Around 375, Basil wrote his

44. Rousseau 239–54; Ayres 225–26; Behr 109–10.

45. George L. Prestige, *St. Basil the Great and Apollinaris* (London: SPCK, 1956); Henri de Riedmatten, "La correspondance entre Basile de Césareé et Apollinaire de Laodicée," *JTS* n.s. 7 (1956): 199–210; 8 (1957): 53–70.

46. Michael A. G. Haykin, *The Spirit of God* (Leiden: Brill, 1994); Hanson 738–90; Ayres 211–18.

47. See the Introduction in Mark DelCogliano, Andrew Radde-Gallwitz, and

own *On the Holy Spirit*, which dealt not only with the divinity of
the Spirit, but also with the Spirit's role in the life of the church
and individual Christians. He dedicated the book to Amphilochius of Iconium, who looked up to Basil as a mentor, much as
Basil had once done with Eustathius. An exchange of letters between them is extant, Basil answering Amphilochius's questions
on matters of ecclesiastical discipline and the finer points of theology. In the correspondence, Basil's affection for his protégé is
evident.[48] Perhaps his friendships with Amphilochius and other
bishops like Eusebius of Samosata that developed during his
episcopacy consoled him for the pain of his estrangement from
Gregory of Nazianzus and Eustathius of Sebasteia, the compan-
ions of his youth.[49]

Though Basil did not mention the Nicene Creed in *Against
Eunomius*, as bishop he became one of the leading pro-Nicene
theologians of his era. Only gradually did he come to accept the
creed as the sufficient means for unifying adherents of diverse
theological positions. Shortly before he wrote *Against Eunomius*,
he had rejected the term *homoousios* in his correspondence with
Apollinarius; shortly after writing the anti-Eunomian treatise,
he admitted his acceptance of the Nicene term in a letter to
Maximus the philosopher.[50] Later, as bishop, he promoted the
Nicene Creed as the expression of standard orthodox teaching,
provided that it was supplemented by a statement about the divinity of the Spirit.[51]

Basil's attempts to build a pro-Nicene alliance required navi-
gating a complex set of relationships among the sees of Rome,
Alexandria, and especially Antioch. By the 370s, there were
three rival bishops in Antioch: (1) Paulinus, leader of the "old-
Nicene" community loyal to Eustathius of Antioch, who had
been deposed around 327; (2) Meletius, the Homoian candi-
date who upon his consecration revealed himself to be more

Lewis Ayres, *Works on the Spirit: Athanasius and Didymus* (Crestwood, NY: St. Vladimir's Seminary Press, forthcoming).

48. See Rousseau 258–69; Ayres 224–25; Hildebrand 27–28.

49. On Eusebius of Samosata, see Rousseau 254–58.

50. *Epp.* 361 and 9.3. On Basil's early doubts over *homoousios*, see Ayres 188–
91; Hildebrand 210–22.

51. See, for example, *Epp.* 52, 113, 125, 128, and 204.

Homoiousian than anything else and in time adopted a pro-Nicene stance; and (3) Euzoius, Meletius's Homoian replacement. Both Paulinus and Meletius were supporters of Nicaea, yet their communities were opposed to one another for a variety of other reasons. Like many other bishops in Asia Minor, Basil supported Meletius, viewed as the best possibility for reconciling the Antiochene factions. Another criterion for reconciliation was the condemnation of Marcellus of Ancyra. Basil realized that his plans could be achieved only by gaining the support of Athanasius of Alexandria and Damasus of Rome, who represented the western bishops. And so, he wrote a number of letters to Damasus and Athanasius (who never answered Basil) and even organized diplomatic missions to Rome. As the western bishops tended to support Paulinus and were reluctant to condemn Marcellus, Basil's plans came to naught.[52]

Basil died before his fiftieth birthday, probably in late September 378.[53] Death robbed him of seeing the groundwork that he had laid come to fruition a few years later. The new emperor, Theodosius, raised to the purple only a few months after Basil's death, was a pro-Nicene Christian from Spain. While some progress had been made in the formation of a viable pro-Nicene alliance in the late 370s and 380, the emperor convened a council in Constantinople in 381 to resolve lingering issues.[54] The

52. For Basil's role in the attempt to build a pro-Nicene alliance, see Rousseau 288–317; Ayres 224–29; Behr 104–17.

53. Though for centuries Basil was thought to have died on January 1, 379, since the 1980s there has been a dispute over the date of his death. Building on earlier scholarship, the most important studies are Pierre Maraval, "La date de la mort de Basile de Césarée," *Revue des Études Augustiniennes* 34 (1988): 25–38 (August 377); J.-R. Pouchet, "La date de l'élection épiscopale de saint Basile et celle de sa mort," *Revue d'histoire ecclésiastique* 87 (1992): 5–33 (late September 378); T. D. Barnes, "The Collapse of the Homoeans in the East," *Studia Patristica* 29 (1997): 3–16 (January 1, 379); and Pierre Maraval, "Retour sur quelques dates concernant Basil de Césarée et Grégoire de Nysse," *Revue d'histoire ecclésiastique* 99 (2004): 153–57 (late September 378). For good reviews of the literature, see Rousseau 360–63 and Vaggione 304–11, who both argue for the traditional date of January 1, 379, as well as Silvas, *The Letters*, 32–39, who reviews the most recent scholarship and argues for a date of late September 378.

54. On the Council of Constantinople, see Hanson 791–823; Ayres 253–60; Behr 117–22.

council fathers ratified a revised version of the Nicene Creed which was more explicit concerning belief in the Holy Spirit as divine and to which many former enemies could subscribe. Imperial legislation throughout the 380s and 390s encouraged acceptance of the council's decrees. It needs to be stressed that "the Council of Constantinople does not mark the end of Trinitarian debate in the eastern empire."[55] In the following years, there were continuing efforts to entice dissidents (such as Heteroousians, Homoians, Pneumatomachians, and Apollinarians) to accept pro-Nicene orthodoxy, by legislation on the part of Theodosius and by theological argument on the part of Gregory of Nyssa, Gregory of Nazianzus, and others. Basil's efforts had not been in vain.

The other so-called "Cappadocian Fathers" acknowledged the impact of Basil, each in his own way. Gregory of Nyssa took up the mantle of his deceased brother in the ecclesiastical and theological realms, defending him against detractors and developing the doctrinal insights of Basil into one of the classic expressions of pro-Nicene Trinitarian theology. Gregory of Nazianzus's Trinitarian theology is not as explicitly indebted to Basil's as Gregory of Nyssa's was, but nonetheless represents a signal achievement in pro-Nicene theology. Shortly after the Council of Constantinople, Gregory of Nazianzus eulogized Basil, still feeling the sting of old hurts but appreciative of the many accomplishments of his one-time friend.[56] He depicted Basil as an exemplary pastor, teacher, and theologian, and bestowed upon him the epithet by which he is still known today: "Basil the Great."[57]

III. THE HISTORICAL CONTEXT
OF *AGAINST EUNOMIUS*

Traditional accounts of the fourth-century Trinitarian debates have tended to corral participants into two competing camps: those in support of the Council of Nicaea and its term

---

55. Ayres 359.
56. *Or.* 43. See Rousseau 18–20; McGuckin, *Saint Gregory of Nazianzus*, 372–74.
57. *Or.* 43.1 and 43.16.

homoousios and those opposed to it. For a long time it was customary to place Basil in the former group and view him, along with and inseparable from his fellow Cappadocians Gregory of Nyssa and Gregory of Nazianzus, as the heirs of the theological and polemical legacy of Athanasius of Alexandria. In turn, Athanasius was seen as the beleaguered champion of an unalterable theological vision enshrined in the Creed of Nicaea in 325 and the indefatigable opponent of the heresiarch Arius and his progeny. Eunomius too was linked with currents from earlier in the fourth century. The title "Neo-Arian" was egregiously used to describe his and Aetius's theology, suggesting a revival and perhaps radicalization of Arius's thought. But these interpretations rely too much on the polemical categories promoted by biased contemporaries of the debates.

Recent revisionist scholarship has taught us that the story of the fourth-century Trinitarian controversies is far more complex and uncertain than such traditional accounts would have us believe—and endlessly more fascinating. Arius and Athanasius are no longer seen as the fountainheads of two irreconcilable and long-lasting streams of theology. The idea of a monolithic Cappadocian theology rooted in Athanasian thought, or of Heteroousian theology as a resuscitation of Arius's doctrine, is now recognized as a fiction, or at least a reductionistic distortion. All of the Cappadocians—Basil of Caesarea, Gregory of Nazianzus, and Gregory of Nyssa—developed distinctive theologies with unique emphases. With this more precise understanding of the fourth-century doctrinal controversies, we can see how the participants in the Eunomian controversy—Eunomius and Basil—do and do not relate to the broader course of the controversies. Accordingly, the two following sections first trace the broad contours of the fourth-century debate and then locate Basil's work *Against Eunomius* in its immediate context in the mid-360s. The final section briefly recounts the fate of Eunomius and the Heteroousian movement after the publication of Basil's groundbreaking treatise.

The Remote Context

The Trinitarian controversies arose in the fourth century when pre-existing theological trajectories clashed.[58] There was little agreement over what it meant to ascribe divinity to the Son, what "Father-Son" language implied, or how the Son was the image of God (Col 1.15). It was questionable whether Father and Son were both "true God," whether one could speak of degrees of divinity. For centuries Christians had used common scriptural terminology for speaking about the Father and Son, but only in the early fourth century came to realize fully that diverse interpretations existed.

The dispute that arose between the presbyter Arius and his bishop Alexander around 318 occurred within this context of theological diversity. Alexander taught that the Father and Son were co-eternal on account of the Father's eternal generation of the Son. In addition, the Son was the "indistinguishable" image of the Father, able to reveal the Father perfectly.[59] To Arius, it seemed as if Alexander's theology implied two "unbegottens," that is, two first principles, which destroyed Christian monotheism. Furthermore, Arius thought that Alexander's insistence on the co-eternity of the Father and Son ignored the hierarchy inherent in the language of 'Father' and 'Son.'[60] Accordingly, Arius stressed the Son's distinctness from and inferiority to the Father.[61]

Many Christians throughout the eastern Mediterranean shared Arius's theology of the unique status of the Father as unbegotten. Besides his allies within Alexandria itself or from nearby Egyptian cities, prominent eastern bishops supported him against Alexander, such as Eusebius of Nicomedia, Euse-

58. Ayres 31–76.
59. Our primary sources for Alexander's theology are Urk. 4b and 14. For discussion, see Ayres 43–45; Behr 124–29; and Hanson 138–45.
60. See p. 78 below in this Introduction for the uses of inverted commas and double quotation marks in the present volume.
61. Our primary sources for Arius's theology are Urk. 1, 6, and 30; Athanasius, *Syn.* 15.3, and *Ar.* 1.5–6. For discussion, see Ayres 54–57; Behr 130–49; Hanson 5–27 and 60–128; and Rowan Williams, *Arius: Heresy and Tradition,* rev. ed. (Grand Rapids: Eerdmans, 2001).

bius of Caesarea, Theodotus of Laodicea, Paulinus of Tyre, Athanasius of Anazarbus, Theognis of Nicaea, and Narcissus of Neronias—an ecclesiastical alliance commonly called the "Eusebians" after its two most prominent leaders.[62] These bishops did not agree with Arius's theology in every detail. Though there were theological differences between them, they rallied around Arius in common cause against what they deemed to be Alexander's doctrinal innovations and his mistreatment of Arius.

After a series of failed attempts to reconcile the feuding factions within the Alexandrian church, the emperor Constantine convened a council at Nicaea in 325 to resolve the controversy—now spread throughout the churches of the East—once and for all. The council ratified a creed designed to exclude the theology of Arius and to secure his excommunication and exile.[63] Thereafter Arius was marginal. Constantine recalled him from exile a few years after Nicaea, but the Alexandrian church repeatedly refused him re-admission to communion. He died outside of the church in the mid-330s, having long ceased to be a factor in ongoing theological debates. He was not the founder of "Arianism" as a theological system or as an ecclesiastical movement.

After Nicaea the theological controversy shifted its focus from Arius and Alexander to the emerging debate between the Eusebians and Marcellus of Ancyra. The leading Eusebians had subscribed to the Nicene Creed, but their actions and writings after the council reveal lingering questions over its meaning. Indeed, the 320s and 330s were the golden age of Eusebian theological development. Foremost among the Eusebians was

62. "Eusebian" is a problematic term, as recently discussed by David M. Gwynn, *The Eusebians. The Polemic of Athanasius of Alexandria and the Construction of the 'Arian Controversy'* (Oxford: Oxford University Press, 2007). We use "Eusebian" here in contrast to the Athanasian usage deconstructed by Gwynn and in line with other recent usage to name the *ad hoc* alliance of eastern bishops and theologians initially formed around the figures of Eusebius of Nicomedia and Eusebius of Caesarea that lasted from ca. 320 to ca. 350. For a definition of the category, see Ayres 52, and Joseph T. Lienhard, *Contra Marcellum. Marcellus of Ancyra and Fourth-Century Theology* (Washington, DC: The Catholic University of America Press, 1999), 34–35.

63. On the events from the outbreak of the controversy to the Council of Nicaea, see Ayres 15–20 and 85–100; Behr 62–69; and Hanson 129–78.

Asterius the Sophist, a layman from Cappadocia (he was permanently debarred from clerical status because of his lapse in the Great Persecution). Around 320–321, he had published a theological handbook entitled the *Syntagmation;* it is even claimed that Arius himself used this little book.[64] Around 323, Eusebius of Nicomedia wrote to Paulinus of Tyre urging him to write to Alexander of Alexandria to protest the excommunication of Arius.[65] Paulinus's letter to Alexander became something of an instant classic, although the theological language used by him became so outdated within a few years of its composition that it was a cause of embarrassment among the Eusebians.[66] Around 327, Asterius wrote a defense of Paulinus's letter. In the early 330s, Marcellus of Ancyra, who had attended the Council of Nicaea and supported its creed and decrees, wrote a book against Asterius's defense of Paulinus. In 337–338 Eusebius of Caesarea issued two anti-Marcellan works: the *Against Marcellus* and the *Ecclesiastical Theology,* the latter of which is in many ways the apex of Eusebian theology. A fragment of an anti-Marcellan work written around 340–341 by Acacius of Caesarea, Eusebius's successor, in defense of Asterius is devoted to explicating what it means to call the Son the image of God.[67]

The Eusebians were by no means characterized by a monolithic theology.[68] Each offers a distinctive perspective within a loosely shared framework that tended to see the differences between the Father and Son as primary, while at the same time affirming the uniqueness of the relationship between the Father and Son. In the early stages of the Trinitarian controversies, there was relatively little reflection by anyone on the divinity of the Holy Spirit or the Spirit's relation to the Father and Son.

Asterius was the intellectual force of his era and the most significant early Eusebian theologian.[69] He distinguished between

64. Athanasius, *Decr.* 8.1.

65. Urk. 8. On the date, see Williams, *Arius,* 58.

66. Urk. 9.

67. Preserved in Epiphanius, *Pan.* 72.6–10. On the date, see Lienhard, *Contra Marcellum,* 185–86.

68. Mark DelCogliano, "Eusebian Theologies of the Son as Image of God before 341," *Journal of Early Christian Studies* 14.4 (2006): 459–84.

69. On Asterius's theology, see Ayres 53–54; Hanson 32–38; Lienhard, *Con-*

the divine power and wisdom that existed in God eternally and the power and wisdom manifested in Christ.[70] He spoke of the Father, Son, and Holy Spirit as three distinct *hypostases*.[71] The Father is always Father, at least potentially so,[72] and the Son is the indistinguishable image of the Father's divinity, substance, will, power, and glory.[73] The unity of the Father and Son is understood in terms of a harmony of wills, not a sharing of nature.[74]

Eusebius of Caesarea is the other major theologian of the ecclesiastical alliance that bears his name.[75] For Eusebius, God the Father is the unbegotten, eternal source of all. The Son derives his existence from the Father: he is the only-begotten of the Father, not co-eternal with him, and a product of the Father's will, not his substance. Eusebius distinguishes between begetting and creating; the Son is not co-ordinate or even pre-eminent among creatures, but, rather, uniquely related to the Father.[76] The Father and Son have independent ontological existences, which Eusebius sometimes calls *hypostases*. Eusebius posits a very close relationship between the Father and the Son. He insists that, as the image of God, it is the nature of the Son to be like the Father with the greatest degree of exactness possible, being in himself the whole form of God.[77]

In contrast, Marcellus's theology was driven by a concern to preserve the unity of God at any cost.[78] He prefers to speak of

---

tra Marcellum, 89–100; and Markus Vinzent, *Asterius von Kappadokien: Die theologischen Fragmente* (Leiden, New York, Cologne: Brill, 1993). Kopecek 29–34 gives a summary of Asterius's theological differences from Arius.

70. Asterius, *Fragments* 64–68 (Vinzent).

71. Asterius, *Fragments* 54–55 and 61–62 (Vinzent).

72. Asterius, *Fragment* 14 (Vinzent).   73. Asterius, *Fragment* 10 (Vinzent).

74. Asterius, *Fragments* 39–41 (Vinzent).

75. On Eusebius's theology, see Ayres 58–60; Hanson 46–59; and Holger Strutwolf, *Die Trinitätstheologie und Christologie des Euseb von Caesarea* (Göttingen: Vanderhoeck & Ruprecht, 1999).

76. Eusebius, *E. th.* 1.10.1.

77. DelCogliano, "Eusebian Theologies," 471–76.

78. On Marcellus's theology, see Ayres 62–69; Hanson 217–35; Lienhard, *Contra Marcellum*, 49–68; Klaus Seibt, *Die Theologie des Markell von Ankyra* (Berlin: De Gruyter, 1994); and Markus Vinzent, *Markell von Ankyra: Die Fragmente [und] Der Brief an Julius von Rom* (Leiden, New York, Cologne: Brill, 1997). On Marcellus's life, see Sara Parvis, *Marcellus of Ancyra and the Lost Years of the Arian Controversy, 325–345* (Oxford and New York : Oxford University Press, 2006).

God and his Word and downplays 'Father-Son' language; the Word can only be called Son and other Christological titles at the Incarnation.[79] He spoke of the Word as eternally intrinsic to God, existing in God much as the power to reason exists within a human being.[80] He denied that there were two of anything in God: two substances, two *hypostases*, two powers, two persons, and so forth. God was understood to be a unitary divine monad that mysteriously expanded into a triad (namely, the Word and Spirit) without losing its essential oneness and indivisibility.[81] Marcellus also taught a distinct eschatology wherein Christ's kingdom comes to an end.[82] His Eusebian contemporaries came to accuse him of Sabellianism, though he denied the charge.[83] Nonetheless, in 336 Marcellus was deposed and exiled for his theological opinions, a victim of Eusebian machinations. He eventually made his way to Rome in 340, where he made common cause with Athanasius.

As a deacon Athanasius had attended the Council of Nicaea in Alexander's entourage.[84] When Alexander died a few years later, Athanasius succeeded him as bishop of Alexandria, though not without controversy and steep resistance from the Melitians, with whom Athanasius struggled in the early years of his episcopacy. Within a few years Athanasius was charged with violence and other crimes, tried and convicted at the Council of Tyre in 335, and exiled to Gaul. For the remainder of his ecclesiastical career, these charges would dog Athanasius, rendering him suspect and tainted in the eyes of many eastern bishops. Before his death in 373, Athanasius would spend five periods of exile outside of Alexandria, about seventeen years in total.

Having returned to Alexandria from his first exile in 337, Athanasius was ousted from Alexandria again in early 339 and fled to Rome, where Marcellus arrived a few months later. Both

79. Marcellus, *Fragments* 3, 5, 7, 65, and 94 (Vinzent).
80. Marcellus, *Fragment* 87 (Vinzent).
81. Marcellus, *Fragments* 48, 73, and 110 (Vinzent).
82. Marcellus, *Fragments* 107 and 109 (Vinzent).
83. Marcellus, *Fragment* 44 (Vinzent).
84. On Athanasius's life, see Timothy D. Barnes, *Athanasius and Constantius: Theology and Politics in the Constantinian Empire* (Cambridge: Harvard University Press, 1993).

exiled bishops were seeking the support of Julius, the bishop of Rome. Julius held a council in early 341 at which Athanasius was found innocent of misconduct and Marcellus's theology was exonerated as orthodox, thus overturning the decisions of the eastern councils. If they had not met earlier, Athanasius and Marcellus most certainly met in Rome, and perhaps Athanasius wrote the *Orations against the Arians* at the suggestion of Marcellus.

Though Athanasius had begun to conceive of his conflict with the Eusebians as a theological debate before he arrived in Rome, the *Orations* marks the transformation of his ecclesio-political struggles with the bishops of the Eusebian alliance into a quest for orthodoxy against the "Arianism" of his opponents. In this treatise, which Lewis Ayres calls "one of the key early anti-Eusebian theological manifestos,"[85] Athanasius sets out to refute the tenets of "Arianism" as taught by Arius, Asterius, and other Eusebians. Nothing much, however, is heard from him on the Nicene Creed as the standard of orthodoxy until the early 350s.[86] It is now recognized that his depiction of the fourth-century church as polarized between his own "orthodoxy" and the "Arianism" of his Eusebian enemies is a polemical misrepresentation aimed at pleading his own case against his many detractors.[87] Despite his distorted polemics, Athanasius is a significant theologian in his own right, and his writings represent a considerable theological achievement that had immediate and long-lasting influence, though perhaps not as pervasive as previous generations of scholars have believed.[88]

85. Ayres 117.

86. Lewis Ayres, "Athanasius' Initial Defense of the Term Ὁμοούσιος: Rereading the *De decretis*," *Journal of Early Christian Studies* 12 (2004): 337–59.

87. David M. Gwynn, *The Eusebians. The Polemic of Athanasius of Alexandria and the Construction of the Arian Controversy* (Oxford: Oxford University Press, 2007).

88. For general introductions to Athanasius's biography and thought, see Khaled Anatolios, *Athanasius* (London: Routledge, 2004), and Thomas G. Weinandy, *Athanasius: A Theological Introduction* (Aldershot: Ashgate, 2007). For overviews of Athanasius's Trinitarian doctrine, see Ayres 45–48, 110–17, and 140–44; Behr 163–259; Hanson 417–58. For more detailed treatments of his theology, see E. P. Meijering, *Orthodoxy and Platonism in Athanasius. Synthesis or Antithesis?* 2d ed. (Leiden: Brill, 1975); Charles Kannengiesser, *Athanase d'Alexandrie. Évêque et Écrivain: Une lecture des traités contre les Ariens* (Paris: Beauschesne, 1983); J. Rebecca Lyman, *Christology and Cosmology: Models of Divine Activity in Origen, Eusebius,*

Summarizing Athanasius's theology is difficult because of the sheer number of his extant writings composed over a fifty-year period. But a few points of similarity and difference with other theologians already discussed can be mentioned. For Athanasius, theological reflection begins with God's eternal Fatherhood. It follows from this that the Son is co-eternal with the Father. As it was for Alexander, the eternal correlativity of the Father and Son was central for Athanasius. Similarly to Eusebius, Athanasius also distinguished between begetting and creating; hence, the Son, as begotten from God, is radically different from the creatures created by God. Against the Eusebians, he repeatedly speaks of the Son as proper to the Father's substance; in other words, the Son's existence is intrinsic to the Father's nature. Therefore, the Son is the Father's very own Word, Wisdom, and Power. There are not two, as Arius and Asterius had claimed. Athanasius was concerned, as was Marcellus, not to compromise the divine unity. Nonetheless, Athanasius taught that the Father and Son are distinct, though he did not employ any technical terminology for distinguishing them as the Eusebians did. Despite their theological differences, Athanasius and Marcellus were able to join together in their ecclesio-political struggles against the Eusebians.

In this initial period of anti-Eusebian collaboration between Athanasius and Marcellus, the Eusebians were not idle. After the Roman council, Julius sent a letter to the Eusebians that is significant because it adopts the polemics of Athanasius and accuses the Eusebians of "Arianism."[89] In response to the Roman council and Julius's letter, the Eusebian bishops held a council in 341 in conjunction with the dedication of the church in Antioch—the so-called Dedication Council. The Eusebians rejected the idea that their theology could be described as "Arian." They considered themselves as representatives of the mainstream tradition

and Athanasius (Oxford: Clarendon Press, 1993); Peter Widdicome, The Fatherhood of God from Origen to Athanasius (Oxford: Clarendon Press, 1994); Khaled Anatolios, Athanasius: The Coherence of his Thought (London and New York: Routledge, 1998); Xavier Morales, La théologie trinitaire d'Athanase d'Alexandrie (Paris: Institut d'Études Augustiniennes, 2006).

89. Preserved in Athanasius, Apol. c. Ar. 21–35.

of theological orthodoxy in the East that avoided the poles of Arius, on the one side, and Athanasius and Marcellus, on the other. The Dedication Council produced two creeds that would become standard in the East for the next twenty years. The Second Creed is a bold statement of Eusebian theology, echoing the theology of Asterius.[90] The Fourth Creed was drawn up a few months after the Dedication Council to summarize the Second Creed and was brought to the West.[91] The latter became the standard creed in the East for more than twenty years and was reissued at many subsequent eastern councils.

The Dedication Council marks the beginning of a period that lasted through the mid-350s, in which various Eusebian councils sought to achieve theological consensus and eliminate the extremes of Arius, Athanasius, and Marcellus. But the situation reached a nadir before the serious work of consensus-building began in earnest: the debacle of the Council of Serdica in 343. Western and eastern bishops refused to meet with each other in the same place because of political maneuvering on both sides and mutual distrust. The western bishops suspected the eastern bishops of "Arianism," and the eastern bishops could not tolerate the western bishops' support of Athanasius and Marcellus. Each side excommunicated the other. The documents issued by each side reveal how far apart they were at this point. The western bishops held that the Father, Son, and Spirit were one in *hypostasis* or *ousia,* whereas the eastern bishops claimed that the *hypostases* of Father, Son, and Spirit were different. The westerners emphasized the eternal correlativity of Father and Son, but the easterners maintained that the Son had some sort of beginning. The westerners distinguished carefully between "begotten" and "created," a distinction which many Eusebians tended to blur.

The failure of Serdica prompted attempts at rapprochement.[92] The so-called Macrostich ["long-lined"] Creed of 345 is the best example. Responding to western Serdican theology, it attempts to moderate the Eusebian theologies of the Dedica-

90. Preserved in Athanasius, *Syn.* 23.
91. Preserved in Athanasius, *Syn.* 25.1–5.
92. Hanson 306–14.

tion Creed and the eastern Serdican statement in order to find common ground with western bishops. Another key council took place at Sirmium in 351. Here Basil of Ancyra (Marcellus's Eusebian replacement) managed to have Photinus of Sirmium, an adherent of Marcellan views, deposed on theological grounds. This set off a series of councils, such as at Arles in 353 and Milan in 355, in both East and West—often at the insistence of Constantius, now the sole emperor—aimed at effecting theological consensus by securing the condemnation of Athanasius, Marcellus, and Photinus.

In these councils of the 350s, we can trace an increasing reluctance to use *ousia*-language, viewed as problematic because of its associations with the positions of Marcellus and Photinus. At the same time, the Eusebian alliance was splintering over this issue. Some rejected *ousia*-language altogether. Adherents of this approach are generally called "Homoians" because they affirmed that the Son was like (*homoios*) the Father without specifying anything about the *ousia* of either. Others endorsed the use of *ousia*, although differently than first-generation Eusebians like Asterius and Eusebius of Caesarea. Adherents of the Nicene theology had of course always used *ousia*-language in their defense of "same in substance" (*homoousios*). This debate over the significance of *ousia* for Trinitarian theology was the undoing of the old Eusebian alliance and constitutes the immediate context of the debate between Eunomius and Basil of Caesarea.

The Proximate Context

At Sirmium in 357 a small council of bishops produced a confession of faith that condemned all use of *ousia*-language when speaking about the relation between the Father and the Son.[93] This Homoian confession clearly exhibits an anti-Nicene and anti-Homoiousian bias, explicitly condemning the use of the terms *homoousios* and *homoiousios*—in fact, the Sirmium Confession of 357 marks the first appearance of the latter term.[94]

93. On this council, see Hanson 343–47 and Ayres 137–40.
94. Hanson 346–47.

The confession's theology also rejects the Dedication Creed of 341, that classic statement of Eusebian theology that had found widespread use throughout the East. The Sirmium Confession of 357 sent shockwaves throughout the East due to its stark subordinationist agenda, and catalyzed all participants in the Trinitarian debates to take stock of their own positions and to formulate responses.

In early 358 Eudoxius of Antioch convened a synod in Antioch that voiced its approval of the Sirmium Confession of 357. Eudoxius also welcomed Aetius to his see, where he propagated his radical "Heteroousian" theology that emphasized that the Son was "different in substance" (*heteroousios*) from the Father.[95] For many, the teaching of Aetius would have appeared to be the logical conclusion of the Homoian theology of the Sirmium Confession of 357. Indeed, in this period there was no clear line of demarcation between Homoian and Heteroousian theology, or for that matter between Homoian and Homoiousian theology. The reticence of Homoian theology allowed for various—and at times widely divergent—interpretations of it.

The Homoiousian alliance developed in response to the Heteroousian theology of Aetius. Its leaders were George of Laodicea and Basil of Ancyra. Alarmed at the developments in Antioch, George wrote to Basil of Ancyra and a number of other bishops who had convened for the dedication of a church in Ancyra, to alert them to the situation in Antioch. George apprised them of Eudoxius's active promotion of Aetius and his teaching and warned them that if Aetius was not checked, his doctrine would spread beyond Antioch and "shipwreck" the entire church.[96] This letter prompted Basil to convene a synod in Ancyra in concert with the dedication of the church to respond to the teachings of Aetius.[97] It met shortly before Easter 358 and produced a long doctrinal statement that constitutes the initial statement of Homoiousian theology.[98]

After the conclusion of the council, Basil of Ancyra headed a

---

95. Sozomen, *h.e.* 4.12. On Aetius, see Kopecek and Vaggione.
96. Sozomen, *h.e.* 4.13.
97. Epiphanius, *Pan.* 73.2.1.
98. Preserved in Epiphanius, *Pan.* 73.2–11.

delegation to Constantius in Sirmium to secure the deposition and banishment of Eudoxius, Aetius, and Aetius's pupil Eunomius, whom Eudoxius had made a deacon. They were successful.[99] Constantius then convened a council in Sirmium at which imperial endorsement was given to Homoiousian theology, though the doctrinal statement produced at this council does not survive.[100] Perhaps thinking that Homoiousian theology could achieve lasting consensus, Constantius planned a large double-council at Nicomedia in late 358. When an earthquake made the city unsuitable, it was decided that the western bishops would meet at Ariminum in Italy and the eastern bishops in Seleucia in Cilicia.[101] The Council of Seleucia met in September 359, and the other met first in late May at Ariminum in Italy and then transferred in mid-summer to Niké in Thrace.

Before this double-council met, however, Constantius convened another council in Sirmium in early 359 to compose a statement of faith that could be presented to both sessions of the double-council. This statement is called the "Dated Creed" because the date of its promulgation has been preserved: May 22, 359.[102] It was intended to be a document that would find acceptance among Homoiousians and Homoians, but exclude Heteroousian and Homoousian theologies. Since the Dated Creed proscribed the use of *ousia*-language, Basil of Ancyra signed it with trepidation, including a note with his signature giving the Dated Creed a Homoiousian interpretation.[103] At this juncture the Homoiousians recognized that Constantius's desire to effect theological consensus threatened to compromise their theology. Hence shortly after this, George of Laodicea, together with Basil, composed a defense of Homoiousian theology against Heteroousian theology, seen as a competing—and mistaken—way of interpreting the Homoian theology of the Dated Creed.[104]

---

99. Sozomen, *h.e.* 4.13.4–14.7; Philostorgius, *h.e.* 4.8. On Basil's response to Aetius, see Hanson 349–57 and Ayres 149–53.

100. On this council, see Hanson 357–62 and Kopecek 172–76.

101. Socrates, *h.e.* 2.39.2–4; Sozomen, *h.e.* 4.16.2–5; Theodoret, *h.e.* 4.16.

102. Preserved in Athanasius, *Syn.* 8.3–7, and Socrates, *h.e.* 2.37.18–24.

103. Epiphanius, *Pan.* 73.22.7–8.

104. Preserved in Epiphanius, *Pan.* 73.12.1–22.4. On its date, see Ayres 158 and Hanson 365–67.

The Council at Seleucia met in September 359, but things did not unfold as Constantius had hoped.[105] The fragile agreement reached between the Homoians and Homoiousians at Sirmium in 358 and early 359 quickly fell apart over political and theological differences. George of Laodicea was one of the principal leaders of the Homoiousians, along with Eleusius of Cyzicus and Sophronius of Pompeiopolis. Basil of Ancyra had been accused of some unspecified misdemeanor that limited his participation in the council.[106] The Homoians were led by Acacius of Caesarea, George of Alexandria, Uranius of Tyre, and Eudoxius of Antioch. Aetius pushed to have Homoian theology interpreted in a Heteroousian manner. After three sessions of fruitless debate, the council president attempted to dissolve the council. But the Homoiousians re-assembled in order to adjudicate the case of Cyril of Jerusalem and other bishops whom Acacius of Caesarea had recently deposed. When Acacius refused to attend, he was deposed, along with some of his Homoian supporters. And so the council ended.

Embassies representing the various positions were then sent to Constantius at Constantinople. The emperor became so exasperated with Aetius during an audience that he threw him out of the palace.[107] Through coercion and trickery Constantius attempted to get the Homoiousians to subscribe to a modified version of the Dated Creed, sometimes called the Creed of Niké because of its place of original composition. While the Dated Creed had declared the Son "like the Father in all respects (ὅμοιον κατὰ πάντα), as the holy Scriptures also declare and teach," and condemned the use of all οὐσία language, the Creed of Niké omitted the phrase "in all respects," an omission that excluded the possibility of its Homoiousian interpretation. Thus the Homoians now had the backing of Constantius; the Homoiousians had been out-maneuvered. The Homoiousian embassy in Constantinople signed the Creed of Niké on December 31, 359.

In January 360 Constantius convened a small council in

---

105. On this council, see Ayres 161–64 and Hanson 371–80.
106. Socrates, *h.e.* 2.39; Sozomen, *h.e.* 4.22.
107. Epiphanius, *Pan.* 76.3.7–10; Philostorgius, *h.e.* 4.12.

Constantinople to ratify the decisions of the twin Councils of Ariminum and Seleucia.[108] As mentioned above, Basil of Caesarea attended this council in the entourage of either Dianius of Caesarea or Eustathius of Sebasteia. Acacius was the council president and ruthless in his attack on his Homoiousian opponents. He managed to depose nearly all prominent Homoiousian bishops on non-theological grounds by accusing them of various crimes.[109] Basil of Ancyra, Eleusius of Cyzicus, Eustathius of Sebasteia, and Sophronius of Pompeiopolis—all hitherto leaders of the Homoiousians—were deposed. Aetius was also banished for his failure to accept the Homoian position. Basil of Caesarea was a minor player and could easily slip away to his Cappadocian homeland. Eunomius's strong connections with Aetius, however, left him suspect to the newly-ascendant Homoians. Near the conclusion of this council, Eunomius probably delivered the speech that would later be issued as his *Apology* in order to demonstrate his agreement with the Homoian theology endorsed at it.[110] He did not merely avoid the fate of his teacher successfully; he was in fact rewarded for his carefully crafted speech with appointment as bishop of Cyzicus. Soon after taking up his post, however, Eunomius enraged the Christians of Cyzicus by flagrantly promoting his Heteroousian theology and by contravening traditional beliefs and practices, such as Mary's perpetual virginity. After prudently fleeing the city, he never again exercised the pastoral oversight of that church or any other church.

Aetius would return from banishment when Julian the Apos-

108. Socrates, *h.e.* 2.42; Sozomen, *h.e.* 4.24–26.

109. See Ayres 164–65 and Hanson 380–82. The Homoiousians could not be deposed on theological grounds since they had recently signed the Creed of Niké.

110. See Lionel R. Wickham, "The Date of Eunomius' *Apology:* A Reconsideration," *JTS* n.s. 20 (1969): 231–40; EW 5–9; and Vaggione 226–27. It is sometimes said that situating the *Apology* of Eunomius at Constantinople in January 360 is made difficult by Basil's denial in *Eun.* 1.2 of its delivery there, especially since Basil himself attended the council. But Basil did not deny that Eunomius delivered his *Apology* at Constantinople; rather, he denied that there was a need for Eunomius to make a defense there. On the basis of the lack of need for defense at Constantinople, Basil dismisses Eunomius's *Apology* as a fiction. See Wickham, "The Date of Eunomius' *Apology*," 238.

tate became emperor, and would even be made a bishop (though without a see). But after the Council of Constantinople of 360, Eunomius eclipsed him as the leader of the Heteroousians. Eunomius's reputation as a theologian grew with the publication of his *Apology* in 360 or 361. The Heteroousians attracted the support of bishops like Serras of Paraetonium, Theophilus the Indian, and Theodulus of Chaeretapa in Phrygia, who promoted Heteroousian theology through missionary activities and otherwise. They created a parallel episcopal hierarchy to minister to Heteroousian Christians.[111] Under Julian, the Heteroousian movement thrived.

The spread and growing strength of Heteroousian theology prompted Basil to issue a refutation of Eunomius in the mid-360s. During his third ascetic retreat at Annisa, Basil had not secluded himself from the wider ecclesiastical world, and despite his insignificant role at the Council of Constantinople, he remained deeply concerned with the issues under debate. He tracked the progress of the theological controversies and even accompanied Eustathius of Sebasteia to the Homoiousian Council of Lampsacus held in the autumn of 364 (but did not himself attend).[112] Some scholars hold that he composed *Against Eunomius* during the period of his third stay at Annisa, probably in its initial form, rather hastily dictated to Eustathius in preparation for the Council of Lampsacus, or at least resulting from conversations between the two churchmen.[113] Raymond Van Dam has suggested that Basil wrote *Against Eunomius* soon after the accession of Valens (which occurred in 364) to ingratiate himself with the new eastern emperor, whose opponent, the usurper Procopius (proclaimed emperor in 365), was supported by Eunomius.[114] Hence a date of 364 or 365 is most likely for the publication of *Against Eunomius*.

111. Vaggione 279. 112. *Ep.* 223.5.

113. J. Gribomont, "Notes biographiques sur s. Basile le Grand," in P.J. Fedwick, *Basil of Caesarea*, 35–38 (364); Fedwick, "A Chronology," 10–11 n. 57 (the second half of 364); Sesboüé, SC 299, 42–45 (before 366, possibly in 364); Rousseau 102 follows Fedwick; Drecoll 45–46 and 145–46 (Bks. 1–2 in 364; Bk. 3 in 365). Other scholars place *Against Eunomius* a few years earlier: Kopecek 364–72 (360–361) and Hildebrand 214–18 (360–362).

114. *Becoming Christian*, 27–28.

Basil's theology in his *Against Eunomius* is not intended to represent the Homoiousian thought defeated at the Council of Constantinople, nor is it meant to refute the Homoian thought victorious at the council, but specifically focuses on countering the Heteroousian theology of Eunomius. Basil was surely influenced by Homoiousian thought, as his mentor Eustathius of Sebasteia identified with this group in Basil's formative years. At the same time, even in this, his earliest doctrinal treatise, Basil reveals himself as an independent and innovative thinker who drew on many theological currents. The teachings of Origen, Eusebius of Caesarea, Athanasius, and the Homoiousians all make appearances in *Against Eunomius*. Basil integrates various streams of thought in such a way that they could later coalesce, through further efforts on his part and those of others, into a viable pro-Nicene theology, that is, a set of doctrines and theological practices aimed at promoting the Nicene Creed as cipher for orthodox Trinitarian theology. But note that in *Against Eunomius* Basil does not appeal to the Nicene Creed at all, and the term *homoousios*, while used, is not central. Therefore, his *Against Eunomius* represents a signal theological achievement. It contains the foundations for the Trinitarian theology that his brother Gregory of Nyssa (and to some extent Gregory of Nazianzus) later developed and clarified in the 380s and beyond, and that became the standard expression of pro-Nicene orthodoxy, sometimes called "the Cappadocian achievement."

Basil was not the only one to respond to the Heteroousians in this period. Heteroousian gains brought other countermeasures in their wake. The Heteroousians started to run afoul of ecclesiastical and imperial authorities because of the disturbances they caused within churches. There was growing discord between Aetius and Eunomius and their former supporter, Eudoxius, who was made bishop of Constantinople at the January 360 council and was now even more influential throughout the East. Their ideas ran counter to mainstream theological developments. They found themselves in trouble with imperial authorities because of their political associations.[115] Nonetheless,

115. See Vaggione 267–311.

the appeal and vitality of the Heteroousian movement in the decades after the Council of Constantinople should not be underestimated. Basil undoubtedly calculated that he would propel himself into prominence by taking on so dangerous an enemy to the church.[116]

The Aftermath of the Debate between Basil and Eunomius

Aetius died in 366. The Heteroousians were increasingly viewed as a nuisance by ecclesiastical and imperial authorities alike. Soon after Demophilus succeeded Eudoxius in 370, Eunomius was banished to Naxos, an island in the Aegean. He would spend the next eight years there, until Gratian allowed the return of exiles after Valens's death in late 378. Probably during this period Eunomius began to write his *Apology for the Apology*, a defense of his original *Apology* in response to Basil's *Against Eunomius*. Why Eunomius waited so long to respond is unclear, but it may well be the case that early on he did not deem it worth his while to respond to a mere presbyter. But in 370 Basil had become the bishop of a major see, and Eunomius could promote his own cause by writing against so prominent an opponent.[117]

The work ran to five books, issued at intervals from 378 until the early 380s. Eunomius circulated the first books soon after his return from Naxos to Constantinople in late 378, making it unlikely that Basil ever received copies of it before his own death in September 378, despite Philostorgius's later claim that Basil died after reading it from the sorrow of being refuted.[118] Throughout his career Basil had remained concerned with combating Heteroousian theology, dealing with it in a number of his homilies and letters. Of particular note is his *Homily against Sabellians, Arius, and the Anomoians,* where he mockingly refers to Eunomius as "Anomius," playing on the popular characterization of Heteroousian theology as teaching that the Son was unlike (*anomoios*) the Father.[119]

116. Van Dam, *Becoming Christian*, 25–30.
117. Ibid., 30–33.
118. Philostorgius, *h.e.* 8.12.
119. *Hom.* 24. Others used the same slur.

The publication of the *Apology for the Apology* seems to have contributed to a resurgence of Heteroousian theology, which nonetheless sparked an immediate reaction.[120] In 380, while in Constantinople, Gregory of Nazianzus delivered three or four of his renowned *Theological Orations,* which were directed against Heteroousians.[121] Further east, news of the *Apology for the Apology* reached Gregory of Nyssa. He managed to borrow a copy of the first two books for only seventeen days.[122] Based on the notes he took, in 380 he wrote the initial installment of his own *Against Eunomius* against Eunomius's first book. In a letter to his brother Peter shortly thereafter, he wrote:

When the holy Basil fell asleep and I received the book of Eunomius, while my heart was still hot with passion and in anguish at this common misfortune of the churches, Eunomius not only wrote on the various topics which might pass as a defense of his own doctrine, but expended the greater part of his energy on laboriously written out abuses against our father (sc. Basil).[123]

Hence Gregory felt compelled to write against Eunomius not only to refute his theology but also to defend his brother against posthumous attacks. He considered himself Basil's heir in the doctrinal controversies of the era and the guardian of his brother's legacy. Gregory responded to Eunomius's second and third books between 380 and 383 (with the second and third books of his *Against Eunomius*). Ironically, Eunomius's *Apology for the Apology* is extant only in the fragments preserved by Gregory. Since Gregory never refuted the fourth and fifth books, nothing from them survives.[124]

Though Eunomius was becoming increasingly marginalized in the late 360s and 370s, the accession of Theodosius in 379 marked the beginning of the end for him. As key architects of pro-Nicene theology in the late 370s and early 380s, Gregory of Nazianzus and Gregory of Nyssa had made the refutation of Heteroousian theology one of their primary concerns. Theodo-

---

120. Kopecek 493–94.

121. *Or.* 27 and 29–30, possibly also 28. See Kopecek 495–503.

122. Gregory of Nyssa, *Ep.* 29.2.

123. Gregory of Nyssa, *Ep.* 29.4; trans. Silvas 207 (modified).

124. On Gregory's rivalry with Eunomius, see Van Dam, *Becoming Christian,* 33–37.

sius, as mentioned earlier, supported pro-Nicene Christianity, orchestrated its official adoption by the bishops at the Council of Constantinople in 381, and gave it imperial sanction. At the council, "Eunomians" were listed as one of the heretical groups, but of course this did not lead to their immediate dissolution. In 383 Theodosius summoned a "council of heresies" in an attempt to reconcile dissident groups deemed heretical at the Council of Constantinople. Representatives from various "heresies" were asked to present a written statement of faith so that it could be judged whether they should be rehabilitated and admitted to communion. Naturally Eunomius represented the Eunomians and composed a profession of faith (which is extant). Soon after, Gregory of Nyssa refuted it in his *A Refutation of Eunomius's Profession*. This would be Gregory's last work specifically against Eunomius. But other theologians of his and subsequent eras also took up the cause against Eunomius as well: Apollinarius, Didymus the Blind, Diodore of Tarsus, Theodore of Mopsuestia, and Theodoret of Cyrus are all said to have written treatises against him.[125] Many others, such as Cyril of Alexandria, refuted him in works on the Trinity.[126] In this era, it is almost as if a pro-Nicene theologian established his credentials by taking on the heresiarch Eunomius.

The "council of heresies" was a miserable failure. Theodosius rejected all but one of the statements of faith drafted by the various groups trying to be reconciled with the official church. Soon thereafter, Theodosius promulgated a number of decrees against the heretical groups, forbidding assembly and construction of churches, threatening confiscation of property if used in worship and even expulsion from the churches.[127] Nonetheless, in Constantinople and its suburbs Eunomius continued to meet with his followers privately and sought to win friends at the imperial court to redeem him.[128] When Theodosius discovered that Eunomius had supporters at his own court, he took swift

125. Richard Paul Vaggione, *Eunomius: The Extant Works* (Oxford: Clarendon, 1987), xiii.
126. Cyril of Alexandria, *Treasury on the Holy and Consubstantial Trinity*, PG 75.9–656.
127. Vaggione 329–30.
128. See Vaggione 350 and 354.

action against Eunomians. Seeing them as a threat to the imperial government, he outlawed the Eunomian community. In the summer of 389, Theodosius had Eunomius arrested, and, in the spring of 390, exiled to Cappadocian Caesarea, though he resided outside the city at an estate called Dacora because of the hatred of Caesarea's citizens for him. Despite his confinement, Eunomius still received visitors and oversaw the Eunomian community.[129] One of his visitors was a twenty-year-old Philostorgius, who later wrote a pro-Heteroousian history of the fourth-century church.[130]

Though it is hard to imagine, Eunomius's fortunes took a turn for the worse when Theodosius died in 395. The new eastern emperor Arcadius, a seventeen-year-old boy, fell under the influence of the eunuch Eutropius, who began a crackdown on Eunomians. In 396 he ordered the expulsion of Eunomians from the cities. Eunomius was transferred from Caesarea to a rustic monastic community in Tyana, where, as an old man now in his seventies, he died soon afterwards, perhaps during the winter of 396–397.[131] By this time all three of his Cappadocian opponents were dead. As mentioned earlier, Basil died in 378. Gregory of Nazianzus died in 390, and Gregory of Nyssa in 394 or 395. Eunomius may have outlived them all, but their efforts had ensured the bleak circumstances of his twilight years and the abiding notoriety of his name after his death.

IV. THE POLEMICAL AND THEOLOGICAL
CONTENT OF *AGAINST EUNOMIUS*

The Genre of Against Eunomius

Basil's *Against Eunomius* is a polemical treatise, a point-by-point refutation of the methodology and main tenets of Eunomius's Heteroousian theology as presented in his *Apology*. Basil proceeds by citing a few lines of Eunomius, then arguing at length against the suppositions or ideas expressed in the quotation. He does not cite every line of Eunomius's text, but only

---

129. Vaggione 355–57.   130. Philostorgius, *h.e.* 10.6.
131. Vaggione 357–60.

those lines needed for an adequate representation of his opponent's viewpoint.[132] In rare cases Basil omits parts of Eunomius's
text,[133] or alters it.[134] But for the most part Basil cites Eunomius
accurately and even paraphrases him fairly.[135] Precedents for
such a methodology in both Christian and philosophical sources include Origen's *Against Celsus*, Marcellus of Ancyra's *Against
Asterius*, Eusebius of Caesarea's *Against Marcellus*, and Iambli-
chus's *On the Mysteries*. Each author conducts his refutations in
the same way as Basil, alternating citation and refutation. After
Basil's death, Gregory of Nyssa refuted Eunomius's *Apology for
the Apology* in much the same manner as Basil had refuted the
original *Apology*. Accordingly, Basil's *Against Eunomius* stands in
a long tradition of polemical literature and needs to be interpreted as such.[136] As a consequence, the doctrine of the Trinity that Basil develops in *Against Eunomius* is not the product
of dispassionate "academic" reflection but an emotionally laden
defense of Christian truth (as Basil perceived it) against one of
its chief detractors.

The polemical character of *Against Eunomius* is most apparent in the sarcasm and *ad hominem* attacks on Eunomius, intertwined with real engagement with his opponent's ideas. While
such invective typically featured in polemical texts from antiquity, Basil displays a certain gusto in his vitriol. According to Basil, Eunomius is nothing more than a scheming, impious char-
latan who attempts to trick people into denying the divinity of
the Son of God. He is "lying, stupid, wanton, dissembling, and
blasphemous."[137] Basil blasts Eunomius again and again for the
arrogance he displays in so many ways: for wanting "to be pro-

132. See Drecoll 48–55 for a discussion of Basil's use of the *Apology*, esp. the
chart on p. 50.
133. E.g., in *Eun.* 2.18, Basil cites *Apol.* 15.3–7 (EW 50–52) but omits parts
of it.
134. E.g., in *Eun.* 2.20, Basil cites *Apol.* 15.14–15 (EW 52) but adds παρὰ
μόνου to Eunomius's text.
135. E.g., in *Eun.* 2.31, Basil paraphrases *Apol.* 20.13–15 (EW 60).
136. Drecoll 58 characterizes the *Eun.* as an "antihäretische Refutations-
schrift." The specific rhetorical-dialectical techniques employed by Basil in his
polemic are discussed by Drecoll 56–63 and Hildebrand 150–60.
137. *Eun.* 1.1.

claimed the pioneer and the patron of the entire heresy,"[138] for having an overblown sense of self-importance,[139] for introducing innovation into the faith of the fathers,[140] for claiming to know the substance of God,[141] and so forth. Basil attacks Eunomius with biting sarcasm. For example, he calls Eunomius's apology "brilliant."[142] He refers to Eunomius as "an unconquerable and clever writer"[143] and addresses him repeatedly as "the wisest of men."[144] He mocks him with such declarations as: "How noble he is for providing us with this theology of the begetting of the Only-Begotten!"[145] and "There is no thought that you don't have a knack for expressing!"[146] According to Basil, Eunomius is a liar in whom the devil speaks.[147] Basil over and over again accuses Eunomius of stupidity, craziness, insanity, madness, derangement, and utter foolishness.[148] On one occasion, Basil even goes so far as to call Eunomius a "whore,"[149] though in this case he couches his abuse in the words of scripture. Perhaps he did so to forestall criticism for using such a nasty expression.

Some modern readers of Basil may find such insults and sarcastic language unsuitable for a person whom some consider a saint and father of the church. Others, however, may find Basil's vituperation, or at least some of it, effective and even hilarious.[150] But, more to the point, Basil's depiction of Eunomius is a willful distortion of the truth, and his ancient readers, familiar with the polemical genre, would have known this, not been surprised by it, and in fact expected it. If Eunomius were so per-

---

138. *Eun.* 1.1.   139. *Eun.* 1.3.
140. *Eun.* 1.1, 1.4, and 1.9.   141. *Eun.* 1.12, 1.13, and 2.30.
142. *Eun.* 1.1.   143. *Eun.* 1.2.
144. *Eun.* 1.2, 1.5, 1.21, 2.10, and 2.24; cf. "noblest of men" (βέλτιστε), *Eun.* 2.23.
145. *Eun.* 2.14.   146. *Eun.* 2.21.
147. *Eun.* 1.3, 1.9, and 1.16.
148. One example suffices: "If this is the case, what need is there to respond to such stupidity? For it would be just as if we were fighting against someone whom delirium has deprived of reason" (*Eun.* 2.21).
149. *Eun.* 1.23: "So, then, let us state a response to him using the words of the prophet: *You've acquired the face of a whore; you have no shame before anyone* [Jer 3.3]."
150. Georgios Tsananas, "Humor bei Basilius dem Grossen," in Anastasios Kallis, ed., *Philoxenia* (Münster: Aschendorff, 1980), 259–79 at 272–73, sees a few of Basil's zingers in *Eun.* as evidence that Basil had a sense of humor.

verse in as many ways as Basil's caricature makes him out to be, it would be hard to account for Eunomius's many successes and his appeal to his followers. Yet the tendency to be uncharitable in polemical literature becomes significant when one interprets such texts. Basil not only depicts Eunomius's character uncharitably, but sometimes he also interprets his *Apology* uncharitably. In other words, even if Basil for the most part cites and paraphrases Eunomius accurately, when he interprets Eunomius, he at times can twist Eunomius's words to indicate something their author never intended. It is difficult to determine whether such misinterpretations are willful or not; it is, however, best in such cases to be prudently suspicious.[151] Therefore, when reading *Against Eunomius,* the interpreter needs to be aware that Basil may be purposely misinterpreting or distorting the meaning of Eunomius's text. Basil does this to score debating points against his opponent, to depict him in the worst possible light, and to set up a "strawman" in contrast to which he can present his own ideas. This is not to say that Basil always or even for the most part interprets Eunomius uncharitably; in many cases, or even most, Basil astutely points out the flaws in Eunomius's arguments. The point here is that the validity of any of Basil's interpretations of Eunomius cannot be judged *solely* on what Basil says but must be supplemented by constant reference to the text of Eunomius's *Apology* itself.

Besides the polemical vitriol, the juridical character of the work also bears upon its interpretation. Basil constructs his treatise as a written response to an oral defense that Eunomius claims to have made before a certain ecclesiastical court. This construction is a mocking response to Eunomius's choice to present his teachings under the form of an apology (ἀπολογία). A common genre in ancient rhetoric, an apology was meant to defend its author when impugned or the author's views when they had come under attack. Basil suspects that Eunomius chose the genre of apology in order to provide a pretext for an exposition of his impious teachings. In claiming to write an apology,

---

151. E.g., in *Eun.* 1.5, Basil cites *Apol.* 7.9–11 (EW 40) and misinterprets the phrase ἀκολουθεῖ τούτῳ. See Anastos, "Basil's *Κατὰ Εὐνομίου*," 78–80.

Eunomius implies that it is legitimate and necessary for him to defend his views against slander.[152] Basil doubts that Eunomius was ever compelled to deliver his apology orally. He compares the *Apology* to an imaginary school exercise and to shadowboxing.[153]

Basil's chief basis for accusing Eunomius of such duplicity is his failure to name his attackers. He denies that Eunomius could have delivered his *Apology* at one of the two recent councils in the East: Seleucia in late 359 or Constantinople in January 360. In each case, Basil argues, Eunomius had no need to defend his views against opponents. Hence, he concludes, the *Apology* is a literary fiction.[154] Despite Basil's denials, Eunomius probably delivered the initial form of his *Apology* at Constantinople in 360.[155] In making contrary claims, Basil is more concerned with depicting Eunomius as a liar than establishing historical fact.

Despite his denial that the *Apology* was actually delivered in a juridical context, Basil "plays along with" the document's apologetic genre and refutes it as such.[156] The treatise is a point-by-point refutation of Eunomius's Heteroousian theology and seeks to convince the reader that Eunomius has distorted the Christian faith and is a danger to believers. As the ancient genre of judicial oratory calls upon the audience to render a judgment in a court of law, *Against Eunomius* is best viewed as a Christian adaptation of the genre.[157] Basil constructs his reader as a member of the jury. He at times even uses the language of the law courts. For example, in a mocking paraphrase Basil puts the following words into Eunomius's mouth to demonstrate his arrogance: "Why do you judge me harshly, gentlemen of the jury? For I have ascended to the very pinnacle of virtue, transcended earthly matters, and transferred my entire way of life to heaven!"[158] In another instance Basil says that he is willing to have

152. *Eun.* 1.2.   153. *Eun.* 2.1.

154. *Eun.* 1.2; cf. 2.9.   155. See n. 110 above.

156. In his *Apology for the Apology*, Eunomius appears to have interpreted this as an admission on the part of Basil that the *Apol.* was not a literary fiction; see Gregory of Nyssa, *Eun.* 1.86 (GNO 1.51).

157. On judicial oratory, see George A. Kennedy, *Greek Rhetoric Under Christian Emperors* (Princeton: Princeton University Press, 1983), 6–19.

158. *Eun.* 1.3.

his entire objection stricken from the record if Eunomius can produce scriptural evidence for his claim.[159] Sometimes Basil refers to Eunomius in the second person singular and directly addresses questions to him, as if he is examining him; sometimes Basil refers to him in the third person singular (or third plural, including his fellow Heteroousians), as if he is speaking about Eunomius to the jury.[160] And so, when reading *Against Eunomius* one must keep in mind that, in line with judicial oratory, Basil is concerned with furnishing incontrovertible proof of Eunomius's impiety. He seeks to highlight Eunomius's errors in logic or doctrine; prove that they are in fact dangerous, impious errors; and refute them. Basil is not primarily presenting his own theology of the Trinity, but developing a Trinitarian theology to disprove the validity of his opponent's.

As for the impieties of Eunomius, Basil is so horrified at them that at times he cannot even bring himself to utter them. On two occasions he refrains from expressing what he considers a terrible blasphemy by purposely omitting to state the apodosis of a conditional or to draw the inference from premises, saying something like: "It is better for us to leave this blasphemous statement incomplete."[161] On other occasions he alerts his reader that he is about to say something irreligious or begs God for mercy for saying such a thing.[162] According to Bernard Sesboüé, "this scruple . . . attests to the strength of the link that exists among theological discourse, the profession of faith, and the adoration of mystery. It witnesses as well to the value of every utterance, even if the one who said it explains that it does not reflect his own thought."[163] It also serves a rhetorical purpose: as a pious Christian, Basil will not even dare to whisper the blasphemies that the impious Eunomius publicizes to the world and blurts out to everybody.[164] Basil's construction of himself as a pi-

---

159. *Eun.* 2.8.

160. E.g., *Eun.* 1.24. Drecoll's analysis of the verbal forms Basil uses to address his audience in part leads him to argue that the *Eun.* is not a unified text, but a hodgepodge of reworked texts (Drecoll 48–55). It seems to us that Drecoll has overlooked that *Eun.* is an adaptation of juridical oratory.

161. See *Eun.* 1.17 and 2.15. The citation is from 1.17.

162. See *Eun.* 2.12 and 2.33.   163. SC 299.233 n. 1.

164. See *Eun.* 1.13.

ous Christian in contrast to the impious Eunomius is but one of his polemical ploys to sway the "jury."

One final element may be operative in Basil's refutation of Eunomius: anti-rhetorical polemic. Richard Vaggione has provocatively argued that echoes of "a war of rival asceticisms" in the fourth century are heard in the vituperation of pro-Nicene, anti-Eunomian polemics.[165] The pro-Nicenes drew on tried-and-true anti-rhetorical tropes that philosophers had leveled for centuries against rhetors. Nicene controversialists who championed the more rigorous, monastic form of asceticism that emerged in the fourth century lampooned as "rhetorical profligacy" the traditional asceticism of "studied moderation" practiced by Eunomius, Aetius, and others of their circle. They present Eunomius and Aetius as rhetorical elites who cultivated the rich and famous and frequented "the cocktail-party circuit," and smear that circle as dedicated urbanites who participated in traditional civic life. But Nicenes claim to have opted out of the traditional structures of power and influence and to have disdained rhetorical fluff, withdrawing from the world to practice strict asceticism in monastic seclusion (even if still a metropolitan bishop!). However more complex the situation was, the invective of this "war of rival asceticisms" drew on themes from the pre-existing debate between philosophy and rhetoric.

Basil may be drawing on the anti-rhetorical features of this debate in his polemical characterization of Eunomius. He repeatedly accuses Eunomius of employing sophisms rather than substantive arguments.[166] Such moves on Eunomius's part are deceptive, a use of trickery and scare-tactics to establish his own teaching.[167] Basil, for example, describes Eunomius's bogus "proof" that God is unbegotten (a concept that even Eunomius said to be self-evident) as tantamount to someone attempting to argue that the sun is the brightest star in the sky

165. See Vaggione 181–97; idem, "Of Monks and Lounge Lizards: 'Arians,' Polemics and Asceticism in the Roman East," in Michel R. Barnes and Daniel H. Williams, eds., *Arianism after Arius: Essays on the Development of the Fourth Century Trinitarian Conflicts* (Edinburgh: T&T Clark, 1993), 181–214.

166. E.g., *Eun.* 2.11.

167. See *Eun.* 2.28.

at high noon.[168] Basil surmises that Eunomius engages in such specious argumentation to enhance his reputation as virtuoso rhetor: "It seems to me that he boasts along with his followers that he is shrewd and subtle in mind, quick to spot an absurdity and even quicker to demolish it once detected, and it is for this reason that he takes pride in how his arguments take twists and turns, and so puts on a fine show."[169] Finally, Basil employs a stock feature of anti-rhetorical polemic when he mocks the fatuity of rhetorical speechifying: "as if dreaming that you're in a forum or addressing an assembly of drunkards, where no one can hear or understand what is being said, you legislate on the basis of your full indemnity, thinking that it is sufficient to say, 'I have spoken,' instead of providing a full demonstration."[170] Accordingly, it appears that Basil has employed features of anti-rhetorical polemic against Eunomius, a polemic that his successors Gregory of Nyssa and Theodore of Mopsuestia employed as well.[171]

Therefore, because of its multiform polemics and juridical oratory, Basil's *Against Eunomius* is not a systematic work on Trinitarian theology, nor should it be interpreted as if it were. The structure of Basil's treatise and the arrangement of topics is for the most part governed by the order of Eunomius's *Apology*.[172] Basil's scorn for Eunomius and the distortions inherent in his character assassination at times carry over to his theological refutations. Basil is more concerned with proving Eunomius wrong than with formulating a systematic account of how the Father and the Son are related. One can still recover a more or less consistent doctrine of the Trinity from *Against Eunomius*, even if it is not as seamless and integrated as a modern researcher would like. Doing so requires an analysis of the accuracy of

168. *Eun.* 1.5.
169. Ibid.
170. *Eun.* 2.9; see Vaggione 184–85, for the anti-rhetorical trope of the rhetor's penchant for drinking parties.
171. On Gregory and Theodore, see Vaggione 185–86; idem, "Of Monks and Lounge Lizards," 184.
172. Only in *Eun.* 2.30–31 does Basil cite Eunomius out of order; see Drecoll 50.

Basil's various interpretations and refutations of Eunomius and how they connect with each other.

Synopsis: The Major Arguments of Against Eunomius

When one considers the contentious and unsystematic character of this text, it is easy to assume that Basil simply talks past Eunomius, making counter-assertions rather than arguments. There is certainly some of that in this text. Indeed, when he denounces Eunomius's ideas as insane and his arguments as based on false pretenses, Basil himself lends support to the notion that the opposition's theology is so warped as to be incommensurable with what Basil takes to be right thinking.

And yet, this line of interpretation only goes so far. The two sides in this debate appeal to the same sources: both claim to base their views on scripture and common notions.[173] As Richard Vaggione has noted, this claim is itself a rhetorical move that one should take with suspicion in that both portray themselves as simply reporting the "obvious" teaching of the Bible and common sense.[174] Nonetheless, it indicates the profound areas of common ground in this debate. Eunomius and Basil share a scriptural vocabulary, interwoven with long-standing traditions in Christian theology such as emphasizing (over against Gnostics and pagans) the idea that God is without origin or "unbegotten." The debate between them is not about whether to use names like Father, Son, and Spirit, or whether to apply the term 'God' to Father and Son (as we will see, the case of the Spirit is trickier). The debate is primarily about how to divide up or, to switch metaphors, how to map the territory: it is about what is meant when God is said to be unbegotten or Father or good, not *whether* one should say these things in the first place. Therefore, the major themes and arguments of *Against Eunomius* are attempts on Basil's part to redraw the map of the common ground shared even with his opponent.

An example can illustrate the "second-order" character of the debate (it is language about language). The substantive por-

173. On common notions, see p. 91 n. 34.
174. Vaggione 85–93.

tion of Eunomius's *Apology* opens with a brief and rather bland creedal statement, which Basil cites.[175] Eunomius claims that this statement is the inerrant rule and criterion governing theological assertions. Accordingly, he claims that the more controversial theological claims are in keeping with this statement. Basil's response is instructive: he does not oppose the content of the creed. Rather, he argues that it is illogical to hold that something is an inerrant criterion *and* that it needs correction or supplementation. Of course, Basil's interpretation is malicious. When Eunomius fleshes out the bare bones of the creed with his theological proposals, he is not claiming to correct or supplement his criterion, but merely to explicate it. Basil surely goes too far in attacking Eunomius on this point. But he is not wrong to perceive that the debate is not about the words of the creed itself, but about how they are interpreted through additional, more controversial claims. The debate is not, then, a clash of creeds, but of interpretations of creeds (which are in turn assumed to be interpretations of scripture). Of course, Basil and Eunomius ultimately endorse different creeds, but we should not be distracted by viewing this as a debate about the famous catchwords like *homoousios* ("same in substance") or *homoiousios* ("like in substance") versus *heteroousios* ("different in substance"). This would mistake the rhetoric of *Against Eunomius*. Basil cites the profession of faith offered by Eunomius as in broad strokes acceptable to both of them.

So how does Basil propose we interpret the complex terrain of scriptural and creedal language? It will be helpful first to give an overview of four fundamental themes in Basil's response to Eunomius:

(1) the role of human conceptualization in theology;

(2) the distinction between positive and negative theological terms;

(3) the distinction between names said in common of the Father and Son and names said specifically of each; and

(4) the distinction between what is true of God *in se* and from eternity and what God has done on behalf of humans whose perspective is inherently temporally structured.

175. *Eun.* 1.4.

After walking through each of these, we will be able to see how these general theological themes enable Basil to articulate a new understanding of the eternal origin or "begetting" of the Son and to reclaim key disputed passages in scripture—his fundamental source—from Eunomius's interpretation of them. We will also see that it is unclear how the Holy Spirit fits into Basil's theological vision at this point in his career.

First, according to Basil, we need to be aware that some of the things we say about God are devised through a process called 'conceptualization' (in Greek, *epinoia*) and that this is not necessarily a bad thing. This observation is in direct contradiction to Aetius and Eunomius, who argued that any theological idea devised via conceptualization must be false. Both sides agree on what it is to engage in conceptualization: it is subsequent reflection on an initial concept. Basil cites the instance of grain. Everyone has the natural concept of grain. But this common notion can be broken down into a variety of concepts based on one's perspective: "It is 'fruit' as the result of farming that has been completed, 'seed' as the beginning of farming to come, and 'nourishment' as what is suitable for the development of the body of the one who eats it."[176]

The term 'conceptualization' comes to denote both the act of reflection and the concepts devised from it. When mythological poets invented the conceptualization of the hippocentaur, they did so by imaginatively combining the concepts of horse and human. Aetius's and Eunomius's worry is that using this kind of reflection in theology will *necessarily* yield fictions along the lines of the hippocentaur. They propose instead that we conform all our thinking about God to God's real, essential attribute, which for them is unbegottenness.

Basil has concerns with the word 'unbegotten.' It is not in scripture, and so it is better to stick with terms like 'Father' and 'Son,' which have biblical pedigree and connote a mutual relation.[177] Moreover, if this is the definition of 'God,' then obviously the *only-begotten* Son is not God, at least not in the same way the Unbegotten is. But, importantly, Basil does not deny

176. *Eun.* 1.6.
177. *Eun.* 1.5.

that God is unbegotten. For him, that would be like denying that the sun is the brightest heavenly body at high noon.[178] He does, however, reinterpret unbegottenness as a concept devised through human conceptualization, rather than as the essence of God.[179] We do not state the definition of God's substance, the *logos tês ousias* of God, when we say God is 'unbegotten.' This term is merely what we say when, reflecting on the life of God and casting our minds backwards, so to speak, we note that this life has no beginning. It makes sense within a temporal framework to deny that God's life has a beginning and an end; such a denial serves a useful function in purifying our minds. But it is mistaken to claim that terms derived from time-bound perspectives state God's very essence. Indeed, Basil famously claims in this text and elsewhere that humans cannot know *what* God is. 'Unbegotten' merely tells us "what God is like"—not "what God is."[180]

Moreover, 'unbegotten' only tells us what God is *not*, not what God is. This brings us to the second major theme in Basil's theological cartography: the distinction of positive and negative theological terms. When we say God is unbegotten, we are simply saying that God is not begotten; we are removing an inappropriate concept from our thinking about God.[181] For Basil, we point to no positive state with this term. This contrasts again with Aetius and Eunomius, who argued that 'unbegotten' is not a privative term in meaning (that is, that the sense of it is not merely 'not-begotten'), but indicates God's substance.

There are of course other negative terms besides 'unbegotten' (such as 'invisible'), but not all adequate theological terms are negative. We call God 'light,' 'good,' 'just,' and so forth. These terms function in a different way than the negative terms because positive terms do not simply remove inappropriate notions from our thinking but somehow give us positive content. There has been a great deal of debate over how to take these terms: are they all derived through conceptualization? Are they predicated of God's substance or merely God's activities (*energeiai*)? These debates must be left to the side for now, except

178. Ibid.
180. *Eun.* 1.15.
179. *Eun.* 1.7.
181. *Eun.* 1.9.

to note that Basil does predicate these positive terms of God's substance in this text, saying that they indicate God's "distinguishing feature."[182]

And that leads to the third theme, which is the division of things we say about God into those that are said in common of the Father and Son (leaving to the side the question of the Spirit) and those that apply uniquely to each. Again, Basil divides up the territory differently from Eunomius, who would deny that there are any terms said in common of the Unbegotten and the Begotten—let alone the Spirit—*with the same signification.* He argues that terms that scripture uses of both the Unbegotten and the Begotten, such as 'light,' mean different things in the two cases. Perhaps Basil's single greatest contribution to Trinitarian theology in *Against Eunomius* is his argument that there are terms predicated of Father and Son in common and with the same sense.[183] These terms name what Basil calls "the commonality of the substance," and they are the same set of terms that, as mentioned above, name the "distinguishing feature" of God's substance.[184] So, when the Bible says that the Father *dwells in unapproachable light* (1 Tim 6.16), and that the Son is the *true light* (Jn 1.9), the term 'light' means the same thing in both instances.

But Basil also holds that some terms refer just to the Son and others just to the Father. For instance, the Son is 'begotten' and the Father 'unbegotten.' These terms name the "distinguishing marks" of the two.[185] The language here can be confusing: Basil uses the same family of terms, all based on the adjective ἴδιος, for both what is unique to a common nature or substance and what is unique to each individual that shares that common nature. The first can be thought of along the lines of what Porphyrian logic (drawing on Aristotle) called *propria.* These are features peculiar to a kind but which do not define the kind. So, for instance, laughing is peculiar to humans, but does not define the essence of humanity. In the same way, the divine power, goodness, light, and life are proper to the divine na-

---

182. *Eun.* 2.29.
183. See Drecoll's account of 'light' as common term, pp. 103–11.
184. *Eun.* 1.19.
185. *Eun.* 2.28.

ture. The second use of terms based on ἴδιος can be thought of roughly along the lines of differentiating features. When Basil is speaking about unique features of the second kind in *Against Eunomius,* he even uses the standard philosophical examples of differentiae of the genus of "animal": being winged or footed, aquatic or terrestrial, rational or irrational.[186] These features distinguish various species within this genus. Of course, Father and Son are not species under a common genus. Nonetheless, the relation of differentiae to common features provides a useful model for thinking about the relation of the distinguishing marks of Father and Son to the properties they share in common. Like all models, it is ultimately inadequate. But it does help us dimly see that there can be distinguishing marks that do not undermine unity of substance.

Basil argues that only when we grasp simultaneously both the common and the distinguishing features do we begin to understand the Father and the Son. So the Father is best thought of as "unbegotten light," while the Son is "begotten light."[187] As begotten light who *qua* light differs in no way from the Father, the Son is able to illumine human minds with the knowledge of the Father.[188]

We come now to our fourth theme, the distinction between those things we say of God that are not direct references to God's provident and incarnate involvement in the temporal and material conditions of the world and those things we say of God that are. This is the sense of Basil's distinction, which is less systematic in his works than in some of his interpreters, between things said in scripture "in the mode of theology" and those in which a biblical author "intimates the reasons of the economy."[189] It is important to be precise here: Basil neither upholds two "phases" of God, nor does he distinguish between an economic and an immanent Trinity. As Lewis Ayres says, "Basil generally uses θεολογία of a mode of insight into the nature of God that comes as a result of an ability to see beyond material reality, or beyond the material-sounding phraseology of some

---

186. Ibid.
188. *Eun.* 1.17; 2.16.

187. *Eun.* 2.28.
189. *Eun.* 2.3.

scriptural passages."[190] So, for instance, when Scripture speaks of the Father "begetting" the Son, it is not referring to a temporal event performed for our sakes; it is speaking "theologically." But when Scripture speaks of Christ taking the form of a slave, being born, and being crucified, it is speaking "economically." Basil uses this scheme to explain the different approaches of the four canonical evangelists. Whereas the authors of the synoptic Gospels (Matthew, Mark, and Luke) focused on Christ's origins "according to the flesh" and "approached the theology by going through the corporeal origins," John began directly with the eternal origin of the Word from God.[191] Since John "left behind all corporeal and temporal notions as lower than his theology, he surpasses the preaching of the preceding evangelists on account of the nobility of his knowledge."[192] With this move, Basil can separate the Gospel accounts of the Son's origins into the economic and the theological and can focus solely on the latter. John's Gospel thus provides an entry-point into speaking of the Word's origin in a way not bound to temporal or spatial sequences. This serves his purpose in arguing against Eunomius, though Basil never suggests that the synoptic Gospels, which narrate Christ's origins "according to the flesh," are less valuable in other regards or that John's masterpiece has rendered them obsolete.

The economy-theology distinction also helps Basil deal with Eunomius's claim that, just as the Father's essential title is 'unbegotten,' the Son's essential titles include the terms 'something begotten' (γέννημα) and 'something made' (ποίημα). The titles are not explicitly scriptural, though they could be drawn from a text like Acts 2.36: *God has made him Lord and Christ, this Jesus whom you crucified.* By a simple grammatical transformation, one could move from "God made him" to calling him "something made." But Basil counters by arguing that the Acts passage has nothing to do with "the subsistence of the Only-

190. Ayres 220. See also Behr 291, and Christopher A. Beeley, *Gregory of Nazianzus on the Trinity and the Knowledge of God* (Oxford: Oxford University Press, 2008), 296.

191. *Eun.* 2.15.

192. Ibid.

Begotten before the ages" or with "the very substance of God the Word." The text is not about "theology," but rather "intimates the reasons of the economy."[193] In other words, the passage is not spinning a metaphysical myth about the Word's origin from the Father, but is speaking about the rule and power of Jesus, which the Father has granted to him in time.

If the begetting of the Son is outside of time and space, then the kind of subordination Eunomius argued for cannot stand. In the context of interpreting the key disputed passage Jn 14.28, in which Christ says, *The Father is greater than I*, Basil concedes that the Father is greater than the Son in the way a cause is greater than its effect. This kind of superiority, however, does not imply that the Father is greater at the level of substance. Nor is the Father greater in power, since, according to 1 Cor 1.24, Christ is the power of God.[194] Basil envisions the Son as standing in a relation of causal dependence upon the Father, but a relation that is outside of time and space and hence utterly incomprehensible to human minds.[195]

In closing, some comment is needed on the theology of the Holy Spirit, which appears principally in the third book of *Against Eunomius*. Just as Basil was prepared to speak of the Son as inferior *qua* caused by the Father, so too does he speak of the Spirit as lesser—or, more precisely, "third"—in dignity and rank than both Father and Son.[196] But he does not believe that this ranking justifies speaking of the Spirit as belonging to a third *nature* "foreign" from the nature of the Father and the Son.[197] To the contrary, the Spirit, just like the Father and the Son, possesses holiness by nature, and not by participation and good deeds, as created, angelic powers possess holiness. It is unclear, however, to what extent here Basil wishes to extend to the Spirit the logic of common terms said of the shared nature of the Father and the Son; later he explicitly does so.[198] For Basil, the Holy Spirit's goodness is clearly not a matter of acquiring a quality from some external source; goodness is simply who the

193. *Eun.* 2.3.
195. *Eun.* 2.11–14.
197. *Eun.* 3.3.

194. *Eun.* 1.22–25.
196. *Eun.* 3.1.
198. *Ep.* 236.

Spirit is. He does not specify how this relates to the Father and the Son, for whom the same can be said. Though the Spirit's inherent goodness separates him from the created realm (Basil is indeed adamant to deny that the Spirit is created through the Word), Basil's vision of the role of the Spirit in the divine activity of creating nonetheless remains unclear. He argues, through a reading of such texts as Ps 32.6, that the Spirit does not create, but perfects the created realm.[199] And yet Basil enumerates several activities the Spirit does perform: adopting the faithful as sons of God, teaching them, distributing spiritual gifts, scrutinizing the depths of God,[200] giving new life to Christians in Christ, and making them the dwelling-place of God. He appeals to the practice of glorifying the Spirit and counting him along with Father and Son, particularly in the baptismal formula. So, in sum, the Spirit's nature is in some sense divine. And yet the Spirit's dignity and rank remain lesser than the Father's and the Son's, and the Spirit's activities are distinct from theirs. There are many questions Basil admits he cannot answer about the Spirit or even about created phenomena. We can end our overview, then, with Basil's own question: "So, then, why is it shocking that we are not ashamed to confess our ignorance even in the case of the Holy Spirit, but we still render him the glorification for which there is undeniable testimony?"[201]

Basil's teaching on the Spirit continued to develop throughout his career. He later distanced himself from Eustathius of Sebasteia, who apparently continued to exclude the Spirit from the divine activity of creating.[202] Yet Basil never went as far as his brother or Gregory of Nazianzus in opposing the "Pneumatomachian" or "Spirit-fighting" followers of Eustathius and affirming the Spirit's divinity and equal involvement in the ac-

199. *Eun.* 3.4.
200. Already in *Eun.* 1.14, Basil states that the Holy Spirit—like the Son and unlike created rational beings—comprehends the substance of God.
201. *Eun.* 3.6.
202. This denial of the Spirit's involvement in the activity of creating is central to the "Pneumatomachian" position that Gregory of Nyssa opposes in the early 380s in his work against followers of the then-deceased Eustathius. See Gregory's works *To Eustathius On the Holy Trinity* (written to a different Eustathius) and *Against the Macedonians On the Holy Spirit.*

tivities of the Father and the Son. Basil always retained something of the reticence and sense of unfathomable mystery we see in the third book *Against Eunomius*. He also retained the conviction that one can go on glorifying the Father, Son, and Spirit, the divine mystery whom the worshiper only imperfectly knows.[203]

V. AN INQUIRY INTO BASIL'S SOURCES

Scripture and Basil's Exegesis of Scripture

One of Basil's primary sources in *Against Eunomius* is scripture. His use of scripture includes explicit citations, verbal reminiscences, and allusions. Like most theologians of his era, Basil develops his doctrine of God by reflecting upon and interpreting scripture. For Basil, good theology consists in explicating what scripture reveals about God and standing in silent adoration before the mystery of what it does not reveal. Scripture not only reveals the content of theology, but also instructs the theologian in how language operates.[204] Scripture dictates what the theologian can and cannot say. This is not to say that Basil did not approach the scriptures with metaphysical assumptions about God. He would have seen these assumptions confirmed by scripture. For Basil, scripture is the foundation and touchstone for all theology.

Scripture for Basil meant of course the Septuagint translation of the Hebrew Bible and the Greek New Testament. Nonetheless, he was aware of other translations of the Old Testament (both Greek and Syriac) and of textual variants in both the Old and the New Testament.[205] Sometimes he preferred one alternative over the other if it suited his purposes; otherwise, he found meaning in both.[206] Only the Gospel of Matthew in Basil has been subjected to a detailed text-critical study and was found to be the earliest known witness to the Byzantine text-

---

203. See *Ep.* 234.

204. See Rousseau 113–14.

205. Other Greek translations: *Eun.* 1.20, 37–44; *Ps.* 59.4; *Ps.* 32.5. Syriac translations: *Hex.* 2.6. Textual variants: *Eun.* 2.19; *Hex.* 4.5; *Ps.* 28.1.

206. See Hildebrand 112–14 for more details.

type, though not in all of its details.[207] Nonetheless, in *Against Eunomius*, Basil's citations for the most part correspond to the standard Greek text as established by modern textual criticism (Rahlfs and Nestle-Aland[27]). At times his scriptural citations are actually conflations of two passages.[208] At times his citations vary in minor ways from the standard texts, but only rarely do they diverge significantly.[209]

Basil placed such a high value on scripture because he viewed it as inspired. Like most patristic authors, he offers little sustained reflection on the meaning and implications of a doctrine of scriptural inspiration. But like most early Christians, he understood inspiration primarily in prophetic terms, meaning that the Spirit inspired the scriptural authors when they spoke or wrote.[210] The scriptures are a product of the Spirit's activity.[211] Basil compares the authors of scripture to flutes played by the Spirit.[212] In *Against Eunomius*, he says that the "saints" (Basil's term for the scriptural authors) spoke "in the power of the Spirit"[213] or "in the Spirit of God."[214] But inspiration for Basil was not only a question of the Spirit's activity in the scriptural writers; it was also a question of the quality of the scriptural text itself. In *Against Eunomius* Basil repeatedly refers to the words of scripture as the very words of the Holy Spirit.[215] Scripture is nothing other than the teachings of the Spirit.[216] What is not explicitly said in scripture indicates the silence of the Spirit, that is, what the scriptures do not intend to teach.[217] Scripture contains no idle syllable; each word is significant.[218] Basil accords

---

207. Jean-François Racine, *The Text of Matthew in the Writings of Basil of Caesarea* (Atlanta: Society of Biblical Literature/Boston: Brill, 2004).

208. See *Eun.* 1.14 (1 Cor 2.10–11 + 1 Cor 2.12); 3.3 (Lam 4.20 + Ps 56.2).

209. See *Eun.* 1.17 (Jn 14.9); 3.3 (Lam 4.20).

210. William A. Tieck, "Basil of Caesarea and the Bible" (Ph.D. diss., Columbia University, 1953), 92–101; Hildebrand 109–10.

211. See *Ps.* 1.1; *Spir.* 21.52; *Hex.* 1.1.

212. See *Ps.* 29.7; see also *Ps.* 45.1 and 48.2; *Hex.* 8.8.

213. *Eun.* 1.21.

214. *Eun.* 2.19.

215. See *Eun.* 1.17, 1.18, 2.7, 2.8, 2.14, 2.15, 2.17, and 2.24.

216. See *Eun.* 1.1, 1.8, 1.9, 1.12, 2.1, 2.7, and 2.16.

217. See *Eun.* 2.2 and 3.7; *Hex.* 9.1.

218. See *Hex.* 6.11; *Hom.* 16.4.

the utmost respect to each word of scripture because it is nothing less than a word of the Spirit.

At the same time, in *Against Eunomius* Basil appears to acknowledge degrees of inspiration. He recognizes that the scriptures are not merely words about God that are inspired by the Spirit, but that the Son speaks for himself in the scriptures.[219] Such passages have extraordinary importance for Basil. He also places Paul and John in a special category of particularly inspired authors.[220] In Basil's understanding of inspiration there remains an unresolved tension between the Spirit's authorship and the role of the human authors.[221] Nonetheless, because Basil believed that the scriptures were inspired, they were for him the authoritative and true "divine scripture,"[222] "divine oracles,"[223] or "divine word,"[224] the basis for all Christian theological reflection and knowledge of God. For him the Bible is "the rule of life, it is the standard of faith and morals, it is the source of doctrine. It constitutes the supreme *regula* in all spheres."[225]

Basil's hermeneutical assumptions and exegetical methodology in *Against Eunomius* have not been the subject of detailed study. It cannot simply be assumed that he subscribed to Origen's principles of exegesis, statements of which constitute the bulk of the texts compiled in the Origenian florilegium, the *Philocalia*. Basil may owe to Origen his belief that proper exegesis can occur only within the context of an ascetic way of life, which ensures the necessary attention for reading and interpreting scripture.[226] And he certainly believes that interpretation demands the assistance of the Spirit.[227] But these atti-

219. Examples from Book 1: *Eun.* 1.17 and 1.18.

220. *Eun.* 1.12 (Paul); *Eun.* 2.15; *Hom.* 16.1 (John).

221. Tieck, "Basil of Caesarea," 98–101 provides insufficient evidence for his claim that "Basil leaves no doubt that he conceives of the inspired authors as being in full possession of their judgment and faculties. The illapse of the Spirit does not displace their individuality and independence" (100).

222. See *Eun.* 2.8.   223. See *Eun.* 1.6 and 2.8.

224. See *Eun.* 1.7 and 2.2.   225. Tieck, "Basil of Caesarea," 127–28.

226. Peter W. Martens, "Interpreting Attentively: The Ascetic Character of Biblical Exegesis according to Origen and Basil of Caesarea," *Origeniana octava* (Leuven: Leuven University Press, 2003), 2.1115–21.

227. Tieck, "Basil of Caesarea," 101–5.

tudes are hardly unique to Basil. Most studies of Basil's exegesis concentrate on other writings in his corpus and focus on the dichotomy between historical and allegorical methods, or Antiochene and Alexandrian schools of exegesis, viewing Basil as a kind of proto-Antiochene who anticipates modern scientific exegesis.[228] But such categories make no sense of Basil's exegesis in *Against Eunomius*. Stephen Hildebrand has attempted an alternative approach of identifying "scriptural centers"—particular sets of passages or scriptural ideas used to interpret others—in *Against Eunomius* as well as *On the Holy Spirit*.[229] Useful investigations of Basil's exegesis have appeared in recent Italian scholarship, which take *Against Eunomius* into account.[230] Nonetheless, a thoroughgoing study of Basil's exegesis in *Against Eunomius* remains a scholarly *desideratum*. Here we mention three brief points about Basil's exegetical assumptions and methodology in *Against Eunomius*.

First, Basil believes in the unity of the scriptures. In other words, the Old and New Testaments narrate a single story of salvation history that begins with creation and culminates in Jesus Christ. But such an assumption is hardly unique to Basil and can be found in most church fathers. Nonetheless, it means that, for Basil, the Father, Son, and Holy Spirit are revealed in both the Old and New Testaments. A few examples suffice to demonstrate this. Ps 109.3 (*From the womb before the daybreak I have begotten you*) is as important for understanding the Son as Jn 1.1 (*In the beginning was the Word*) is: the former speaks of his begetting,

228. Hugo Weiss, *Die grossen Kappadocier Basilius, Gregor von Nazianz und Gregor von Nyssa als Exegeten* (Braunsberg: A. Martens, 1872); Tieck, "Basil of Caesarea," 157–78; Richard Lim, "The Politics of Interpretation in Basil of Caesarea's *Hexaemeron*," *Vigiliae Christianae* 44 (1990): 351–70; Hildebrand 122–39. For further bibliography, see Charles Kannengiesser, *Handbook of Patristic Exegesis* (Leiden and Boston: Brill, 2006), 740–47.

229. Hildebrand 160–72 and 178–87.

230. Mieczysław Celestyn Paczkowski, *Esegesi, teologia e mistica. Il prologo di Giovanni nelle opere di S. Basilio Magno* (Jerusalem: Franciscan Printing Press, 1995), and Mario Girardi, *Basilio di Cesarea interprete della Scrittura. Lessico, principi ermeneutici, prassi* (Bari: Edipuglia, 1998). The former incorporates *Eun.* in its study of Basil's exegesis of Jn 1.1–18; the latter comments on Basil's exegesis of Prv 8.22 in *Eun.*

the latter of his eternity.[231] In addition, following an exegetical tradition already ancient in Basil's day, he interprets the Old Testament theophanies as appearances of the Only-Begotten.[232] Furthermore, Basil cites Ps 32.6 (*By the Word of the Lord the heavens were made firm, and by the Spirit of his mouth all their power*) as a statement about the creative activities of the Son and the Spirit.[233] Second, Basil takes part in exegetical traditions. The Trinitarian controversies of the fourth century, whatever else they may have been, were at their core debates over the correct exegesis of scripture. Adherents of the various theological trajectories collected scriptural passages that were thought useful for arguing their position, and it was incumbent upon their opponents to refute their interpretations.[234] Some of these exegetical traditions preceded the fourth century; others emerged in the early part of it. Basil is a participant in both the older and the more recent traditions. His indebtedness to the former is seen, for example, in his interpretation of the Old Testament theophanies (mentioned above); his awareness of the latter is detected in his interpretation of disputed texts such as Acts 2.36[235] and Prv 8.22.[236]

Third, Basil continually applies scriptural passages to Eunomius himself and his fellow Heteroousians. This sort of interpretation sees the scriptures as prefigurations or predictions of his opponents, their activities, and their attitudes. For example, when Basil rebukes the Heteroousians for disbelieving what was beyond their own powers of reasoning, he says:

Why did the nations *become futile and their senseless heart darkened* [Rom 1.21]? Wasn't it because they followed only what was apparent to their reasoning and refused to believe the proclamation of the Spirit? Whom does Isaiah mourn for as lost? *Woe to those who are wise in their own eyes and smart in their own sight!* [Is 5.21] How can it not be men such as these?[237]

---

231. *Eun.* 2.17.   232. *Eun.* 2.18.

233. *Eun.* 3.4.

234. Vaggione, 383–95, collects theologically significant passages of scripture used by non-Nicenes.

235. *Eun.* 2.2–3.

236. *Eun.* 2.20. See Mark DelCogliano, "Basil of Caesarea on Proverbs 8.22 and the Sources of Pro-Nicene Theology," *JTS* n.s. 59 (2008): 183–90.

237. *Eun.* 2.24.

According to Basil, the Heteroousians are like the "nations" about whom Paul spoke; they are those upon whom Isaiah pronounced woe. In another good example, Basil chides Eunomius for basing himself on Aristotle instead of scripture:

> To prove that he speaks not on the basis of the Spirit's teaching, but according to *the wisdom of the rulers of this age* [1 Cor 2.6], it is enough that we quote a psalm verse against him: *Transgressors told me garrulous tales, but it is not as your Law, Lord* [Ps 118.85 LXX]. Realizing that his statement is not based on the teachings of our Lord Jesus Christ, it suffices to recall that saying of his: *Whenever he tells a lie, he speaks on his own authority* [Jn 8.44].[238]

Both the psalmist and Paul predicted the non-scriptural methodology of the Heteroousians. Basil even goes so far as to compare Eunomius (implicitly) to the devil, who is the subject of Jn 8.44 in its original context. Such a use of scripture is polemically and rhetorically effective because it situates the controversy between Basil and Eunomius within the biblical world, within the cosmic conflict between God and the powers of evil that culminates in the passion, death, and resurrection of Christ. Basil paints his dispute with Eunomius as but another instance of the oppression of the holy by ungodly men, so often lamented in scripture. The scriptures are actualized and realized before Basil's eyes in the person, activities, and opinions of Eunomius and the Heteroousians.

Ecclesiastical Authors

In *Against Eunomius*, Basil does not name his ecclesiastical influences. Therefore, tracing his sources is a matter of identifying parallels between him and earlier authors and determining the likelihood of Basil's usage of them. Building upon the work of earlier scholars, we have detected Basil's use of Origen, Eusebius of Caesarea, Athanasius of Alexandria, and the Homoiousians Basil of Ancyra and George of Laodicea. As this list shows, the sources of Basil's theology in *Against Eunomius* are eclectic.

In contrast to his practice vis-à-vis the sources of his own theology, Basil does name several notorious heretics when he

238. *Eun.* 1.9.

finds connections between their views and Eunomius's. He specifically likens Eunomius to Mani, Marcion, and Montanus.[239] Such passages are merely polemical and designed to insinuate that Eunomius is nothing more than a disciple of such impious heretics. Nonetheless, they reveal Basil's familiarity with the church's anti-heretical literature. In addition, Basil identifies a vague creed cited by Eunomius as that which Arius presented to Alexander.[240] Yet the creed is not found in any of Arius's extant writings or fragments. Nor does Basil display much knowledge of Arius's theology itself, though perhaps he alludes to Arius's infamous jingle: "He was not before he came to be."[241] Basil is also well aware of Aetius's influence upon Eunomius and possibly alludes to his work, the *Syntagmation,* in one passage.[242]

Origen In his survey of Origen's influence upon Basil in *Against Eunomius,* Bernard Sesboüé makes two general points.[243] First, Basil uses Origen quite selectively and prudently because theology had developed significantly in the century that separated Origen and Basil. Second, it is difficult to establish precise textual reminiscences between the two authors. In most cases, it is impossible to determine whether Basil draws upon Origen directly or through intermediate sources. The following ideas listed by Sesboüé and found in *Against Eunomius* are broadly Origenian: the Creator can be known through his creatures,[244] the Son as image of God reveals the Father,[245] the eternal begetting of the Son,[246] the necessity of a purified understanding of divine begetting,[247] and the unity of angelic nature despite differences in ranks.[248] With the exception of the last of these, all these Origenian themes are found in many theologians between Origen and Basil and thus could have come to Basil through intermediate channels.

In other cases, however, we can discern Basil's direct use of Origen, particularly in Basil's understanding of conceptualization

---

239. *Eun.* 2.8 and 2.34.
241. *Eun.* 2.14.
243. SC 299.65–74.
245. *Eun.* 1.18, 1.26, and 3.1.
247. *Eun.* 2.22–24.

240. *Eun.* 1.4.
242. *Eun.* 1.1 and 2.22.
244. *Eun.* 1.12, 1.14, and 2.32.
246. *Eun.* 2.14–17.
248. *Eun.* 3.1.

(*epinoia*). Basil affirms the positive role of conceptualization in theology in response to Eunomius's denigration of it.[249]According to Basil, conceptualization allows real knowledge of objects, especially simple objects, without comprehension of their essence. Like Origen, he views the conceptualizations of Christ as naming the ways in which Christ acts toward and relates to humanity; they do not reveal Christ's substance.[250] Origen and Basil interpret names for Christ like 'light' and 'bread' similarly, but differ over 'vine.'[251] Basil, however, adapts Origen considerably. While Origen identifies the scriptural names for Christ with the conceptualizations of Christ, Basil uses the scriptural names for Christ and God to derive conceptualizations about them. For example, according to Basil 'unbegotten' is a conceptualization derived from the scriptural designation of God as 'life.'[252] Scriptural terms are productive of conceptualizations; they themselves do not refer to them. Hence Basil's appeal to Origen's positive use of conceptualization is, at least in part, polemical, an attempt to situate his doctrine fully within longstanding ecclesiastical traditions against the innovations of Eunomius.

There are several more examples of Basil's use of Origen: the argument for the eternity of God's Fatherhood based on the fact that the goodness and blessedness of God require it;[253] the use of Jn 1.1—and specifically the verb 'was,' as in *In the beginning was the Word*—to argue for the eternity of the Word;[254] the praise of John as the most profound of the evangelists based on an examination of the opening lines of all four gospels;[255] and the interpretation of a lacuna in Eph 1.1 found in some manuscripts.[256] Even in these four examples, Basil shows himself to be well versed in Origen's writings and able to weave arguments and interpretations of his theological forebear seamlessly into his own.

---

249. *Eun.* 1.6–11. Basil's understanding of conceptualization is discussed in more detail on pp. 48–49 and 68–70.

250. See especially *Princ.* 1.2.1, 1.2.13; *Jo.* 1.52–57, 1.118–28, and 1.153–57.

251. *Eun.* 1.7. 'Light': *Jo.* 1.158–80, 1.267, 2.133–70. 'Bread': *Jo.* 1.130–31, 1.205–8, 6.223, 10.99–101. 'Vine': *Jo.* 1.130–31, 1.205–8.

252. See *Eun.* 1.15 and 2.29.   253. *Eun.* 2.12; *Princ.* 1.2.9–10.

254. *Eun.* 2.14–15; *Jo.* 2.8–11.   255. *Eun.* 2.15; *Jo.* 1.21–22.

256. *Eun.* 2.19; *Fragments from the Commentary on the Epistle to the Ephesians* 2.

Eusebius of Caesarea The influence of Eusebius upon Basil has attracted little, if any, scholarly attention. But in *Against Eunomius* we have detected a striking example of Basil's use of Eusebius in his interpretation of Prv 8.22. The interpretation of this verse was one of the most fecund sites of theological reflection and debate in the course of the Trinitarian controversies. Various members of the Eusebian alliance based their claim that the Son could be called a 'creature' on this verse, as Eunomius did as well. But Eusebius is conspicuous among his fellow Eusebians for generally avoiding calling the Son a 'creature' and rejecting this interpretation of Prv 8.22. In refuting Eunomius's interpretation of this verse, Basil draws upon Eusebius of Caesarea, not upon Athanasius as one might have expected.[257] Basil advances three separate arguments against calling the Son a 'creature' by appeal to Prv 8.22: (1) when the teaching of a scriptural *hapax legomenon* contradicts the predominate teaching of the rest of scripture, it should be ignored; (2) because of the genre of Proverbs, no interpretation of a verse from this book can be convincing; and (3) the Greek phrasing is an incorrect translation of the Hebrew. Basil adopts the first and third points directly from Eusebius's *Ecclesiastical Theology*.[258] When citing Gn 4.1 as part of his argument, Basil even misattributes the verse, as Eusebius did, to a masculine speaker (Adam) when in fact it is Eve who speaks it.[259] The fact that Basil has so closely followed Eusebius in his interpretation of Prv 8.22 should prompt us to reassess more widely the influence of Eusebius on Basil.

Athanasius Recent scholarship has increasingly contested the traditional assumption that Athanasius was a major influence upon Basil.[260] We concur with this assessment. Basil's reliance

257. *Eun.* 2.20.
258. *E. th.* 1.10.2, 3.2.15, and 3.2.21–23. See Mark DelCogliano, "Basil of Caesarea on Proverbs 8:22 and the Sources of Pro-Nicene Theology," *JTS* n.s. 59 (2008): 183–90.
259. Basil makes the same error in *Spir.* 5.12, explicitly attributing the verse to 'Adam.'
260. See Ayres 221, and Stephen M. Hildebrand, *The Trinitarian Theology of Basil of Caesarea* (Washington, DC: The Catholic University of America Press, 2007), 80 n. 10.

upon Athanasius needs to be demonstrated rather than assumed. One of the difficulties in assessing Athanasius's influence upon Basil is that Basil draws heavily upon the Homoiousians, who in turn drew heavily upon Athanasius. Indeed, it is easier to demonstrate ideas that Basil does not derive from Athanasius than to prove that Basil did in fact borrow from Athanasius. We have noted above that Basil preferred Eusebius's approach to Prv 8.22, completely ignoring Athanasius's interpretation. In addition, Marina Silvia Troiano has argued that the third book of *Against Eunomius,* which is devoted to the Holy Spirit, bears no trace of influence from Athanasius's *Letters to Serapion.*[261]

Nonetheless, we have detected one instance of Basil's direct use of Athanasius. Basil draws upon Athanasius's interpretation of Acts 2.36, a verse cited by the early Eusebians and Eunomius as the basis for calling the Son 'something made.' Like Athanasius, Basil claims that the text does not refer to the substance of the eternal Son, but to the incarnate Christ.[262] Hence, though Athanasius's influence upon Basil is no longer held to be axiomatic, there is some evidence for Basil's knowledge of Athanasius's writings and undoubtedly more to be found.

The Homoiousians: Basil of Ancyra and George of Laodicea   The influence of the Homoiousians upon Basil of Caesarea has long been recognized, although subject to misunderstanding. The connection between them was initially made in the course of debates over the meaning of the Nicene *homoousios.* As mentioned above, traditionally the Cappadocians were thought to have rooted their theology in Athanasius. Reacting against this, the nineteenth-century scholars Theodor Zahn and Friedrich Loofs placed a wedge between Athanasius and the Cappadocians, arguing that they understood *homoousios* differently. Building upon their work, Adolf von Harnack argued that the "neo-Nicene" position of the Cappadocians amounted to a re-

261. Marina Silvia Troiano, "Il *Contra Eunomium* III di Basilio di Cesarea e le *Epistolae ad Serapionem* I–IV di Atanasio di Alessandria: nota comparativa," *Augustinianum* 41.1 (2001), 59–91. She refutes the claims of Athanasian influence in *Eun.* 3 made by Drecoll 138–39.

262. *Eun.* 2.3; Athanasius, *Ar.* 2.11–18.

jection of the "old-Nicene" position of Athanasius in favor of Homoiousianism, which in its turn was a modified form of Arianism. Harnack provocatively stated that the church's official doctrine of the Trinity, as understood in the 380s, owed more to Basil of Ancyra than to either Athanasius or Basil of Caesarea.[263] The Harnack thesis has continued to be debated in scholarship to the present day, and scholarship shaped by Harnack's categories has portrayed Basil as more or less making a choice between Athanasian and Homoiousian positions. This approach is flawed, however, not least of all because of its inaccurate assessment of Homoiousian theology and its view of Cappadocian theology as a unity.

In reaction to Harnack and other nineteenth-century currents, Jaakko Gummerus took a more nuanced, though lesser known, approach to the question. He argued that Cappadocian theology did not simply restate Athanasius but modified the Alexandrian bishop along Homoiousian lines.[264] Taking Gummerus's thesis as his starting point, Jeffrey Steenson, in an unpublished dissertation, explored Homoiousian theology in relation to both Athanasius and Basil of Caesarea's *Against Eunomius*.[265] He concluded that the Homoiousians are greatly indebted to Athanasius, and Basil to the Homoiousians. We concur with Steenson's general assessment. Basil is influenced by the Homoiousians in significant ways but not beholden to all features of their thought. Furthermore, while Basil engaged Athanasius directly, the Athanasian tradition is for the most part mediated to him through the modifications of the Homoiousians.

An introduction is not the place to conduct a detailed analysis of the relations between Basil of Caesarea and the Homoiousians because of the complicated methodology that it demands. It requires distinguishing between Basil's direct use of Athanasius, his mediated use of Athanasius through Homoiousians, his direct

---

263. Adolf Harnack, *History of Dogma*, translated from the 3d German ed. by Neil Buchanan (New York: Russell and Russell, 1958), 4.80–107. On the "Harnack thesis," see Ayres 237–38.

264. Jaakko Gummerus, *Die homöusianische Partei bis zum Tode des Konstantius* (Leipzig: Helsingfors, 1900).

265. Jeffrey N. Steenson, "Basil of Ancyra and the Course of Nicene Orthodoxy" (DPhil. diss., Oxford University, 1983).

use of the Homoiousians, and his use of sources common to him and Homoiousians. Though Steenson has posited thirteen areas of theological connection between Basil and the Homoiousians, he focuses only on similarities between Basil and the Homoiousians and sidesteps more complicated source-critical issues.[266] Despite the usefulness of Steenson's contribution, a detailed analysis of the relation between Basil's thought in *Against Eunomius* and Homoiousian theology remains a scholarly *desideratum*. Nonetheless, we offer a few areas in which Basil's direct dependence on the Homoiousians seems likely. First, the names 'Father' and 'Son' give rise primarily to notions; that is, they do not reveal substance as the Heteroousians had taught.[267] Similarly, Basil's understanding of 'Father' and 'Son' as relative terms—a fairly widespread position—seems more indebted to the Homoiousians than anyone else.[268] Basil's argument against 'Unbegotten' and in favor of 'Father' has a Homoiousian provenance even though the Homoiousians themselves drew upon Athanasius for this argument.[269] This is a classic example of the Homoiousian modification of Athanasius. Athanasius had advanced three distinct arguments preferring 'Father' to 'Unbegotten' as names: (1) scriptural usage, (2) the ambiguous meaning of 'unbegotten,' and (3) the greater accuracy of correlatives 'Father-Son' than 'Unbegotten-Begotten.'[270] Basil of Caesarea adopts George of Laodicea's three arguments: 'Unbegotten' (1) is unscriptural, (2) lacks the comprehensiveness of 'Father,' and (3) is not a relative term. Both Basil of Caesarea and George rejected two of Athanasius's three arguments, declining to view 'Unbegotten-Begotten' as relative terms and 'Unbegotten' as ambiguous. Basil even cites some of George's scriptural testimonies for 'Father' and 'Son.'[271] Future research should reveal further points of contact between Basil and the Homoiousians.

---

266. Steenson, "Basil of Ancyra," 313–31.
267. *Eun.* 2.4, 2.9–10, 2.28–29; Epiphanius, *Pan.* 73.3.1–3.
268. *Eun.* 2.9; Epiphanius, *Pan.* 73.3.4–5 and 73.19.3–4.
269. *Eun.* 1.5; Epiphanius, *Pan.* 73.14.5–6, 73.19.1–3, and 73.20.1–2.
270. Athanasius, *Ar.* 1.30–34; *Decr.* 28–31; *Syn.* 46–47.
271. *Eun.* 2.7; Epiphanius, *Pan.* 73.20.3–4.

Philosophical Authors

When asking about Basil's debt to non-Christian philosophical traditions in *Against Eunomius*, an initial distinction must be made. On the one hand, Basil explicitly refers to philosophers, their texts, or their ideas. He does this rarely in the three books, and while these explicit references reveal Basil's acquaintance with philosophy, they tell us little about his use of it. Moreover, these references to philosophy in this treatise are uniformly hostile, intended to link Eunomius with modes of thinking foreign to unperverted biblical faith.[272] Accordingly, Basil accuses the Heteroousians of relying on the syllogistic methods of Aristotle and Chrysippus to prove a point that is perfectly obvious, namely, that the God who is without origin is unbegotten.[273] Later in the treatise, he shows that Eunomius's notion of privation is dependent on Aristotle's *Categories*, referring to the treatise by name and summarizing its account of privation.[274]

These are the only explicit references to philosophical traditions in the three books *Against Eunomius,* and they give us exactly the impression Basil wishes to convey: that non-Christian philosophy has influenced only one participant in the debate, namely, Eunomius, in any significant way. But, on the other hand, Basil cannot but be influenced by the traditions he knows quite well. Indeed, in his later treatise *On Faith,* which was addressed to a sympathetic monastic audience, he admits—in a likely reference to the books *Against Eunomius*—that

while I was compelled to fight the heresies that arose from time to time, I thought it appropriate to the specific nature of the impiety sown by the Devil that I should check or confute if I could the blasphemies which were brought forward [by the opposing side]—and in this I was imitating my predecessors—by arguments gleaned from various sources as the need of those weak in faith required; and in many cases these were not written, yet were not out of harmony with sound Scriptural teaching.[275]

272. For another example in Basil's rhetoric of the incompatibility of scripture and philosophy, see *Ps.* 32.7 (PG 29.341a3–b4).
273. *Eun.* 1.5.
274. *Eun.* 1.9.
275. Basil, *Fid.,* trans. Sr. M. Monica Wagner, C.S.C., *St. Basil: Ascetical Works,*

Basil does not tell us exactly which arguments he has in mind, or what his sources were in developing these arguments. Still, this statement certainly justifies us in looking for the influence of philosophical concepts within *Against Eunomius,* even where they are not explicitly attributed. The following paragraphs survey philosophical influence in four areas of Basil's thinking: his defense of conceptualization (ἐπίνοια), his understanding of substance, his theory of the semantics of names, and his refutation of Eunomius's definition of time.

Basil's dependence upon philosophy is perhaps easiest to ascertain in the first area. In *Against Eunomius* 1.6, he appeals to the way in which "conceptualization" is defined in "customary usage of language" (συνήθεια) or "common usage" (κοινὴ χρήσις). Basil is clearly less interested in ordinary layman's language than in reflective philosophical usage of the term "conceptualization," though not necessarily in any single school's account of the term. Basil believes that Eunomius is careless in his denunciation of "conceptualization" since he never clearly defines it and the way he uses it runs afoul of how it is used both in "common usage" (that is, philosophy) and in the tradition of interpreting the Christian scriptures.

In spelling out what "conceptualization" means in common usage, Basil focuses on the phrase "through conceptualization alone" (ἐπινοίᾳ μόνῃ), which was quite common in late ancient philosophy. The phrase was used most frequently in connection with two ideas: (1) to be divisible and (2) to exist. Let us take the two in turn. As for (1), something can be divisible in reality or merely in thought; if the latter, then it is divisible "through conceptualization alone." For instance, every body has resistance and color. In fact, no body can continue being a body without these, and so they are naturally inseparable from it. One can, however, mentally separate these qualities from the body and reflect upon them on their own. Hence, the body can

FOTC 9 (Washington, DC: The Catholic University of America Press, 1962), 58.
"Not written down" means "not mentioned explicitly in scripture": Emmanuel Amand de Mendieta, *The 'Unwritten' and 'Secret' Apostolic Traditions in the Theological Thought of St. Basil of Caesarea,* Scottish Journal of Theology Occasional Papers, no. 13 (Edinburgh: Oliver and Boyd, 1965), 17–21.

be subdivided or dissolved into such qualities "through conceptualization alone." The appearance of this phrase together with
verbs of division or distinction is quite common in the third-
century Aristotelian Alexander of Aphrodisias,[276] and appears
in Platonists like Plotinus[277] and Dexippus[278] and the fourth-
century Aristotelian Themistius.[279] In all such cases, the phrase
is used, as it is by Basil, to point out that even naturally inseparable items or properties can be distinguished mentally.

As for (2), Basil does not speak, as philosophical tradition had
done, of items *existing* "through conceptualization alone." But he
does speak of similar cases, referring to the items under question
as being "*considered* by conceptualization" (κατ' ἐπίνοιαν θεωρητά).
This includes imaginary beings such as centaurs, but it also includes diverse perspectives on the concept of a real item. He
gives as examples the ideas of "fruit" and "seed" as perspectives
on the basic notion of "grain." When Basil says that all these,
the imaginary creatures of mythology and the uses of grain, are
"considered by conceptualization," he means that they are all
mind-dependent; that is, they depend for their existence on
creative human reasoning. While one cannot identify a single
source for Basil's usage, there are many parallels in philosophical texts. For instance, at the beginning of his introduction to
Aristotelian logic, the *Isagoge*, the Neoplatonist philosopher
Porphyry refers to the nominalist position that universals (that
is, genera and species) "depend upon bare conceptualizations
alone."[280] Often, existing "by conceptualization" and "in reality" are contrasted—the latter being specified with words like
hyparxis, hypostasis, and *energeia.*[281]

---

276. *In Metaph.* 661, 6; 683, 1–2 Hayduck; *de An.* 6, 20 Bruns.
277. *Enn.* 6.2.3.23; cf. 6.3.7.8 and 2.9.1.40ff.
278. *In Cat.* 26, 6; 50, 13ff.; 59, 33 Busse.
279. *In Ph.* 125, 31 Schenkl.
280. Porphyry, *Intr.* 1 Busse; trans. Jonathan Barnes, *Porphyry: Introduction*
(Oxford: Oxford University Press, 2003), 3 [altered]; see Barnes's helpful comments on conceptualization at pp. 40–43. Cf. Alexander of Aphrodisias, *in
Metaph.* 483, 27; 636, 20; 677, 2; 792, 20 Hayduck.
281. See Philo Judaeus, *Migr.* 192; Sextus Empiricus, *M.* 8.453; Origen,
Fragmenta in evangelium Joannis, ed. E. Preuschen, *Origenes Werke,* vol. 4, GCS 10
(Leipzig: Hinrichs, 1903)), fr. 121; Diogenes Laertius (reporting Posidonius),

In sum, to say that some idea depends upon conceptualization did not necessarily mean that it is false, but merely that it is an idea dependent on human reasoning. Basil has drawn on the philosophical *koine* of his day, rather than on any particular school's doctrine, for his positive assessment of conceptualization within theology.

In *Against Eunomius* Basil also subtly draws upon non-Christian thought in his use of the language of "substance" (*ousia, hypostasis,* and *hypokeimenon*). This language is of obvious importance given its controversial status in the Trinitarian debates. But what does it mean? It has been claimed that Basil's understanding of substance is fundamentally and exclusively Stoic, but here again we see far greater complexity in the way Basil handles philosophical traditions than such a source-hypothesis would allow.[282] The "Stoic" interpretation of Basil is based largely on Basil's equation of "substance" (οὐσία) with "material substrate" (τὸ ὑλικὸν ὑποκείμενον) twice in *Against Eunomius*.[283] The Stoics used the latter phrase to denote both the first and the second categories or genera of their metaphysics: unqualified matter and commonly-qualified material objects.[284] That is, they used the phrase when describing objects simply as lumps of matter without specification or as lumps of a certain kind of matter—for instance, clay. A jar *qua* material substrate is a bit of matter or a bit of clay.

According to Reinhard Hübner, the principal proponent of the "Stoic" interpretation of *Against Eunomius*, Basil intends readers to think of the shared properties of the Father and the Son along the lines of Stoic material substrate, simply stripped of the

---

Vitae philosophorum 7.135; Themistius, *in Ph.* 125, 31; 157, 17–18; 162, 25–26 Schenkl.

282. Reinhard Hübner, "Gregor von Nyssa als Vorfasser der Sog. Ep. 38 des Basilius: Zum unterschiedlichen Verständnis der οὐσία bei den kappadozischen Brüdern," in Jacques Fontaine and Charles Kannengiesser, eds. *Epektasis: Mélanges Patristiques Offertes au Cardinal Jean Daniélou* (Paris: Beauschesne, 1972), 463–90. For criticism, see David G. Robertson, "Stoic and Aristotelian Notions of Substance in Basil of Caesarea," *Vigiliae Christianae* 52 (1998): 393–417.

283. *Eun.* 1.15; 2.4.

284. See David Sedley, "Hellenistic physics and metaphysics," in Keimpe Algra, et al., *The Cambridge History of Hellenistic Philosophy* (Cambridge: Cambridge University Press, 2005), 355–411 at 407–8.

matter. For Hübner, Basil is intentionally rejecting the generic account of shared properties found in the broadly Aristotelian tradition that includes much of late ancient Platonism. This tradition accounted for shared properties among members of a kind by invoking an immaterial genus or species. When Basil uses the phrase "material substrate" in *Against Eunomius*, however, it is unclear whether he intends his readers to think of Stoic metaphysics as a suitable tool for describing the relation of the Son to the Father. In both passages where the phrase occurs, Basil is speaking of human beings. In one, the "material substrate" of the biblical character Adam is supposed to provide the answer to the question "What is he?" The other instance of "material substrate" is ambiguous, referring either to the particular man Peter or to the common human nature.[285] Finally, thinking of material substrate as one of the senses of "substance" is not at all foreign to Aristotle or late ancient Platonism.[286] The assumption that the mere appearance of the phrase is meant to signal Stoicism is question-begging.

Basil also invokes language drawn from the Aristotelian and Platonist tradition in explicating his notion of common substance. First, he speaks of something's substance as answering the question "What is it?" In Aristotle and the tradition of interpreting him, an object's genus or species was the uniquely appropriate answer to this question.[287] "What is Socrates?"—the best answers would be "a human being" or "an animal." Moreover, Basil uses Aristotelian language in speaking of a "formula of being" (λόγος τοῦ εἶναι) or "formula of substance" (λόγος τῆς οὐσίας) as the content of one's response to the question "What is it?"[288] Basil believes that the "formula of substance" is identical for the Son and the Father, which accounts for their "commonality of substance."[289] Finally, when Basil attempts to explain the

---

285. *Eun.* 2.4. For discussion, see Paul Kalligas, "Basil of Caesarea on the Semantics of Proper Names," in Katerina Ierodiakonou, ed., *Byzantine Philosophy and its Ancient Sources* (Oxford: Clarendon Press, 2002), 31–48.

286. See, e.g., Aristotle, *Metaph.* 8.1, 1042a26–b8.

287. On the "question test," see Jonathan Barnes, *Porphyry: Introduction*, 65, 85–92.

288. See, e.g., Aristotle, *Cat.* 1a2ff.

289. *Eun.* 1.19.

"distinguishing marks" (ἰδιώματα), which account for the distinctness of the Father and the Son without undermining their shared formula of substance, he invokes the properties that had been discussed in the Platonist and Aristotelian tradition as the exemplary differentiae of the genus of "animal": being winged or footed, aquatic or terrestrial, rational or irrational.[290] So there is much of the broadly Aristotelian notion of substance in *Against Eunomius*. But just as it would be wrong to see Basil as simply reproducing Stoic metaphysics in his Trinitarian theology, we must beware of a similarly reductionist account of Basil's Aristotelianism. Basil has appropriated language that could be used in both traditions for his own purposes and with little regard for fidelity to either tradition.

Basil also discusses the semantics of proper, relative, and absolute names.[291] He develops a unique theory of proper names that reflects an eclectic and heavily adaptive use of earlier philosophical theories concerning what differentiates individuals and what information proper names communicate about the individuals that bear them. He advances this theory for the sole purpose of refuting Eunomius's theory of names. According to Basil, proper names reveal, not substance as his opponent claimed, but an individual's distinctive features (ἰδιότητες).[292] An individual's name brings to mind a concurrence of distinctive features that enables one to distinguish that individual from others. Basil's "bundle theory of individuals" has precedents in Platonist sources. While Porphyry viewed individuals as both constituted and identified by distinctive characteristics, Basil maintained that individuals were only recognized by means of them.[293] Thus it is highly unlikely that Basil was influenced by the Stoic theory of the proper name, wherein a proper name communicates the single peculiar quality that defines the indi-

290. *Eun.* 2.28. Plato, *Sph.* 220a–222b, *Ti.* 39e–40; Aristotle, *Cat.* 1b18–19, 14b38, 15a2–3, *Part. an.* 697b2–3. For the commentary tradition, see Jaap Mansfeld, *Heresiography in Context: Hippolytus' Elenchos as a Source for Greek Philosophy*, Philosophia Antiqua 56 (Leiden: Brill, 1992), 80–81.

291. See DelCogliano, *Basil of Caesarea's Anti-Eunomian Theory of Names*, 189–260.

292. *Eun.* 2.4.

293. Porphyry, *in Cat.* 129, 9–10 Busse; Porphyry, *Intr.* 7.19–26 Busse.

vidual.[294] His theory of proper names is crucial for his understanding of what 'Father' and 'Son,' which Basil treats as proper names, mean when applied to God.

Basil also writes about relative and absolute terms, another perennial topic of philosophers.[295] Once again, he formulates his theories to undermine Eunomius's theory of names. Reinforcing the point he made concerning proper names, he teaches that relative terms—like 'father' and 'son'—do not communicate substance, but rather distinctive features, namely, a relative property. In other words, each term entails the other. 'Son' implies 'father' and vice versa. Nor do absolute terms— like 'horse' and 'ox'—communicate substance, even though these terms might seem to indicate substances. Rather, they disclose distinctive features much like Porphyrian *propria*.[296] Basil's understanding of relative terms is ultimately indebted to Stoic-inspired grammatical discussions rather than Aristotelian sources.[297] At the same time there was by Basil's day a long Christian tradition of viewing 'Father' and 'Son' as relative terms. Basil's own theory of relative terms has much in common with that of the Homoiousians.[298]

The final major passage we shall discuss in which philosophical concepts have surreptitiously shaped the argument of *Against Eunomius* is the explication of time in Book One. At 1.19, Basil quotes Eunomius's definition of time as "a certain kind of motion of the stars." For present purposes, there is no need to examine the context of this claim, merely its philosophical pedigree and the nature of Basil's response. Eunomius's definition of time closely parallels one given in the fourth-century *Commentary on Job* attributed to a Julian whose precise identity is unknown,

294. Paul Kalligas, "Basil of Caesarea on the Semantics of Proper Names," in Katerina Ierodiakonou, ed., *Byzantine Philosophy and its Ancient Sources* (Oxford: Clarendon Press, 2002), 31–48; David G. Robertson, "A Patristic Theory of Proper Names," *Archiv für Geschichte der Philosophie* 83 (2002): 1–19.

295. *Eun.* 2.9; cf. 1.5 and 1.22.

296. See pp. 50–51.

297. David G. Robertson, "Relatives in Basil of Caesarea," *Studia Patristica* 37 (2001): 277–87. Sesboüé SC 299.78–86, Drecoll 65 n. 56, and Ayres 202 n. 53 suggest an Aristotelian background for Basil's theory of relatives.

298. On Basil's indebtedness to the Homoiousians, see pp. 64–66.

the contents of which reflect a Heteroousian theology. Julian says that "time is a certain kind of motion of the stars going along with the sun and the moon" and explicitly attributes this view, which he obviously endorses, to Plato.[299] The definition does not appear verbatim in Plato. Nonetheless, it faithfully reflects one of three major interpretations of the account of time found in Plato's *Timaeus*. According to this "astral interpretation," time begins with the formation of the world, since time is closely identified with the motion of the stars, which in some sense cause time. Critics of this reading of the *Timaeus* noted that Plato speaks of a kind of disorderly time before the world's formation, that is, before the orderly time governed by the stars' regular motions. Moreover, Aristotle had criticized the identification of time with motion. Even if time *measures* motion, the two are not identical.

Basil draws on this tradition of criticizing the idea that the stars cause time and that their motion is identical with time in *Against Eunomius* 1.21. He asks how this could be, since the heavenly bodies are not said to be created until the fourth day: how could there be time before their creation if they are responsible for time? Moreover, Basil argues that motion is not identical with time, since time measures motion. He offers his own definition of time as "the extension coextensive with the existence of the cosmos." He specifies the interrelation of motion and time: it is not that the stars' (or anything else's) motion causes time, but that "all motion is measured in time." In defining time as "extension" (διάστημα), Basil links himself with Middle Platonic authors like Philo Judaeus and Alcinous, who themselves drew on an eclectic mix of sources including the Stoics.[300] In spelling out the interrelation of time and motion as he does, Basil is remarkably similar not only to Middle Platonic tradition but also to his contemporary, the Aristotelian Themistius, who was himself influenced by Platonism.[301]

299. Julian, *Commentary on Job* 38.7, ed. Dieter Hagedorn, *Der Hiobkommentar des Arianers Julian*, Patristische Texte und Studien 14 (Berlin: De Gruyter, 1973), 254.

300. Philo, *Aet.* 54; Alcinous, *Intr.* 14.6; Chrysippus *apud* Stobaeus 1.106, 5–23; Aëtius, *Plac.* 1.21.2.

301. Themistius, *in Ph.* 154, 8–13 Schenkl.

Perhaps what is most interesting, however, is not identifying exactly which philosophical position Basil held on time, but how he responds to Eunomius's definition. He does not point out that Eunomius's notion is beholden to Plato and leave it at that. In fact, he does not mention any source at all. Rather, he engages in the same kind of philosophical refutation of the "astral interpretation" of the *Timaeus* that he has encountered in the philosophical tradition without explicitly linking his project with this tradition. This brief survey does not exhaust the subject of philosophical influence in *Against Eunomius*.[302] But it suffices, we hope, to delineate in broad strokes *how* philosophy has influenced the treatise. Without question, many of the important passages invoke philosophically significant terms, and it is crucial for the interpreter to ask which sense(s) of these terms Basil has in mind. Yet answering this question involves more than a simple source-critical appeal. It is not merely that Basil's philosophical lexicon is too diverse for this. It is also that he has transformed the doxographical heritage for his own purposes. His refutation of Eunomius is, at least at times, a philosophical exercise in its own right, rather than merely a report on previous thinkers.

VI. A GLOSSARY OF TECHNICAL VOCABULARY IN *AGAINST EUNOMIUS*

ἀγεννησία, τὸ ἀγέννητον: unbegottenness
ἀγέννητος: unbegotten
ἀΐδιος: eternal
ἀϊδιότης: eternity
αἰτία: cause
αἴτιον: cause
αἰών: age
αἰώνιος: everlasting

ἄναρχος: without beginning, without origin
ἀνόμοιος: unlike
ἀνομοιότης: unlikeness
ἀπαράλλακτος: indistinguishable
ἀπαραλλάκτως: indistinguishably
ἀρχή: beginning, origin

302. See, e.g., his account of the proper objects of the five senses at *Eun.* 1.12, which owes something to Aristotle's *De anima* 2.6–11 or commentaries or handbooks summarizing it. Also see his rejection at *Eun.* 2.17 of the classical etymology that derives the term 'age' (*aiōn*) from 'always existing' (*aei einai*), found in both

ἀσύγκριτος: incomparable
ἀσύνθετος: incomposite
ἄχρονος: non-temporal
ἀχρόνως: non-temporally
γεννάω: to beget
γέννημα: something begotten
γέννησις: begetting
γεννητός: begotten
δημιούργημα: created work
δημιουργός: creator
διάστημα: interval, extension
δύναμις: power
ἐναντίος: contrary, opposite
ἐνέργεια: activity
ἔννοια: notion
ἐπίνοια: conceptualization
θεότης: divinity
ἰδιότης: distinctive feature
ἰδίωμα: distinguishing mark
κοινός: common
κοινωνία: communion
κτίσις: creation
κτίσμα: creature
μείζων: greater than
λόγος τοῦ εἶναι: formula of being

λόγος τῆς οὐσίας: formula of substance
Μονογενής: Only-Begotten
οἰκειότης: affinity
οἰκείωσις: affinity
οἰκονομία: economy
ὅμοιος: like
ὁμοιότης: likeness
ὄνομα: name
οὐσία: substance
ποίημα: thing made
ποιητής: maker
προσαγορεύω: to designate
προσηγορία: designation
στέρησις: privation
συναΐδιος: co-eternal
σύγκρισις: comparison
σχέσις: relation
τάξις: order, rank
ὑποκείμενον: substrate, subject, referent
ὑπόστασις: subsistence
φύσις: nature
χαρακτήρ: character
χρόνος: time

VII. A NOTE ON THE TEXT AND TRANSLATION

Our translation is based on the critical edition of the text established by Bernard Sesboüé and his collaborators Georges-Matthieu de Durand and Louis Doutreleau for Sources Chrétiennes in 1982–1983.[303] We have also had recourse to the Mau-

---

Aristotle, *Cael.* 1.9 (279a27–28), and Plotinus, *En.* 3.7.4, 43 (cf. 3.7.6), 32–33, and often repeated by Aristotelian and Neoplatonist commentators.

303. Bernard Sesboüé, Georges-Matthieu de Durand, and Louis Doutreleau, *Basile de Césarée, Contre Eunome suivi de Eunome Apologie*, SC 299 and 305 (Paris: Cerf, 1982–1983).

rist edition by Julien Garnier, which was first published in 1721 and reprinted by J.-P. Migne in his *Patrologia graeca*.[304] In rare cases we diverge from Sesboüé's text, preferring the readings of the manuscripts or Garnier. We note these departures in the footnotes. In our translation we have at times been assisted by both Garnier's Latin translation and Sesboüé's French translation. Ours is the first complete translation to appear in English.

In the "Note to the Reader" that precedes his translation of Porphyry's *Isagoge*, Jonathan Barnes writes: "My translation purports to be written in English. It also purports to be faithful to the Greek—that is to say, to convey in English all and only what Porphyry conveyed in Greek. These two commonplace ambitions are, as every translator knows, mutual enemies...."[305] Barnes' words well express our own experience. Basil's *Against Eunomius* is in content a treatise of technical theology and in form a rhetorical tour de force. It is not easy reading. At times Basil is obscure. In our translation we have attempted to render Basil as clearly as possible in English without making him clearer than he is in Greek. At the same time we have tried to capture Basil's nuanced explanations, his theological distinctions, his polemical tone, and the sarcasm with which he treats Eunomius and his ideas.

In our translation we have aimed to satisfy two distinct audiences at opposite ends of the reading spectrum. The first is the reader without knowledge of Greek who reads our translation without recourse to the original. The second is the reader who knows Greek and reads our translation while constantly comparing it to the original. For our first reader, we strived to produce English prose that is understandable, idiomatic, and felicitous. We have added explanatory footnotes to help when Basil is murky. For our second reader, we endeavored not to stray into paraphrase so that the words and phrases of our translation could be matched with the Greek on which they are based. Even though our second reader may not always agree with our choices, we believe that he or she will understand them. We

304. PG 29.497–670.
305. Barnes, *Porphyry: Introduction*, xxv.

hope that the combination of these principles satisfies readers at both ends of the spectrum as well as the majority who fall somewhere between these two extremes. A few words on the style and format of our translation are necessary. While the division of the treatise into three books goes back to Basil himself, the subdivision into numbered sections stems at least from Garnier's edition and was adopted by Sesboüé. In our translation these are signaled by a number within square brackets, for example [2.4], which indicates Book 2, section 4. Sesboüé further divided the numbered sections into unnumbered paragraphs. Our translation also subdivides each numbered section into unnumbered paragraphs, but not always in accordance with Sesboüé's divisions. Our paragraphing aims to follow modern English practice.

Italics are used in the translation for scriptural citations or reminiscences; these are always followed by the scriptural reference in square brackets, for example, [Jn 1.1]. References to scriptural allusions are given in the footnotes. Note that the Psalms are referenced according to the Septuagint version. On rare occasions *italics* are used for emphasis or for other purposes explained in the footnotes. In a few places words are inserted in square brackets to improve the sense. Double quotation marks (",") signal a non-scriptural citation; long citations appear as block text without quotation marks. Since Basil's treatise is so concerned with terminology, inverted commas (',') are used to signal when he is talking about a linguistic term as opposed to the thing or concept to which the term refers. For Basil, there is a difference between Father and 'Father.'

AGAINST EUNOMIUS

From our holy father Basil, Archbishop of Caesarea in Cappadocia, the refutation of the *Apology* of the impious Eunomius

BOOK ONE

F ALL THOSE UPON WHOM the name of our God and Savior Jesus Christ had been invoked had preferred not to tamper with the truth of the gospel and to content themselves with the tradition of the apostles and the simplicity of the faith,[1] there would be no need for our present treatise. Instead, we would have maintained even now the complete silence we have honored from the beginning. But the enemy of truth ceaselessly proliferates evil, adding to the weeds he sowed in the church of God at the beginning.[2] Finding at present instruments for executing his entire scheme[3] all at once, he introduces on the pretext of Christianity the denial of the divinity of the Only-Begotten. With this empty external wisdom[4] he disturbs what is pure and simple in the teaching of the divine Spirit and misleads the innocent through the use of plausible arguments.[5] So, on account of Your Charity, who enjoins us to do this,[6] and

1. Gr. ἡ ἁπλότης τῆς πίστεως. See also *Ep.* 258.2 and *Fid.* 1. Similarly, τὸ ἁπλοῦν τῆς πίστεως at *Hex.* 1.10 and *Eun.* 1.4.
2. See Mt 13.25. 3. Gr. τέχνη.
4. That is, external to ecclesial teaching.
5. See Col 2.4. Note that "the use of plausible arguments" (πιθανολογία) lacks the rigor and certitude of "logical demonstration" (ἀπόδειξις).
6. "Your Charity" is a title of politeness, found often in Basil's letters and usually employed to address bishops (e.g., *Ep.* 47); see Agnes C. Way, *The Language and Style of the Letters of St. Basil* (Washington, DC: The Catholic University of America Press, 1927), 161. The recipient of the treatise is probably Eustathius of Sebasteia, and it probably took its initial form as stenographic notes taken when Basil dictated objections to Eunomius when Eustathius was preparing for the council of Lampsacus in 364 (see Introduction, p. 33 above).

81

for the sake of our own well-being,[7] it is necessary for us to accept the responsibility of allying ourselves with the truth and refuting this falsehood. Giving no heed to our weakness for this task and although we are altogether untrained in such a form of speaking, we undertake this task insofar as the Lord apportions knowledge to us.[8] In our opinion, we will not fail to attain at least one of three goods. Our refutation will either remedy the evil for those already taken in by it or provide an adequate safeguard for the healthy. Failing that, we ourselves will earn the reward for offering our brothers the best things.[9]

As far as I can tell, the first one who dared to declare openly and teach that the only-begotten Son was unlike the God and Father in substance was Aetius the Syrian. I will not mention in what sort of customs he was reared from the beginning of his life and how, when he grew up, he intruded perniciously into the churches of God, lest I seem to focus on abusing him and appear to neglect the refutations.[10] But the one who has taken up the impiety and brought it to perfection is Eunomius the Galatian.[11] He has acquired for himself a notoriety of the most shameful sort—for it says *their glory is in their shame* [Phil 3.9]—preferring the infamy of writing things that no one else ever dared to say rather than the goods reserved for the pious. In this brilliant handbook[12] he

7. On Basil's "well-being," see n. 9 below.

8. See Mt 7.2; Mk 4.24; Lk 6.38.

9. Interestingly, both Basil and Eunomius (see *Apol.* 1, esp. 4–5 and 13–14) justify their treatises as being for the good of both themselves and others. A few lines above, Basil speaks of his own "well-being" (τὸ ἀσφαλές) and Eunomius speaks of the "well-being" (ἀσφάλεια) of others when they enumerate their reasons for writing. Sesboüé (SC 299.143 n. 4) attributes this parallel to a similar formation in the laws and themes of rhetoric.

10. Basil may have known about the early life of Aetius from a letter by George of Laodicea (d. 359) that was later used by Gregory of Nyssa, *Eun.* 1.37.

11. Eunomius was actually a Cappadocian like Basil, from the town of Oltiseris in the extreme northwest of the province near the border of Galatia. Vaggione surmises that Basil's tagging of Eunomius as a "Galatian" is an instance of Cappadocian chauvinism (Vaggione 2). Van Dam suggests that Basil was trying to keep Cappadocia free from the stain of Eunomius's heresy (*Becoming Christians*, 29). Eunomius complained of the epithet, but Gregory of Nyssa defended it (*Eun.* 1.105).

12. Here Basil adopts a mocking, sarcastic tone toward Eunomius, a tone which continues throughout the treatise.

was roused to publicize the blasphemy so long spoken under his breath,[13] striving with all his might to be proclaimed the pioneer and the patron of the entire heresy. Therefore, he is the one we propose to set straight in the present work. But since there is a single evil in the pair,[14] it is clear that if we refute the fully-trained disciple[15] we also refute along with him his teacher, the sower of the seeds of the impiety. May it be possible for us through your prayers to receive such a great power for argument that, like the zealot Phinehas, we can strike down both of them—this pair intertwined with one another in impiety—with the single stroke of refutation.[16]

So, then, even though I have plenty of material to demonstrate in this treatise that Eunomius is lying, stupid, wanton, dissembling, and blasphemous, I will consider mentioning all these as secondary and focus on the blasphemy he has uttered regarding the grandeur of the glory of the Only-Begotten. After I have revealed the devices he uses to conceal his scheme, I will attempt to make his blasphemy as clear as day for all.

[1.2] So now I will proceed to the refutations, beginning with the very title of his work. He contrived the first of all his tricks to be the very genre he gives to his arguments, in that he organizes his teaching in the form of an apology. He does this to avoid the appearance of intentionally giving an exposition of the doctrines of his impiety and to give the impression of coming to these arguments out of necessity. By any means whatsoever he wanted to circulate this evil and godless proclamation and bring into public view the blasphemy which he long ago conceived and gave birth to. Yet he realized that if he openly sat in the teacher's chair, besides being most vulgar and distasteful to his audience, he would still remain unconvincing and suspect to many on the grounds that he had come to innovate out of a desire for glory. But if he puts these arguments of his in the form of an apology, he escapes the suspicion of innovation. Instead, his audience is somewhat drawn to him, as by nature all human beings are accustomed out of kindness to side with those at a disadvantage. This is why he alleges that he has accus-

---

13. Lit., "under his teeth."
15. See Lk 6.40.

14. That is, Aetius and Eunomius.
16. See Nm 25.7–8.

ers and denouncers, and lays the blame for his treatise on them. There is no better way of making his scheme plain to all than by listening to the prologue of his text. This is what it says:

We know that denouncing and slandering people because of a loose tongue and a senseless mind is the business of knaves and squabblers. Yet when deemed wicked out of slander, attempting with all zeal to ward off the falsehood with refutations is the task of discreet men and those who by means of their own prudence place a high value on the well-being of the many.[17]

So, then, the form of the treatise is such as would come from someone who acts neither straightforwardly nor without dishonest intent. For he obscures the suspect character of his innovation under the cloak of an apology and seeks favor from his audience, making it seem as if he came to make these arguments under the compulsion of being slandered.

Yet his deceptive tactic of employing apology is refuted because the drama of his apology is staged without any characters, as he cannot name the accuser against whose charge he makes a pretense of fighting. It is not on account of magnanimity that he refrains from mentioning his harassers by name. If this were the case, how could he cudgel his opponents with such abuse? Rather, suspecting that his falsehood would become manifest, he is ashamed to name definite persons as his accusers. If he had been able to name anyone, he certainly would have spoken up and stated who they were. Even if doing this would not have allowed him to give free rein to his own anger, at least he would have provided for "the well-being of the many"—those for whom he proclaims to have such great care. After all, a concealed wickedness is more damaging than one revealed. Hence if we had known who his denouncers were, we would have easily escaped "their loose tongues and senseless minds"—yes, I will use the very words of that wisest of men.

Since he has maintained silence until the present (whatever his reason may have been), it is now time for him to be interrogated. It is now time for him to answer some questions. Who are the accusers that compelled him to make an apology by first

17. Eunomius, *Apol.* 1.1–5 (EW 34).

slandering him? From what part of the world do they come? Who are the judges before whom he brought his case? In what court of justice did he enter this document? At what place on earth or sea did it convene? Indeed, what would he say? At Seleucia?[18] But those convicted there were convicted by their silence. For they did not appear in court when the assembly summoned them time and again to inquire into the charges they had made against some of its members. They were promptly condemned on these grounds.[19] My explanation is equally applicable to the entire group:[20] due to their communion with impiety they were cut off from the church as a diseased limb is amputated from a healthy body. Perhaps at Constantinople?[21] But at that council there was no need for either an apology or a discourse. For after winning over to their side the imperial courtiers and the rest of the most influential figures, they dealt with the council's agenda from a position of great superiority. They themselves were the accusers, the judges, the executioners, and everything whatsoever they wanted to be. Some bishops they deposed. Others they installed in their place. They threatened the lives of others. They divided up the cities among themselves, making the most of their great power. One of them who had been ousted from the cities of Syria seized control of Constantinople to tyrannize it.[22] That unconquerable and clever writer with whom we are

18. The Council of Seleucia was held in September 359; see Introduction, pp. 30–31. There is no evidence that Eunomius was present at Seleucia. Aetius, however, was present with Eudoxius either during or shortly after the council: see Philostorgius, *h.e.* 4.11, with Kopecek 202–5 and 225–27 and the corrective of Vaggione 223 n. 140.

19. Acacius of Caesarea and his supporters had accused Cyril of Jerusalem and other deposed bishops of various crimes. When the council decided to review the depositions and to hear the accusations as a kind of court of appeal, Acacius and his supporters refused to attend and were themselves summarily deposed.

20. Basil means all the supporters of Acacius, not all the bishops at the council.

21. The Council of Constantinople met in January 360; see Introduction, pp. 9–11 and 31–32. For Basil's view of the council, see his *Epp.* 9.3 and 51.2. Eunomius first delivered his *Apology* here; see EW 5–9 and Vaggione 226–27.

22. Basil is here referring to Eudoxius, bishop of Antioch since 358, who was made bishop of Constantinople at the council, replacing the deposed Macedo-

concerned carried off Cyzicus as the prize of his impiety.[23] The church of Sardis was presented to Theosebius after his refutations in defense of the unutterable blasphemies.[24] I pass over in silence Bithynia, Pamphlagonia, Cilicia, and all the lands upon which this evil, swirling all around, encroached. So, then, at that time was there still anything to be gained by making some sort of apology? I think it was impossible for a gain to be made by him presenting one: he is intentionally lying. Hence it is truest of all that he devised the form of the treatise for the purpose of deceit. So much for this subject.[25]

Advancing a little, let's look at what he writes. Before refuting his impiety, it would perhaps not be useless to give a few indications of how conceited he is.

[1.3] Above all I implore you, both my current audience and those who will read this work later: do not attempt to distinguish truth from falsehood by numbers, associating what is better with the majority party; do not cloud your judgment by focusing on positions of dignity; do not close your ears to those who come after by giving more attention to the contingent of those who have gone before.[26]

What are you saying? That we should not give more attention to those who have gone before? That we should not respect the multitude of those who are currently Christians and those who have been Christians from the time when the gospel was first proclaimed? That we should not consider the honor of those enlightened with manifold spiritual gifts? You have indeed inaugurated this road of impiety as an act of hatred and hostility against people such as these! Or should each of us do this: shut

---

nius. He had "been ousted from the cities of Syria" soon after becoming bishop of Antioch when Basil of Ancyra convinced Constantius to expel him, but he was rehabilitated at the Council of Seleucia.

23. Eunomius, still a deacon, replaced the deposed Eleusius of Cyzicus; see Sozomen, *h.e.* 4.25. Aetius met the opposite fate: he was banished.

24. From Sozomen, *h.e.* 4.24, we learn that Heortasius, bishop of Sardis, was deposed at the Council of Constantinople on the grounds that he had been ordained without the sanction of the bishops of Lydia, but Sozomen does not record his replacement, for which Basil is our sole source.

25. Gr. καὶ ταῦτα μὲν εἰς τοσοῦτον. This is one of Basil's usual phrases for signaling the completion of one section and the beginning of another.

26. Eunomius, *Apol.* 2.1–6 (EW 36).

the eyes of our soul once and for all, banish from our mind the memory of every saint, and then each of us take his own heart, now *empty* and *swept-clean* [Mt 12.44; Lk 11.25], and hand it over to your misleading and sophistical arguments? You would indeed have obtained great authority, if it turned out that by a word of command you obtained what the *devil* could not attain by his various *wiles* [Eph 6.11]! Furthermore, if we were persuaded by you, we would have to judge the tradition that has prevailed in every time past due to so many saints as of less worth than your impious fabrication.[27] In addition, he is not only satisfied with snatching away the thoughts of his current audience, but he also expects those who will later read his treatise to hold the same opinion. What arrogance! He thinks that his treatise will endure for posterity and that his memory will be cherished as immortal for all time to come!

And then, a little further on, he adopts an affected tone before his audience, pretending that he does not care at all about self-conceit. It is thus that he speaks to the judges in his imagined drama and dares to say the following:

In addition, do not judge us harshly, if we do not care about self-conceit and fear, seeing that we value indemnity in the world to come more highly than present favor or security, and we deem the punishments determined for the impious a cause for more fear than any earthly misery or temporal death, and so we expound the truth stripped of every covering.[28]

Could any arrogance be more excessive than this? Could any arrogance surpass this bombast? He compounds his dissimulation by being insolent toward his judges. For he implies that what is good displeases them, making them scarcely able to refrain from harshly judging someone who does not care about stubbornness and self-conceit, who values indemnity in the world to come more highly than security in the present, and who deems punishment hereafter a cause for more fear than temporal death. But this amounts to: "Why do you judge me harshly,

---

27. Gr. ἐπίνοια. For the dispute over this term, see *Eun.* 1.6–11. Since Eunomius argues against *epinoia*, there is some irony here in Basil accusing Eunomius of having one.

28. Eunomius, *Apol.* 3.1–5 (EW 36).

gentlemen of the jury? For I have ascended to the very pinnacle
of virtue, transcended earthly matters, and transferred my entire way of life to heaven!" Who has ever heard such arrogance!
With the very words he uses to pretend that he does not care
about self-conceit he exalts himself to the height of pride. For if
he is claiming that his actions merit forgiveness on the grounds
that he is merely observing the chief points of the gospel way of
life, he is letting himself be portrayed as the kind of man appropriately numbered among those who act rightly. So, then, such
statements give clues to his overall purpose. Though we have
passed over many of them in silence, enough has been said for
us to recognize that when he lies, it is *the father of lies* [Jn 8.44]
who speaks in him and to ascertain from his arrogance the one
with whom he is condemned. For the Apostle plainly says that
whoever is swollen with pride falls into the condemnation of the devil [1
Tm 3.6]. At long last, then, let us pass to the refutations of the
impiety.

[1.4] First, he sets out a faith composed of simple and undefined terms that even some of the fathers used. They did not concern themselves with the questions suggested by the terms, but
spoke in this way imprecisely for themselves[29] in their simplicity
of heart. And even if it is said that Arius proposed this faith to
Alexander in order to deceive him (for this is what is claimed),
Eunomius nonetheless proposes this faith as if it agrees with his
own opinion. He does this for two reasons: (1) that he might escape the suspicion of innovation by accepting the faith of the fathers as being correct, and (2) that all who place their trust in the
simplicity of these terms might unexpectedly fall into the snares
of his sophisms. But at the same time he also knows that he can
introduce his opinion in an attractive manner by expounding the

---

29. Gr. ἐφ᾽ ἑαυτῶν. The sense of this phrase seems to be that each father who
used such "simple and undefined terms" spoke informally and privately, intend-
ing neither theological precision nor public, binding statements, but rather
"off the cuff" or "off the record" comments, as it were. Thus their statements
were not authoritative "for others." See Rousseau 118–19. Garnier suggests (PG
29.509d) that the phrase means "*sponte naturae,* hoc est, primo mentis impetu,
id quod agitur quasi non cogitantes," but translates it as *a seipsis.* Sesboüé apparently follows Garnier: "selon leur premier mouvement."

very words of the fathers, and especially that he can be impious without it being noticed. Therefore, even if he were to be detected, he would appear to be blameless seeing that he has said nothing of his own or on his own authority, but was expounding the ideas of someone else. Yet in doing this he did not notice that he actually makes an utter fool of himself. For after he showered so much praise upon the faith, a little further on, he in turn heaped upon it the most shameful reproaches.

To make my point clearer, I will examine his text by dividing it into sections. Let's first consider the faith he puts forward, by citing his very words:

Having already set forth the pious tradition, which has prevailed from the beginning and has come down from the fathers, as a kind of norm and rule, let us use this precise criterion for judging what is said.[30]

To these words he adds the faith which goes as follows:

We believe in one God, the almighty Father, *from whom are all things* [1 Cor 8.6], and in one only-begotten Son of God, God the Word, our Lord Jesus Christ, *through whom are all things* [1 Cor 8.6], and in one Holy Spirit, the Paraclete.[31]

Then immediately he adds:

This, then, is the faith that is simpler and common to all who are concerned with either appearing to be or actually being Christians, so that one can say the more important points in a summary.[32]

A little later on we will talk about the contradictions in his statements and how they battle shamelessly against each other. But first let us remember that he is the one who in his above-mentioned words promised us so pompously "to expound the truth stripped of every covering." Now somewhere it is written: "We believe that unbegottenness is the substance of the God of the universe," or "We believe that the Only-Begotten is unlike the Father in substance."[33] Such is what he would have written if he

---

30. Eunomius, *Apol.* 4.6–9 (EW 36–38).

31. Eunomius, *Apol.* 5.1–5 (EW 38).

32. Eunomius, *Apol.* 6.1–3 (EW 38).

33. Here Basil is summarizing what he thinks are the two main theses of the Heteroousian doctrine advanced by Aetius in his *Syntagmation;* see L. R. Wickham, "The *Syntagmation* of Aetius the Anomean," *JTS* n.s. 19 (1968): 532–69.

had kept his promise and not obscured his ideas with a veil of deceit. I think everything he says is part of his plot. On the one hand, he keeps silent about his own ideas lest he make himself unconvincing and hard to accept by actually presenting them to untrained ears. On the other hand, he puts forward the faith of the fathers as a defense. Because this faith contains ambiguous words, it will not be an obstacle to the argument of his own treatise and will easily lend itself to having its meaning changed by him, under the guise of explaining it, to whatever he wants.

The truth of this is evident from the fact that as soon as he has set forth the faith of the fathers, he immediately rushes into its interpretation on some other pretext, [namely,] that it is insufficient for the resolution of the accusation made against him. Why, then, did you bother to cite this faith rather than directly advancing to those precise statements which would have cleared you of the accusations? Instead he offers this faith as an inerrant criterion, then in turn corrects it as if it were unsound. Now everyone can recognize that he is wrapping the simplicity of this faith around his ideas like bait around a fish-hook that drags its catch to death. And so, when the less experienced run after the appearance of good, they are caught off-guard and hooked by the evil of impiety. Wanting to avoid the appearance of attempting, without being compelled, to correct the faith which he himself extolled with extravagant praise, it is as if he forgot his own words. Look at how he ridicules it: "This, then, is the faith that is simpler and common to all who are concerned with either appearing to be or actually being Christians, so that one can say the more important points in a summary."

Tell me: is the pious tradition of the fathers, the rule (as you yourself have called it), the norm, and the inerrant criterion, now to be designated in turn an instrument of deceit, a scheme of pretense, and things such as these? If it is not such a thing, then what else ought we understand it as? For it does not apply to those who are really Christians, but to those who place more value on seeming to be rather than actually being Christians! Who, then—unless he is completely crazy!—would claim that the rule of correctness applies to those whose souls are perverted? That the norm of truth applies to enemies of the truth?

After all, those who place more value on being called Christians rather than truly being Christians, who don this false mask to deceive the many, are far from all correctness and truth. So, then, as the Preacher says, *neither will what is perverted be made correct* [Eccl 1.15], nor will the criteria of the truth apply to those who have chosen falsehood during their life, as Eunomius thinks it will.

[1.5] For the reasons I just mentioned he has been led into such blatant contradictions. In some statements he praises the faith so that he might seem to be in a communion of piety with the fathers. In other statements he in turn finds fault with it so that he might sneak open for himself a way to his own interpretation. This is why he asserts that the faith is both a rule and stands in need of something more precise to supplement it. But this assertion will be a sign of the utmost stupidity if anyone would like to analyze it. For, surely, O wisest of men, the rule and the norm, as long as they do not fall short of being the rule and the norm, do not need any supplementation for their precision. Additions are made, after all, when something is missing. But if the rule and the norm should be imperfect, there would be no justification for designating them as such. So much for this subject.

But now let us examine for ourselves the arguments that Eunomius sets out concerning God:

Therefore, it is in accordance with both the natural notion[34] and the teaching of the fathers that we have confessed that God is one and that

34. In Stoic and Epicurean epistemology, a "common notion" (κοινὴ ἔννοια) or a "natural notion" (φυσικὴ ἔννοια) is any ordinary, naturally well-founded concept that is available to the mind as a "preconception" (πρόληψις). A preconception is the innate concept of a thing that makes discussion, investigation, and understanding of it possible. Preconceptions are the necessary foundations and principles of all further knowledge that arises from rational inquiry. For ancient testimonies, see Cicero, *ND* 2.43 and *Acad.* 2.30; Diogenes Laertius 7.54; Epictetus, *Disc.* 1.22; and Sextus Empiricus, *M.* 8.331a–332a. According to Michael Frede, common notions "provide us with an antecedent general understanding or grasp of the things which as rational beings we perceive and think about, and which even in perceiving them we represent in terms of these conceptions" ("Stoic epistemology," in K. Algra et al., eds., *The Cambridge History of Hellenistic Philosophy* [Cambridge and New York: Cambridge University Press, 1999], 295–322, at 319).

he did not come into existence either from himself or from another. Each of these alternatives, you see, is equally impossible, since according to truth the maker must pre-exist what comes into existence, and what is made must be secondary to the maker. A thing cannot be prior or posterior to itself, and no other thing can be prior to God. If there were such a thing, it, rather than the second, would surely have the dignity of divinity.[35]

Why have I cited all this text of his? To expose the garrulity of the man throughout the entirety of his discourse. After claiming that on account of the common notions of all people it is self-evident[36] that God is unbegotten, he makes an attempt to supply us with the proofs for this. In doing this, he resembles the man who at high noon wants to use rational argumentation to teach those who can see things quite well for themselves that the sun is the brightest of the stars in heaven. Now if someone who uses rational argumentation to prove what is already quite well known through sense perception is considered to be utterly absurd, how could the person who teaches what common preconceptions[37] enable us all to agree upon not be considered guilty of the same foolishness? For people of sound judgment give far more credence to these realities than to those visibly manifested. Therefore, if anyone were shamelessly attacking this truth and adamantly insisting that the unbegotten was begotten either by himself or by another, then perhaps the vanity of Eunomius's words should be pardoned. But of all those who are unconcerned with our doctrine or who have risen up

---

35. Eunomius, *Apol.* 7.1–7 (EW 40).

36. According to some Hellenistic philosophers, "self-evidence" (ἐναργεία) was the basis for all knowledge, and no argument could be discovered that would be clearer than what was ἐναργές, "self-evident." See Cicero, *Acad.* 2.17; Sextus Empiricus, *M.* 7.216–218. Hence, any argument attempting to prove what was claimed to be self-evident would be considered superfluous.

37. In Stoic and Epicurean epistemology, a "preconception" (πρόληψις) is related to natural notions (see n. 34 above), and is the innate notion of a thing that makes discussion, investigation, and understanding of it possible. See Cicero, *ND* 1.43; Diogenes Laertius 7.54; Epictetus, *Disc.* 1.22. On the difference between a notion and a preconception, see F. H. Sandbach, "Ennoia and prolepsis," in A. A. Long, *Problems in Stoicism* (London: The Athlone Press, 1971), 22–37, and Matt Jackson-McCabe, "The Stoic Theory of Implanted Preconceptions," *Phronesis* 49/4 (2004): 323–47.

against the truth from within the church itself, if until today not even one of either group has become so severely paralyzed in his mind that he holds the unbegottenness of the unbegotten in dispute, I do not see what he seeks to gain by making these arguments. Do we really need the syllogisms of Aristotle and Chrysippus[38] to teach us that the unbegotten was not begotten, either by himself or by another? That he is neither older nor younger than himself? So what is he trying to do when he makes these statements?

It seems to me that he boasts along with his followers that he is shrewd and subtle in mind, quick to spot an absurdity and even quicker to demolish it once detected. Hence he takes pride in how his arguments take twists and turns, and so puts on a fine show in proving that the unbegotten was begotten neither by himself nor by another. In what follows, however, he has not forgotten his schemes. In the course of wasting his time discussing what everybody already agrees on, he slips in for his own purposes certain things as the building blocks for the arguments that follow. For it is not without purpose that he makes the point that "according to truth the maker must pre-exist what comes into existence." He hopes in his arguments about the Son that everyone will have already conceded that the Son comes into existence secondarily and posterior to the Father, since the maker is older than the one who comes into existence. Moreover, he wants to have it taken as a consequence of this that the Son was begotten from nothing. But our refutation of this impiety toward the Son will be postponed for now and conducted later in the suitable place.[39]

For my part, I would say that we would be justified in passing over the designation 'unbegotten' in silence, even if it seems to harmonize particularly well with our notions, on the grounds that it is nowhere to be found in Scripture and furthermore is the primary building block of their blasphemy. The term 'Fa-

38. Aristotle (384–322 BCE) was the founder of the Peripatetic school of philosophy, while Chrysippus (c. 282–206 BCE) was considered to have developed the Stoicism he inherited from his teachers into its classic form. Both were held in high regard for their contributions to logic.

39. Book Two refutes Eunomius's views on the Son.

ther' means the same as 'unbegotten,' yet it has the additional advantage of implying a relation, thereby introducing the notion of the Son. For the one who is really Father is the only one who is from no other, and being 'from no one' is the same as being 'unbegotten.' Accordingly, we should not designate him the 'unbegotten' instead of 'Father,' at least if we are not going to claim a wisdom superior to the teachings of the Savior, who said: *Go, baptize in the name of the Father* [Mt 28.19], but not in the name of the unbegotten.[40] So much for this subject.

Now let's look at what comes next in his treatise. If we advance a few lines, we see that he writes the following as if making a summary of what he has already said:

So then, if it has been demonstrated that God neither pre-exists himself nor that anything else pre-exists him, but that he is before all things, then it follows from this[41] that he is unbegotten, or rather, that his unbegottenness[42] is unbegotten substance.[43]

We detect in these words a captiousness quite easy to recognize, I think, even for one with slight knowledge. But making this captiousness evident to the many proves to be no easy task. Nevertheless, we must make an attempt, placing our hope in the one who gives *a word to those who proclaim good news with great power* [Ps 67.12]. After saying "if neither God pre-exists himself nor anything else pre-exists him, then God's being unbegotten is consequent to him,"[44] Eunomius then realized that the conse-

---

40. Cf. Athanasius, *Ar.* 1.34; *Decr.* 31; George of Laodicea, *Ep. Dogm.* (*apud* Epiphanius, *Pan.* 73.14.5–6 and 73.19.1–2).

41. Gr. ἀκολουθεῖ τούτῳ, "it follows from this." By "this" Eunomius means the three premises he has set out in the protasis of the conditional whose truth he thinks he has already demonstrated. Below Basil misinterprets (mistakenly or otherwise) the τούτῳ as a reference to God.

42. Gr. αὐτό. Eunomius had written αὐτός, "he."

43. Eunomius, *Apol.* 7.9–11 (EW 40). Cf. Aetius, *Synt.* 28: "If everything that has come to be has come to be from another, but the unbegotten subsistence (ὑπόστασις) has not come to be either from itself or from another subsistence, then unbegottenness must reveal substance (οὐσίαν)" (Wickham 543). Basil would say that the Aetian passage has the same problem as the Eunomian passage: it concludes too much from its premises. Aetius, like Eunomius, only proves that God is unbegotten, but Aetius, like Eunomius, claims that it also proves that unbegottenness is the substance of God.

44. Gr. ἀκολουθεῖ αὐτῷ, "is consequent to him." See n. 41 above. Because Ba-

quences of his propositions had brought his line of reasoning around to the opposite of what he intended. For if "God's being unbegotten is consequent to God,"[45] it is clear that his unbegottenness is externally concomitant to him. And what is external to God is not his substance—this is the reason why his ploy is destined to fail.

What does he do to avoid suffering this fate? Giving little thought to the ridicule to which he would subject himself for stating non-sequiturs, he corrected what he previously had said in order to redirect his line of reasoning toward his intended conclusion, saying: "rather, that his unbegottenness is unbegotten substance." But this does not agree at all with what precedes it! For how can God have unbegottenness as consequent to him and simultaneously not consequent to him and contained in the formula of his substance?[46] Even so, he still does not admit that we have completely destroyed his sophism. For if he had brought his arguments to an end after saying that "God's being unbegotten is consequent to God," he would then have had no way of saying that unbegottenness is the substance of the God of the universe, or of proving that the only-begotten Son is alien to him according to substance. The reason for this is that nothing externally consequent to Father and Son is able to rupture their affinity according to substance. As a matter of fact, by adding: "rather, that his unbegottenness is unbegotten substance," Eunomius indicated that unbegottenness is precisely what God is. How this prepares his road to impiety, I shall demonstrate a little further on in my treatise.[47]

So, then, there are two things in this passage: one which he claimed from the outset and showed on the basis of the truth

---

sil has construed Eunomius's τούτῳ as a reference to God, it necessitates translating ἀκολουθεῖ a bit differently to capture his interpretation of Eunomius.

45. Gr. ἀκολουθεῖ τῷ Θεῷ, "is consequent to God." See n. 41 above.

46. Gr. λόγος τῆς οὐσίας. Basil uses this phrase and its synonym, "formula of being" (λόγος τοῦ εἶναι), to denote the account that defines a thing's substance. Objects that are of the same substance have the same formula of substance. This terminology comes from Aristotle: see *APo.* 97a19; *Cat.* 1a1–12; *GA* 715a5, 731b19; *GC* 335b7; *Metaph.* 998b12 and 1018a10.

47. In *Eun.* 1.16–18, Basil speaks of how the views of Eunomius result in blasphemy.

of the matter and according to the logical consequence of his propositions,[48] the other which this so-called writer tossed in with a heretical intention as his concluding statement when he demonstrated unparalleled shamelessness in suddenly shifting his position in order to correct his argument.[49] For how is the same thing both consequent to God and identical with him, seeing that it is already obvious to everyone that what is consequent is different from that of which it is a consequence? As if committing himself to travel along a certain road, he starts with a line of reasoning meant to deceive, and advances toward establishing the proposition that unbegottenness is the substance of the God of the universe, so that, once this has been demonstrated, it may be conceded that the Only-Begotten is unlike the Father in substance.

But let's have a look at what he says:

> When we say 'unbegotten,' we do not intend to honor God in name alone by human conceptualization; rather, we intend to repay him the most necessary debt of all, namely, confessing that he is what he is. Things said by way of conceptualization, you see, have an existence in name alone and when they are being pronounced, and by nature are dissolved together with the sounds used to say them.[50]

He denies that unbegottenness can be considered in the case of God by way of conceptualization. For he thinks that this denial will make it easy for him to prove that unbegottenness is his substance, and, once this is proved, to demonstrate incontrovertibly that the only-begotten Son is unlike the Father in substance. This is the reason why he attacks the term 'conceptualization' as signifying absolutely nothing but having subsistence only when it is being pronounced. Also, he pretends that honoring God with conceptualizations is unworthy of God. As far as I am concerned, any affirmation or denial of whether unbegottenness can be considered through conceptualization must wait until an inquiry into the word itself has taught us something about it.

[1.6] So I am glad to raise the question: what in the world is a conceptualization? Does this term signify absolutely noth-

---

48. That is, that God is unbegotten.
49. That is, that God's substance is unbegottenness.
50. Eunomius, *Apol.* 8.1–5 (EW 40–42).

ing, being merely a noise escaping from the tongue? But such a thing is not called conceptualization, but rather craziness and babbling![51] Now what if Eunomius were to concede that a conceptualization does in fact signify something, but something completely false and non-existent, like the fictional centaurs and Chimaera that appear in the mythologies? If this were the case, how does the falsehood, once it is spoken, dissolve together with the noise of the tongue, seeing that the false concepts remain in the mind after the voice is entirely dissipated into the air? For whenever the soul has become filled with utterly false and vacuous fictions, either the impressions received during sleep or simply the idle movements of the mind, and the soul retains these fictions in its memory but then willingly chooses to make them known with the voice, it is not the case that these mental impressions dissolve together with the words that expressed them. Speaking falsehoods would in fact be very worthwhile if it truly were the nature of a falsehood to be destroyed with the spoken words. But a falsehood does not have such a nature.

It still remains to demonstrate not only how and for what sort of realities customary usage of language[52] employs the term 'conceptualization,' but also how the divine oracles admit of its usage. Therefore, let us first look at common usage: whatever seems simple and singular upon a general survey by the mind,[53] but which appears complex and plural upon detailed scrutiny and thereby is divided by the mind—this sort of thing is said to be divided through conceptualization alone. For example, at first glance the body may seem to be simple, but when reasoning is used it reveals that the body is complex, dissolving

51. Basil here plays on *epinoia* and *paranoia* ("craziness").

52. In Stoic language theory, the "customary usage" (συνήθεια) and "common usage" (κοινὴ χρῆσις) of language referred to natural operations of the mind by which human beings communicate.

53. Gr. ταῖς ἀθρόαις ἐπιβολαῖς τοῦ νοῦ. The phrase "general survey" (ἀθρόα ἐπιβολῇ) has a long philosophical pedigree. In Epicurean epistemology an ἐπιβολῇ referred to the application or focusing of the mind upon an external image that resulted in a sensory or mental impression (e.g., Epicurus, *Ep. Her.* 46–53 [Diogenes Laertius 10.46–53]; cf. Lucretius 4.722–822). Epicurus himself used the phrase ἀθρόα ἐπιβολῇ, meaning "general survey," in a context similar to Basil, making a distinction between a detailed investigation of a subject and a general overview (*Ep. Her.* 35 [Diogenes Laertius 10.35]).

it through conceptualization into the things out of which it is constituted: color, shape, solidity, size, and so forth. Another example would be completely non-existent things envisioned only by a sort of conceptual portrait-painting and imagination, such as is marvelously done by myth-writers and painters to astound their audience: according to customary usage of language, such things are said to be considered by way of conceptualization.

Eunomius has made no mention of these points, either through ignorance or captiousness, and has confined the philosophical account he gave us only to the topic of the conceptualization of non-existent things—and he does not even explain this as it really is. He does not claim, you see, that a conceptualization signifies something, albeit something false, but that the term is completely meaningless and has subsistence only when it is being pronounced. The term 'conceptualization,' however, is far from being restricted only to vain and non-existent imaginations. After an initial concept has arisen for us from sense perception, the more subtle and precise reflection on what we have conceived is called conceptualization. For example, the concept of grain exists in everybody as something simple, by means of which we recognize grain as soon as we see it. But when we examine grain in detail we come to consider more things about it and use different designations to indicate the different things that we have conceived. For the same grain can be called at one time 'fruit,' at another time 'seed,' and again at another time 'nourishment.' It is 'fruit' as the result of farming that has been completed, 'seed' as the beginning of farming to come, and 'nourishment' as what is suitable for the development of the body of the one who eats it. Now each one of these things mentioned is considered by way of conceptualization: each of these is not dissolved together with the noise of the tongue, but rather the concepts remain settled in the soul of the one who has conceived them. Generally speaking, all things recognized through sense-perception and which seem simple in substrate but which admit of a complex account upon further consideration are said to be considered through conceptualization.[54]

54. At *Eun.* 1.6, 57 (SC 299.188), we read ἐπινοίᾳ for ἐπινοία, clearly a misprint.

[1.7] The usage of conceptualization that we have learned from the divine word is actually quite close to the way of using the term that we outlined above. Though there is much I could say, I will only mention a single case, the most pertinent, leaving all the others aside. When our Lord Jesus Christ spoke about himself to make known both the Divinity's love of humanity and the grace that comes to humanity from the economy,[55] he did so by means of certain distinguishing marks[56] considered in connection with him. He called himself 'door,' 'way,' 'bread,' 'vine,' 'shepherd,' and 'light,'[57] even though he is not a polyonym.[58] All these names do not carry the same meaning as one another. For 'light' signifies one thing, 'vine' another, 'way' another, and 'shepherd' yet another.[59] Though our Lord is one in substrate, and one substance, simple and not composite, he calls himself by different names at different times, using designations that differ from one another for the different conceptualizations. On the basis of his different activities and his relation to the objects of his divine benefaction, he employs different names for himself. For instance, when he calls himself 'the light of the world,' he points out the inaccessibility of the glory in the divinity. He also calls himself this because he illuminates those who have purified the eye of their soul with the splendor of his knowledge. He calls himself 'vine' because he nurtures those who have been planted in him by faith so that they may bear the fruits of good works. And 'bread' because he turns out to be a

55. Gr. τὴν ἐξ οἰκονομίας χάριν τοῖς ἀνθρώποις. The "economy" refers to God's saving acts in the world, especially those acts performed (and suffered) in the incarnation of Christ. See also *Eun.* 1.12, 2.3, and 2.15. For discussion, see Ayres 220–21 and Behr 290–93.

56. Gr. ἰδιώμασί τισι. This is the first occurrence of a term crucial for Basil's Trinitarian theology in *Eun.*

57. See Jn 10.9, 14.6, 6.51, 15.1, 10.11, and 8.12, respectively.

58. Porphyry (*in Cat.* 69, 1f. Busse) explains that "polyonyms are things that have several different names, but one and the same account, such as 'sword,' 'sabre,' and 'blade,' and in the case of clothing, 'coat' and 'cloak'" (trans. Strange 50). Christ is not a polyonym for Basil because the diverse names given to him have different accounts.

59. Cf. Origen's discussion of the conceptualizations of Christ in the first two books of his *Commentary on the Gospel of John*, especially *Jo.* 1.22, 1.52–57, 1.126, 1.154; see also *Cels.* 2.64 and 7.16.

rational being's most appropriate nourishment, since he maintains the soul's constitution, preserves its distinguishing mark, and, always filling up from himself what is lacking, does not allow it to be dragged down to the weakness that enters it from irrationality. And if anyone should examine each of the names one by one, he would find the various conceptualizations, even though for all there is one substrate as far as substance is concerned. Who, then, has so sharpened his tongue for blasphemy that he dares to say that these conceptualizations are dissolved together with the sound of the words?

So, then, what is absurd about having a similar understanding of terms used by way of conceptualization for the God of the universe, even the very term that first motivated our entire treatise?[60] We will discover that the name 'unbegotten' is said in no other way. For we say that the God of the universe is 'incorruptible' and 'unbegotten,' designating him with these names according to various aspects.[61] Whenever we consider ages past, we find that the life of God transcends every beginning and say that he is 'unbegotten.' Whenever we stretch our mind forward to the ages to come, we designate the one who is without boundary, infinite, and comprehended by no terminal point as 'incorruptible.' Therefore, just as 'incorruptible' is the name we give him because his life is without an end, so too is 'unbegotten' the name given because his life is without a beginning, when we consider each through conceptualization.[62] What reason could there be, then, for denying that each of these names is conceptualized and that they constitute a confession of what truly belongs to God? But Eunomius separates the two—what is said "by way of conceptualization" and what repays God the confession he is due, namely, "that he is what he is"—as if they were opposed to one another and utterly incompatible.

[1.8] Let's not pass by the fact that he makes a show of reverent caution only to bring those who listen to him to ruin. For he says that we do "not honor God by human conceptualization"

60. That is, 'unbegotten.'

61. Gr. κατὰ διαφόρους ἐπιβολάς.

62. Gr. τῇ ἐπινοίᾳ θεωρούντων ἡμῶν ἑκάτερα. We follow the reading of CVBFKRXZ and other mss., a reading also witnessed to by Gregory of Nyssa, *Eun.* 2.507.

when we designate him 'unbegotten,' but rather that we "repay him the most necessary debt of all" when we "confess that he is what he is."[63] What could we say that would fittingly describe this wily duplicity? He attempts to alarm the more simple by claiming that they fail to render what is owed to God unless they confess that unbegottenness is his substance. In addition, he calls his own impiety the payment of a debt, so that he appears not to be saying something on his own authority, but to be fulfilling the debt we are constrained to pay to God. And to others he indicates that, once they have placed unbegottenness in the substance of God, they will be discharged as innocent. But if they understand the matter differently, in the pious way, they should expect inexorable wrath, on the grounds that they failed to repay the most important and the most necessary of all obligations.

Gladly, then, would I scrutinize him to see if he similarly sticks to this prudence in the case of all that is said about God, or if he does so only in the case of this word.[64] For if he does not consider anything at all by way of conceptualization so as to avoid the appearance of honoring God with human designations, then he will confess this: that all things attributed to God similarly refer to his substance. But how is it not ridiculous to say that his creative power is his substance? Or that his providence is his substance? Or the same for his foreknowledge? In other words, how is it not ridiculous to regard every activity of his as his substance? And if all these names converge upon a single meaning, each one has to signify the same thing as the others, such as is the case with polyonyms, as when we call the same man 'Simon,' 'Peter,' and 'Cephas.'[65] In the same vein, whoever has heard that God does not change will also be led to his unbegottenness, and whoever has heard that he has no parts will also be brought to his creative power. What is more absurd than this confusion? Each of the names is deprived of its proper signification, and conventions are established that contradict both common usage and the teaching of the Spirit. And yet, when we hear it said about God that *in*

63. Eunomius, *Apol.* 8.1–3 (EW 40–42).
64. That is, 'unbegotten.'
65. See n. 58 above.

wisdom he made all things [Ps 103.24], we learn of his creative art. When it is said that *he opens his hand and fills every living thing with delight* [Ps 144.16], it is a question of his providence that extends everywhere. When it is said that *he made the darkness his hiding-place* [Ps 17.12], we are taught that his nature is invisible. Furthermore, when we hear what was said by God himself, *As for me, I am and do not change* [Mal 3.6], we learn that the divine substance is always the same and unchanging. So, then, how is it not sheer madness to deny that a proper signification underlies each of the names, and to claim in contradiction to their actual meaning that all names mean the same thing as one another?

Nevertheless, even if we were to concede this point, not even then will they come any closer to reaching their goal. For if all these names which are used for our God and Father signify his substance—I mean 'unchangeable,' 'invisible,' and 'incorruptible'—then it is basically clear that they will also be indicative of substance in the case of the only-begotten Son and God. For we also call the only-begotten Son 'invisible,' 'unchangeable,' 'incorruptible,' 'partless,' and all such names. And thus will their cleverness come back to refute them. For they will be no more capable of demonstrating that the Son is unlike in substance because of a single different designation than compelled by the very necessity of the terms admitted to confess his likeness because of many shared designations. If he were to say that he has employed this reverent caution only in the case of the term 'unbegotten,' whereas in the other cases he is careless, let us once more put a question to him: why this arbitrary selection? When there are so many things that are said about God, why does he opt to be exact in this one case alone? And if in the case of this name he is paying his debt of "confessing that he is what he is," why in the case of other names does he not refrain from honoring him with the whole multitude of human conceptualizations? For the one who has many debts but repays only one is not prudent for repaying this one but rather exceedingly imprudent for withholding the repayment of all the rest. Therefore, as if they were traps set for wild beasts, Eunomius is caught by his own wiles: the more he attempts to escape from them, the more he is refuted by them.

[1.9] Look at what comes next in his treatise. After he thinks he has demonstrated that it is impossible to comprehend unbegottenness through conceptualization, he adds:

Moreover, in no way [is God said to be unbegotten] by way of privation, if privations are in fact privations of natural attributes, and secondary to possessions.[66]

It is not difficult to show that he chatters on and on about these matters based on the wisdom of the world. Perverted by this wisdom, he proposes innovative arguments such as these. The claims about possession and privation come from Aristotle, as those who have read him can attest, in his book entitled *Categories*, where he says that privations are secondary to possessions.[67] To prove that he speaks not on the basis of the Spirit's teaching, but according to *the wisdom of the rulers of this age* [1 Cor 2.6], it is enough that we quote a psalm verse against him: *Transgressors told me garrulous tales, but it is not as your Law, Lord* [Ps 118.85 LXX]. Realizing that his statement is not based on the teachings of our Lord Jesus Christ, it suffices to recall that saying of his: *Whenever he tells a lie, he speaks on his own authority* [Jn 8.44].[68] In this way we are able to curtail the bulk of our own arguments, as we have now made it plain to all with these statements that we have no communion with them. *For what agreement does Christ have with Belial? Or what does a believer share with an unbeliever?* [2 Cor 6.15] But lest lack of refutation imply that we are taking refuge in silence, come, let's briefly discuss these matters.

Note, Eunomius, that many of the things said about God are expressed with terms of a similar formation, for example, 'incorruptible,' 'immortal,' and 'invisible.' We maintain that 'unbegotten' has the same formation.[69] So, then, if some call such names 'privatives,' this way of speaking is of no concern to us. For we know nothing about the technical jargon for terms, nor are we envious of those who do know. Nonetheless, in whatever category

66. Eunomius, *Apol.* 8.7–8 (EW 42).

67. Aristotle, *Cat.* 10, 12a26–13a37.

68. Basil is implicitly comparing Eunomius to the devil, who is the subject of Jn 8.44.

69. In Greek all these terms are formed with an alpha-privative, the Greek equivalent of the prefixes *in-* or *un-*.

one may put the other terms we have listed, we say that the designation 'unbegotten' also belongs in the same. Just as 'incorruptible' signifies that no corruption is present to God, and 'invisible' that he is beyond every comprehension through the eyes, and 'incorporeal' that his substance is not three-dimensional, and 'immortal' that dissolution will never happen to him, so too do we also say that 'unbegotten' indicates that no begetting[70] is present to him. So, then, if none of the former terms is privative, then neither is the latter. But if you grant that the former terms are privatives without conceding this for the designation 'unbegotten,' then tell me, what is the preceding possession whose privation is revealed by 'incorruptible'? Why can't 'unbegotten' have the same force? He practices his evil art on this term alone because the foundations of his impiety depend upon it.

To make his deception plain, do this: take the arguments that he uses for 'unbegotten' (that it is not reasonable to speak about God either "by human conceptualization" or "by way of privation"), and notice what happens when you transfer them to some of the other things said about God. You will discover that the arguments he uses are perfectly suited for each term. If you like, we can do this for 'incorruptible,' substituting it into his own text: "When we say 'incorruptible,' we do not intend to honor God by human conceptualization; rather, we intend to repay him the most necessary debt of all, namely, confessing that he is what he is. Moreover, in no way [is God said to be incorruptible] by way of privation, if privations are in fact privations of natural attributes, and secondary to their possessions." Why is it more fitting to give this philosophical account for 'unbegotten' than for 'incorruptible' and in general for each

---

70. Gr. γέννησιν. Mss. BKRXZ witness to the alternative reading γένεσιν, "coming to be." The alternative reading accords much better with Basil's thought elsewhere. At *Eun.* 1.7, 43 and 1.15, 25–26, Basil argues that unbegottenness is synonymous with "without origin" (ἄναρχον). In other words, it is a term that rules out the notion that God came to be in any way, not simply through begetting. Perhaps more importantly, Basil elsewhere affirms that there *is* begetting (γέννησις) in God in the sense that the Father generates the Son, who is God: see, e.g., *Eun.* 2.6. At *Eun.* 1.10, 37, however, Basil repeats his claim that the term 'unbegotten' is a denial of begetting (γέννησις), which leads us to believe that the alternative reading of γένεσιν in the present passage is a learned correction.

term with the same formation? None of the others assists him in achieving his impiety! For this reason he does not mention the rest of them, notwithstanding the fact that there are countless things that we say about God.

[1.10] Such is the situation. There is not one name which encompasses the entire nature of God and suffices to express it adequately. Rather, there are many diverse names, and each one contributes, in accordance with its own meaning, to a notion that is altogether dim and trifling as regards the whole but that is at least sufficient for us. Now some of the names applied to God are indicative of what is present to God; others, on the contrary, of what is not present. From these two something like an impression of God is made in us, namely, from the denial of what is incongruous with him and from the affirmation of what belongs to him.

For example, whenever we call him 'incorruptible,' we are implicitly saying to ourselves or to those who hear us: "Do not think that God is subject to corruption." Whenever we call him 'invisible': "Do not suppose that he can be comprehended by the perception that comes through the eyes." Whenever we call him 'immortal': "Do not think that death happens to God." It is the same whenever we call him 'unbegotten': "Do not believe that the being of God depends on any cause or principle." On the whole, we learn from each of these names not to fall into inappropriate notions in our suppositions about God. So, then, in order that we may come to know the particular distinguishing mark[71] of God, in our statements about God we forbid each other to lower our thoughts to the level of what is not appropriate. We do this so that human beings will never consider God to be one of the things that are corruptible, or one of the things that are visible, or one of the things that are begotten. Forbidding all these names results in something like a denial of what is foreign to him, since our minds articulate distinctly and cast aside the suppositions concerning what is not present to him.

Again, we say that God is 'good,' 'just,' 'Creator,' 'Judge,' and all such things. So, then, as in the case of the terms we just spoke about which signified a denial and rejection of what is foreign

71. Gr. τὸ ἐξαίρετον ἰδίωμα.

to God, so here they indicate the affirmation and existence of
what has affinity with God and is appropriately considered in
connection with him. Accordingly, we learn from each of the
two forms of designation either that what is present is present
or that what is not present is not present. Now 'unbegotten' is
indicative of what is not present. For it reveals that there is no
begetting present to God. But it makes no difference to us if
someone wants to designate this a 'negation' or a 'rejection' or
a 'denial' or some such thing. I think that what I have said has
sufficiently demonstrated that 'unbegotten' is not indicative
of what belongs to God. Now the substance is not one of the
things not present, but is rather the very being of God; indeed,
it is the pinnacle of insanity to count it among that which does
not have being. For if the substance is among that which does
not have being, then it could hardly be the case that any of the
other things we have mentioned has being. So, then, it has been
demonstrated that 'unbegotten' is classed with what is not present.[72] Therefore, whoever holds that this term is indicative of
the substance itself is a liar.

[1.11] Since he cannot bear that anything is said about God
by way of privation, on the grounds that it is absurd, he has recourse to something more pious: he situates unbegottenness in
the substance itself. Here is how he summarizes his argument:

So then, if [God is unbegotten] neither by way of conceptualization,
nor by way of privation, nor in part (for he is without parts), nor as
something else in him (for he is simple), nor as something else alongside him (for he is the one and only unbegotten), then it[73] must be
unbegotten substance.[74]

His argument is now exactly where he wants it to be. After drag-
ging unbegottenness away from all other senses, he shoves it

72. Basil's statement here is elliptical: in light of what he has just argued, he
must mean that 'unbegotten' is among those terms that signify what is not present. It signifies that being begotten is not present. Basil is not saying that being
*un*begotten is not present.
73. Gr. αὐτό. The referent of αὐτό should probably be understood as τὸ ἀγέννητον, "unbegottenness." Eunomius is claiming that the only way in which one
can make sense of calling God 'unbegotten' is as a definition of the substance of
God, that is, that unbegottenness is the substance of God.
74. Eunomius, *Apol.* 8.14–18 (EW 42).

(so he thinks) into the substance itself and says concerning the God of the universe that "it must be unbegotten substance." As for me, I too would say that the substance of God is unbegotten, but I would not say that unbegottenness is the substance. Moreover, it is worthwhile to remind him that partlessness and simplicity are the same thing as far as the notion is concerned. For that which is not composed from parts is partless; similarly, that which is not constituted from many elements is simple. Yet Eunomius divides these two from one another as if their referents were different. Then he issues an injunction, saying that we ought not divide God, supposing that some part of him is unbegotten and another begotten. Nor ought we think that unbegottenness is located in him as one thing in another.

I hesitate to describe the foolishness of these claims. For whoever speaks against foolishness somehow or other seems to resemble the one uttering such nonsense. I think this is why the wise Solomon recommends *not replying to a fool according to his folly* [Prv 26.4]. At any rate, Eunomius has classified some words, which have been neither said nor spoken at any time, in order to appear to be making this discovery: that of the many ways he has enumerated, there is only one appropriate way to say 'unbegotten.' We would perhaps need a longer argument to expose his fallacy and show that unbegottenness is not the substance of God, if we had not already provided a clear refutation of the ways enumerated by him in his classification. For even if one were to grant his claim that 'unbegotten' is understood "neither by way of conceptualization, nor by way of privation," his conclusion would still not follow. Why would unbegottenness have to fall under one of the ways he enumerated? The truth, however, is otherwise: since he introduces this statement as if it necessarily follows from what went before—"therefore, if neither by way of conceptualization, nor by way of privation," nor according to another one of the ways he enumerated, "then it must be unbegotten substance"—let us retort: "Therefore, since 'unbegotten' is considered by way of conceptualization and is privative, unbegottenness is not the substance of God." You see, as long as he does not refute what we have said and does not confirm his own propositions, his conclusion will have no place to stand.

[1.12] Generally speaking, how much arrogance and pride would it take for someone to think he has discovered the very substance of God above all? For by their bragging[75] they nearly eclipse even the one who said: *Above the stars I will set my throne* [Is 14.13]. Yet these men are not insolently attacking the stars or heaven, but are bragging that they have penetrated the very substance of the God of the universe! Let's ask him from which source he claims to have comprehended it. So, then, from a common notion?[76] But this tells us that God exists, not what God is.[77] Perhaps from the Spirit's teaching? Which one? Where is it located? Isn't it clear that the great David, to whom God manifested the secret and hidden things of his own wisdom,[78] confessed that such knowledge is inaccessible? For he said: *I regard knowledge of you as a marvel, as too strong—I am not able to attain it* [Ps 138.6]. And when Isaiah came to contemplate the glory of God,[79] what did he reveal to us about the divine substance? He is the one who testified in the prophecy about Christ, saying: *Who shall tell of his begetting?* [Is 53.8] Then there's Paul, *the vessel of election* [Acts 9.15], who had *Christ speaking in him* [2 Cor 13.3] and *was snatched away up to the third heaven and heard inef-*

75. That is, the bragging of Eunomius and his associates.

76. On common notions, see p. 91 n. 34 above.

77. According to both the Epicureans and Stoics, one of the common notions was that God exists; for the Epicurean view, see Epicurus, *Ep. Men.* 123–24 (Diogenes Laertius 10.123–24); Cicero, *ND* 1.43–49; Sextus Empiricus, *M.* 9.43–47; for the Stoic view, see Cicero, *ND* 2.12–16 and 75–76; Plutarch, *Comm. not.* 1075e; Diogenes Laertius 7.147; Sextus Empiricus, *M.* 9.133–36. For both Epicureans and Stoics, the common notion of God was not limited to the content that God exists but included a set of specific attributes of God. According to the Epicureans, God was, for example, eternal, blessed, immortal, and imperishable; according to the Stoics, immanent, providential, rational, and active. These attributes were discerned through reason and a general observation of the universe. Basil expresses a similar view in a letter (*Ep.* 234) written to Amphilochius of Iconium in January 376, where he says that the notion (ἔννοια) of God is formed by reflecting on God's attributes revealed in scripture, such as his greatness, power, wisdom, goodness, providence, and justice, but that God's substance is incomprehensible. Hence, for Basil, while the notion of God tells us far more than simply that God exists, it still does not grant us knowledge of the divine substance.

78. See Ps 50.8.

79. See Is 6.1–3.

fable words which are impossible for a person to utter [2 Cor 12.2–4].[80]
What teaching did he bequeath to us about the substance of
God? He is the one who peered into the particular reasons for
the economy[81] and cried out with this voice, as if the vastness of
what he contemplated made him dizzy: *O the depth of the riches
and wisdom and knowledge of God! How inscrutable are his judgments,
and how unsearchable are his ways!* [Rom 11.33] If these things
are beyond the understanding of those who have attained the
measure of the knowledge of Paul, how great is the conceit of
those who profess to know the substance of God?

I would like to ask them about the earth upon which they
stand and from which they come—what do they say? What do
they tell us is its substance?[82] If they were to argue incontrovertibly about what lies on the ground and under their feet, we

---

80. Gr. ἃ οὐκ ἐξὸν ἀνθρώπῳ λαλῆσαι [2 Cor 12.4]. While this passage is nor-
mally translated "which no one is permitted to speak," ἐξὸν can also mean "it is
possible" and the context in which Basil cites this verse warrants understanding
it in this way. It is not the case that Paul grasped the "ineffable words" he heard
regarding the substance of God but was not permitted to speak them; rather,
since Paul did not even understand what he heard, it was impossible for him
to say anything definite about the substance of God. Such is precisely how both
Gregory of Nyssa (*Hom. in Cant.* 3 and 5) and Gregory of Nazianzus (*Or.* 27.9,
28.3, and 28.20) understand this verse.

81. Gr. τοὺς μερικοὺς τῆς οἰκονομίας λόγους. On the economy, see n. 55 above.

82. Basil here is not thinking primarily of what we call the planet earth, but
of the element earth; if he is thinking of the former, it is because it is made
of the latter. The present passage is a close parallel to Basil's *Hex.* 1.8: "Let us
make the same resolutions for ourselves concerning earth: not to inquire med-
dlesomely what its substance might be, nor to spend our time investigating by
reasoning its very substrate, nor to seek some nature devoid of qualities, existing without qualification in its own account, but rather to know well that all the
things which are observed in connection with it are set down in the formula of
its being, being complements of its substance. If you tried to remove by reason
each of the qualities that exist in it, you would end up with nothing. For if you
take away blackness, coldness, heaviness, solidity, the qualities that exist in it
with respect to taste, or any others which are observed in connection with it, the
substrate will be nothing" (Giet 122–24; our translation). The point is that one
cannot through reasoning abstract an unqualified substance (οὐσία) for earth,
since the qualities of earth are its essential complements: take them away and
you destroy earth. A further assumption seems to be that an essential definition
would exclude qualities on the grounds that they are accidental. These notions
inform the logic of the argument Basil makes in *Eun.* 1.12–13.

would believe them even when they concern themselves with the things beyond every notion. What, then, is the substance of the earth? What is its mode of comprehension?[83] Let them respond and tell us whether it is a rational account or sense-perception that attains comprehension.[84] If they claim sense-perception, by which of the senses is it comprehensible? By sight? But sight apprehends colors. Perhaps by touch? But touch can distinguish between hardness and softness, between hot and cold, and such things, none of which anyone would call substance—unless he had been carried away to the utmost insanity! As for taste and smell, what do we need to say about these senses? The former apprehends flavors; the latter, odors. And as for hearing, it is perceptive of noises and voices, things which have no relationship to the earth.[85] Therefore, the only option left to them is to say that they have discovered the substance of the earth by a rational account. What sort of rational account is this? Where is it located in the scriptures? Which of the saints handed it down?

[1.13] The one who gave us an account of creation taught us only this much: *In the beginning God made the heaven and the earth; now the earth was invisible and without form* [Gn 1.1–2]. Think-

---

83. Gr. κατάληψις, "comprehension." According to Stoic epistemology, "comprehension" is the kind of knowledge that stands between "opinion" (δόξα) and "scientific understanding" (ἐπιστήμη). Opinion is the grasp of an individual proposition in such a way that it could be false and is thus a kind of knowledge that is unreliable and subject to error. Comprehension is the grasp of an individual proposition in such a way that it cannot be false and is thus a kind of knowledge that is certain, reliable, and impregnable to any reasoning aimed at producing a change of mind. Scientific knowledge is based upon comprehension, in that it is a systematic comprehension of a whole body of interrelated propositions. For ancient testimonies, see Cicero, *Acad.* 1.41–42; 2.145; Sextus Empiricus, *M.* 7.151–57; Stobaeus 2.73.16–74.3. Here and in *Eun.* 1.13–14, Basil is using the Stoic technical term "comprehension" to demonstrate that Eunomius does not have certain, reliable knowledge of the substance of the earth, to say nothing of the substance of God.

84. Here the disjunction is between achieving comprehension of something by "sense-perception" (αἴσθησις) or by a "rational account" (λόγος). The term λόγος here has the sense of "reason" but also the sense of an expression of reason, such as one might find in the Scriptures; hence our translation, "rational account."

85. Basil's enumeration of the proper objects of each of the five senses is ultimately based on Aristotle, *de An.* 2.6–11.

ing it sufficient to state who made the earth and set it in order, he has refused to waste his time investigating what the earth's substance is, on the grounds that such an endeavor is pointless and useless to his audience. Hence, if knowledge of the earth's substance is established neither by the testimony derived from sense-perception nor by the teaching derived from the rational account, on what basis do they still claim to possess comprehension of it? Insofar as the earth is perceptible to the senses, it is either color or mass or lightness or heaviness or density or rarity or hardness or softness or coldness or hotness, or the qualities pertaining to flavor, or shape or magnitude—none of which they can say is its substance, not even if they were to affirm all of them readily. Yet none of the wise and blessed has provided a rational account which has made it possible to consider the earth's substance. Therefore, what mode of knowledge still remains? Let them answer us, seeing that they despise all things under their feet, transcend the heaven and all the supercosmic powers, and join themselves to the first substance itself through their intellect.[86] But it seems that self-conceit is the most difficult of all the passions in human beings since in actual fact it envelops those whom it affects in the condemnation of the devil.[87] Hence those who have no understanding of the nature of the earth on which they trample go so far as to brag that they have penetrated the very substance of the God of the universe!

God said that he was *the God of Abraham and the God of Isaac and the God of Jacob*, for *this is my everlasting name and my memorial to generations of generations* [Ex 3.15]. When he said this, he was placing a high value on being named the God of such men due to their perfection in all virtue, considering being thus named as something proper and fitting to his majesty. Yet God did not even disclose his name to these saints, namely, to Abraham and to Isaac and to Jacob, and much less[88] did he reveal what his

---

86. Basil's rant against the intellectual arrogance of Eunomius and his followers is reminiscent of Plotinus's against Gnostics in *En.* 2.9. The accusation of arrogance became a *topos* in anti-Eunomian literature; see Gregory of Nazianzus, *Or.* 27.

87. See 1 Tm 3.6. Basil makes a similar point in *Eun.* 1.3.

88. At *Eun.* 1.13, 32 (SC 299.218), we read ἤπου for ἥπου.

substance is! For he said: *I am the Lord, and I appeared to Abraham and Isaac and Jacob, as I am their God, and I did not disclose my name to them* [Ex 6.2–3]. Clearly, he said this because his name is too great for human ears. Yet it seems that to Eunomius God has manifested not only his name, but also his very substance! This great secret, which was not manifested to any of the saints, he makes public by writing it in his books, and blurts it out to all people recklessly. While the promised blessings stored up for us[89] are beyond all human knowledge, and *the peace of God surpasses all intelligence* [Phil 4.7], he does not admit that the very substance of God is beyond all intelligence and beyond all human knowledge.

[1.14] I think that comprehension of God's substance transcends not only human beings, but also every rational nature. Now by "rational nature" here, I mean one which belongs to creation. For the Father is known by the Son alone, and by the Holy Spirit, because: *No one knows the Father except the Son* [Mt 11.27], and: *The Spirit searches everything, even the depths of God. For no one knows what belongs to a man except the spirit that is in him, and no one knows what belongs to God except the Spirit that is from God* [1 Cor 2.10–11].[90] What, then, will remain distinctive about the knowledge that the Only-Begotten or the Holy Spirit has, if indeed they[91] themselves have comprehension of the very substance? Even though they do not attribute to the Only-Begotten the contemplation of the power and goodness and wisdom of God, they have nonetheless made the apprehension of God's substance commensurate with themselves.[92] In fact, the exact op-

89. This expression is often repeated elsewhere by Basil, but only here are the promised blessings said to be beyond human understanding; cf. *Epp.* 2.1, 8; 23.1, 16; 277.1, 29; 314.1, 11; *Spir.* 15.36.7.

90. Gr. εἰ μὴ τὸ Πνεῦμα τὸ ἐκ τοῦ Θεοῦ, "except the Spirit that is from God." This wording is borrowed from 1 Cor 2.12 and conflated with 1 Cor 2.10–11, which in the standard text reads: εἰ μὴ τὸ Πνεῦμα Θεοῦ, "except the Spirit of God." Basil makes the same conflation in *Spir.* 16.40.

91. That is, Eunomius and his followers.

92. The thought here is that while Eunomius and his followers grant to the Only-Begotten neither the contemplation of God's substance nor even the contemplation of the attributes of that substance, they themselves arrogantly claim to have apprehended God's substance.

posite is the case. It is to be expected that the very substance of God is incomprehensible to everyone except the Only-Begotten and the Holy Spirit. But we are led up from the activities of God and gain knowledge of the Maker through what he has made, and so come in this way to an understanding of his goodness and wisdom. For *what can be known about God is that which God has manifested* [Rom 1.19] to all human beings.

Since whatever the theologians seem to have recorded about the substance of God has been expressed in figurative language or even in allegories, the words transport us to other notions. Hence if someone should contentiously stand by the mere letter, taking it in its obvious interpretation without duly examining it, he has strayed into *the myths of the Jews* [Ti 1.14] and *silly old wives' tales* [1 Tm 4.7], and he will grow old in abject poverty, devoid of worthy concepts about God. For in addition to thinking that the substance of God is something material and thereby agreeing with the Greek atheists, he will also suppose that it is complex and composite. For example, the prophet describes God as *like amber from his loins upward and composed of fire below* [Ezek 8.2]. Whoever does not ascend, by means of the letter, to the loftier notions and somehow sticks to the corporeal descriptions of the passage learns from Ezekiel that this is what the substance of God is like. Then again, he will hear from Moses that *God is fire* [Dt 4.24]. In addition, the wise man Daniel will lead him to other suppositions.[93] Hence when he reads the scriptures he will find in them images which are not only false but also in conflict with one another.

Therefore, putting aside this idle curiosity about the substance since it is unattainable, we ought to obey the simple advice of the Apostle, who said: *One must first believe that God exists and that he rewards those who seek him* [Heb 11.6]. For it is not the investigation of what he is, but rather the confession that he is, which prepares salvation for us. Therefore, since it has been demonstrated that the substance of God is incomprehensible to human nature and completely ineffable, it remains that we must thoroughly examine unbegottenness itself, both what it is

93. See Dn 7.9–10.

and how it is considered in the case of the God of the universe.
[1.15] So, then, when we reflect upon the matter, we find that
our notion of unbegottenness does not fall under the examination of 'what it is,'[94] but rather—and here I am forced to speak
this way—under the examination of 'what it is like.'[95] When our
mind scrutinizes whether *God who is over all* [Rom 9.5] has some
cause superior to himself, then, unable to conceptualize any, it
designates the fact that his life is without beginning as 'unbegotten.' When we talk about human beings and say that this person
has come from that person, we are not relating the 'what it is' of
each but the 'from where he has come.' Similarly, when we talk
about God, the term 'unbegotten' does not signify his 'what'
but that he is 'from no source.'

My point can be clarified as follows. When Luke the evangelist recounted the genealogy of our God and Savior Jesus Christ
according to the flesh, he worked his way backwards from the
last to the first.[96] He began with Joseph, saying that he was the
son of Heli, who was the son of Matthan. He traced the lineage
similarly all the way back to Adam. When he reached the end,
he said that Seth came from Adam but that Adam came from
God, and stopped there. In narrating the begetting of each person, he did not indicate the substances of those enumerated but
recounted the proximate origin from which each one came. So,
just as Luke said that Adam came from God, let us ask ourselves:
"Did God come from anyone?" Isn't it obvious in each one of
our minds that God came from no one? Clearly, that which is
'from no one' is 'without origin,' and that which is 'without origin' is 'unbegotten.' Therefore, just as being 'from someone'
is not the substance when we are talking about human beings,
so too when we are talking about the God of the universe it is
not possible to say that 'unbegotten' (which is equivalent to saying 'from no one') is the substance. Whoever says that being
'without origin' is the substance equates himself with someone

---

94. Gr. τὸ τί ἐστιν. The expression is Aristotelian, and refers to the substance
of a thing (see, for example, *Metaph.* Z, 4); the phrase was translated into Latin
as *essentia*, whence our English word 'essence.'

95. Gr. τὸ ὅπως ἐστιν.

96. See Lk 3.23–38.

who, when asked, "What is the substance of Adam? What is his nature?" replies that he is not formed from the copulation of a man and a woman, but rather by the divine hand. The recipient of such a reply may object: "I am not seeking the manner of his subsistence but rather the material substrate of the man himself. Your response has not answered my question."[97] So, then, this is how it is for those of us who have learned from the term 'unbegotten' what God is like rather than his very nature.

[1.16] Generally speaking, if anyone wants to understand the truth of what we are saying, let him examine what he does when he wants to get some idea of the things concerning God and see if he arrives at whatever is signified by 'unbegotten.' As I see it, when we stretch our mind toward the ages to come, we say that the life not limited by any boundary is 'without end.' Similarly, when we ascend in our thoughts to that which is beyond the ages and peer upon the boundlessness of the life of God as if upon some vast ocean, we are unable to apprehend any origin from which he has come. Rather, we think of the life of God as always outside of and exceeding whatever we can conceive, and call the fact that his life is without beginning 'unbegotten.' For the notion of 'unbegotten' is this: that it does not have the origin of its being from another source.

But since 'unbegotten' is considered only with respect to the God of the universe, Eunomius has seized upon the most harmful thing of all for his blasphemy against the Only-Begotten. What does he say next?

But if God is unbegotten as in the preceding demonstration, he could never admit a begetting which would result in his giving a share of his own proper nature to the one who is begotten, and he would escape all comparison or fellowship with the one who is begotten.[98]

What a shameless and wicked blasphemy! What hidden *deceit* and subtle *villainy* [Acts 13.10]! It is exactly as though he speaks with the very *wiles of the devil* [Eph 6.11]! Since he wants to show that the only-begotten Son and God is unlike the God and Father, he keeps silent about the names of 'Father' and 'Son,' and

97. On "material substrate," see *Eun.* 2.4, and the note there.
98. Eunomius, *Apol.* 9.1–3 (EW 42).

simply discusses the 'unbegotten' and the 'begotten.' He conceals the names that belong to the saving faith and hands over the doctrines of his blasphemy unveiled. He does this so that, once he has practiced his impiety first with things and then shifted to persons,[99] he might not seem to have said anything slanderous while maintaining that his blasphemy has been proven, as if it follows as a consequence of his reasoning.

"But if God is unbegotten," he says, "he would escape all comparison or fellowship with the one who is begotten." He did not say 'Father' and 'Son' but 'unbegotten' and 'begotten.' This great misdeed of his is one thing, but look at what the second is like: "But if God is unbegotten," he says, "he could never admit a begetting." And he adds: "which would result in his giving a share of his own proper nature to the one who is begotten." The phrase "he could never admit a begetting" has two meanings: (1) that begetting is not applicable to his proper nature, since it is impossible for an unbegotten nature to come under begetting, and (2) that he does not admit of generating another. Eunomius used the phrase according to the second meaning, but he seizes the masses by the first notion. That this is his plan is clearly shown by what follows. For after he said that "he could never admit a begetting," he added: "which would result in his giving a share of his own proper nature to the one who is begotten." This is the consequence of the second notion: he does not admit of becoming Father, and so he does not "give a share of his own proper nature to the one who is begotten." What could be more bitter than this impiety? Who has ever *spoken* such *wickedness to heaven*? [Ps 72.8]

[1.17] For my part, I fear that if we put another's blasphemies on our lips, we might defile our own mind and come to share in their condemnation. But there is a passage in the gospels that comforts me. When the Holy Spirit reports the blasphemy of the Jews against the Lord, he does not refuse to transmit it to future generations and publicly records their blasphemy for all time without inflicting any blasphemy on the immaculate glory

---

99. In other words, Eunomius first speaks in terms of "things" or "impersonal objects" (πράγματα), that is, the 'unbegotten' and the 'begotten,' and then switches to speaking in terms of persons (πρόσωπα), that is, 'Father' and 'Son.'

of the Only-Begotten.[100] So if "he could never admit a begetting which would result in his giving a share of his own proper nature to the one who is begotten," then God is not Father and there is no. . . . It is better for us to leave this blasphemous statement incomplete.[101] For the former has nothing to do with begetting, and the latter does not have a share in the nature of the one who has begotten him.

He next tries to outdo himself, inventing a new way to prove his blasphemy. He does not issue anything close to a retraction, but contentiously uses what comes after to conceal what he mentioned before. What did he dare to say? "He would escape all comparison or fellowship with the one who is begotten." If there is no comparison of the Son with the Father and no fellowship with the one who has begotten him, the apostles are liars and the gospels are liars. But our Lord Jesus Christ is the Truth itself. As for me, I once again shudder at the blasphemy, yet it is easy for everyone to recognize it. If he has no comparison whatsoever with the Father, how could he say to Philip: *Have I been with you for so long a time and you do not see me, Philip* [Jn 14.9]?[102] How could he say: *The one who sees me sees the one who sent me* [Jn 12.45]? How could the Son show in himself the one who neither admits comparison nor possesses any fellowship with him? That which is unknown is not comprehended through that which is unlike and foreign to it, but it is natural for something to become known by what has affinity with it.[103] In this way the features of a seal are perceived by means of its impression, and the archetype is known through its image, since by comparing them, it is clear that there is identity in each.[104]

100. See Mt 26.65, Mk 14.64, Lk 5.21, and Jn 10.33.
101. See *Eun.* 2.15 for another example of Basil's horror at expressing what he considers a terrible blasphemy.
102. Basil's citation replaces the standard reading "you do not know me" (οὐκ ἔγνωκάς με) with "you do not see me" (οὐχ ἑώρακάς με).
103. Basil is not merely stating the ordinary meaning of the idea that "like is known by like," in which the knowing agent must be like the object of knowledge in order for the agent to acquire knowledge of the object. Here Basil is saying that that which makes the unknown thing known *to us* must be like that thing.
104. Gr. δηλονότι τὴν ἐν ἑκατέρῳ ταυτότητα. The phrase means either that there is something identical in each or that they are identical. We prefer to retain the ambiguity of the Greek.

[1.18] Hence, through this one blasphemy he rejects all the terms handed down by the Holy Spirit for the glorification of the Only-Begotten, even though the gospel teaches that *the Father, God, has set his seal upon him* [Jn 6.27], and the Apostle that *he is the image of the invisible God* [Col 1.15]. He is not a lifeless image, nor handmade, nor a product of art or conceptualization, but a living image, or rather self-existent life which always preserves the indistinguishability, not by likeness of shape, but in his very substance. In my opinion, I say that *existing in the form of God* [Phil 2.6] means the same as "existing in the substance of God." For just as *having taken up the form of a slave* [Phil 2.7] signifies that our Lord was begotten in the substance of humanity, so too saying *existing in the form of God* [Phil 2.6] certainly reveals the distinctive feature of the divine substance. *The one who sees me*, he says, *sees the Father* [Jn 14.9].

When Eunomius alienates the Only-Begotten from the Father and utterly separates him from fellowship with the Father, he cuts off (insofar as he can) the way upward to knowledge[105] that occurs through the Son. While the Lord says: *All that the Father has is mine* [Jn 17.10], Eunomius says that the Father has no fellowship whatsoever with the one who comes from him. In addition, the Lord himself has taught us that *as the Father has life in himself, so he has granted also to the Son to have life in himself* [Jn 5.26]. But what has Eunomius taught us? That the one who is begotten has no comparison with the one who has begotten him. Through this one statement he once and for all does away with the account of the image and denies that the Son is the Father's *radiance* and *the character of his subsistence* [Heb 1.3]. Now it is impossible to conceive an image of something that is incomparable or for there to be a radiance of something with which it has no fellowship by nature. But once again, he persists in the same kind of scheme, saying that "the unbegotten has no comparison with the begotten." He does not say "the *Father* has no comparison with the one from him" in order to demonstrate

105. Gr. τῆς γνώσεως ἄνοδον. There are possible allusions here to Plato, *R.* 517b5 (the upward journey from the cave to the sun of the intelligible realm) and Jn 14.6 (Christ is "the way, the truth, and the life").

the opposition between these words,[106] thereby transferring this opposition to the very substance of the Father and the Son.

[1.19] In order to keep our treatise from becoming excessively long by going through each of his blasphemies and trying to correct everything he said, we will omit those passages whose impiety is obvious and immediately manifest to those who read them. Instead, we will adduce those passages which need some argument for their refutation. After he established in manifold ways that the Father's substance has no fellowship with the Son and demonstrated the absurdity in every way (or so he thinks),[107] he adds:

> Now they would certainly not say the following: that while the substance is common to both, it is due to order and to superiorities based on time that the one is a first and the other a second. This is because the cause of pre-eminence must be present in that which is pre-eminent, but neither time nor age nor order has been joined with the substance of God. For order is secondary to the orderer, but nothing which belongs to God has been ordered by another. Time is a certain kind of motion of the stars, but the stars came into being not only later than the substance of the unbegotten and all the intelligibles, but also later than the primary bodies. Do we even need to speak about ages? For scripture clearly declares: *Before the ages God exists* [Ps 54.20].[108]

In the course of the treatise he has presupposed whatever he wanted and drawn what follows from his presuppositions. Then, diving headlong into absurd notions, he thinks that from this reasoning he has demonstrated the necessity of accepting his own doctrines. He says: "they would not say the following: that while the substance is common to both, it is due to order and to superiorities based on time that the one is a first and the other a second." So, then, if he is speaking of the commonality of the substance, conceiving it to be a kind of doling out and division of pre-existent matter into the things that come from it, this

---

106. That is, 'unbegotten' and 'begotten.'

107. That is, the absurdity Eunomius believes to result from attributing commonality of substance to Father and Son. In the part of *Apol.* 9 which Basil skips, Eunomius sets up the consequences that follow from making the substance common, which according to him results in "many absurdities, or rather, blasphemies" (*Apol.* 9.6–7 [EW 42]).

108. Eunomius, *Apol.* 10.1–9 (EW 44).

understanding is unacceptable to us. God forbid! We declare that those who speak in this way (if indeed anyone really does) are no less impious than those who affirm the 'unlike.'[109] But if someone takes the commonality of the substance to mean that one and the same formula of being is observed in both, such that if, hypothetically speaking,[110] the Father is conceived of as light in his substrate, then the substance of the Only-Begotten is also confessed as light, and whatever one may assign to the Father as the formula of his being, the very same also applies to the Son. If someone takes the commonality of the substance in this way, we accept it and claim it as our doctrine. For this is how divinity is one. Clearly, their unity is conceived to be a matter of the formula of the substance. Hence while there is difference in number and in the distinctive features that characterize each, their unity is observed in the formula of the divinity.

[1.20] Now that we have determined in what way we need to understand the commonality of the substance, let's closely examine what comes next to see if it has any connection with what came before. He says: "it is due to order and to superiorities based on time that the one is a first and the other a second." In the case of things whose substance is common, why is it necessary for them to be subject to order and to be secondary to time? For it is impossible that the God of the universe has not co-existed from eternity with his image who has radiated light non-temporally, that he does not have a connection with him that is not only beyond time but also beyond all ages. And so he is called the *radiance* [Heb 1.3] that we may understand his connection,[111] and the *character of his subsistence* [Heb 1.3] that we may learn that he is of the same substance.[112]

Furthermore, there is an order which is natural and another which comes about by deliberation. On the one hand, order is natural when it is a question of the order which is arranged for created beings according to the rationales of their creation, the

109. Basil here refers to Eunomius and his Heteroousian associates.
110. Gr. καθ' ὑπόθεσιν.
111. Gr. τὸ συνημμένον. That is, the Son's connection with the Father.
112. Gr. τὸ ὁμοούσιον. This is the only place in *Eun.* where Basil describes the Son as *homoousios* with the Father.

position of countables,[113] and the relation of causes to their effects. (Now it has already been agreed upon that God is Maker and Creator of nature itself.) On the other hand, order comes about by deliberation and art when it is a question of structures that are built, subjects of learning, logical propositions,[114] and such things. But Eunomius concealed the first kind of order and mentioned only the second kind, saying that one ought not to posit order in the case of God since "order is secondary to the orderer." He has either not understood or purposely concealed the fact that there is a kind of order which is not established by our imposing it but which is found in the natural sequence of things. An example of the latter is the kind of order between fire and the light which comes from it. In these cases we say that the cause is prior and that which comes from it is secondary. We do not separate these things from one another by an interval, but through reasoning we conceptualize the cause as prior to the effect. So, then, in the case of things in which there is a prior and a secondary, how is it reasonable to deny that there is an order which exists not by our imposing it, but from the natural sequence that exists in them?

Why, then, does he refuse to accept that there is order in God? He thinks that if he has demonstrated that priority in God is conceivable in no other way, then he is demonstrating that the only remaining option is that God has pre-eminence according to the substance itself. But we say that the Father is ranked prior to the Son in terms of the relation that causes have with what comes from them, not in terms of a difference of nature or a pre-eminence based on time. Otherwise, we will deny even the very fact that God is the Father since difference in substance[115] precludes their natural connection.

[1.21] Since this man who is wise in everything has proceeded to give us a definition of the nature of time, let's investigate whether his thinking on the matter is solid and circumspect. He says that "time is a certain kind of motion of the stars," clearly meaning the sun, the moon, and the rest of the stars in which

---

113. That is, the numbers used to count have a natural sequential order.

114. Gr. ἀξιώμασι. Or, "axioms."

115. Gr. κατὰ τὴν οὐσίαν ἀλλοτριότης.

there is the power to move by themselves. What, then, will this expert in astronomical phenomena declare is the interval from the coming-to-be of heaven and earth until the making of the stars? For the one who in the power of the Spirit recorded the cosmogony clearly said that the great lights and the rest of the stars came to be on the fourth day.[116] Therefore, it seems as if there was no time during the preceding days. The stars, you see, were not moving yet. For how could they, when they had not come to be at the beginning? And again, when Joshua the son of Nun was waging war against the Gibeonites, and the sun, constrained by a command, remained unmoved, and the moon stood still,[117] was there not time in these circumstances? What, then, should we call the interval of that day? What designation have you dreamt up for it? If the nature of time has failed, clearly an age[118] takes its place. But if you designate a small part of the day as an age, is there any excess of folly left to surpass? It seems that because of his great sagacity he thinks that day and night happen by a certain kind of motion of the stars, but that these are parts of time. For this reason he declared that "time is a certain kind of motion of the stars," not realizing what he said. It was more appropriate to say, not "a certain kind of" motion,[119] but rather (if I may) "a certain amount of" motion.[120] But who is so completely childlike in his thinking so as not to know that days and months and seasons and years are measures of time, not parts? Rather, time is the extension coextensive with the existence of the cosmos. All motion is measured by time, whether of the stars, of living creatures, or of anything else that moves. On the basis of time we say that one thing is quicker or slower than another. The quicker is what traverses a longer interval in less time; the slower is what moves a shorter interval in more time. But since the stars move in time, he declares that they are the creators of time. Therefore, it follows from the reasoning of this wisest of men that, since dung-beetles also move in time, we should define time as a certain kind of movement of dung-

116. See Gn 1.14–19.
118. Gr. αἰών.
120. Gr. ποσήν.

117. See Jos 10.12–13.
119. Gr. ποίαν.

beetles.[121] For what he says is no different from this, except for the dignity of the names. So much for this subject. Let's look at what follows:

[1.22] Moreover, it is not possible for anything to exist within the substance of God,[122] such as form or mass or size, on account of the fact that God is completely free from composition. But if it neither is nor ever could be lawful to imagine any of these things or others like them as being linked with the substance of God,[123] what sort of account will still allow for likening the begotten to the unbegotten? For neither likeness nor comparison nor fellowship in substance allows for any preeminence or difference, but rather they clearly bring about equality, and along with the equality they show that one likened or compared is unbegotten. But no one is so stupid or so defiant of piety as to say that the Son is equal to the Father! For the Lord himself explicitly declared: *The Father who sent me is greater than I* [Jn 14.24 and 28].[124]

And again, a little later:

But even though many points have been left in abeyance, I believe that what I have already said is sufficient for demonstrating that the one God of all things is unbegotten and incomparable.[125]

Whenever he is about to launch into some wicked argument, he anticipates it by making statements with which everyone agrees so that through his prudence in these matters no one will disbelieve him with regard to the rest of what he says. He says: "Nothing can exist within the substance of God, neither form nor mass nor size, on account of the fact that God is completely free from composition." Up to this point he is prudent, but in what follows he returns to himself.[126] For he tacks on his blasphemy as necessarily following from what he has set forth: "But if it neither is nor ever could be lawful to imagine any of these things or others like them as being linked with the substance of God, what sort of account will allow for likening the begotten to the

---

121. Dung-beetles were widely detested in antiquity; see, for example, Porphyry, *Abst.* 4.9, 46–48.

122. Gr. τῇ οὐσίᾳ τοῦ Θεοῦ. As Garnier noted (PG 29.561 n. 56), Basil has simply specified the referent of Eunomius's ταύτῃ (*Apol.* 11.1 [EW 46]).

123. Basil adds "of God" to the text of Eunomius (*Apol.* 11.5 [EW 46]).

124. Eunomius, *Apol.* 11.1–12 (EW 46).

125. Eunomius, *Apol.* 11.15–17 (EW 46).

126. In other words, "he takes up his old tricks once again."

unbegotten?" What sort of logical sequence do these statements have with each other: "if God is incomposite, then the Son does not admit of likeness to him"? Well, tell me: will you not more or less also be affirming that the Son has neither form nor mass nor size in himself and that he is completely free from composition?

[1.23] For my part, I do not think that even you are so crazy that you would defiantly affirm that the Son is anything other than incorporeal and without form and without figure and all things whatsoever you would affirm in the case of the Father. How, then, is it not in line with piety to compare the one without form to the one without form? The one without size to the one without it? The one without composition to the one without composition? But Eunomius considers likeness to be a question of form, and equality a question of mass; as for size, whatever he thinks it is besides mass he will have to explain more properly.[127] "For this reason," he says, "he is neither equal nor like, since he is both without quantity and without form."[128] But for my part, I consider their likeness to consist in this very thing,[129] since just as the Father is entirely free from composition, so too is the Son altogether simple and without composition. Furthermore, one does not consider likeness according to the identity of form, but rather according to the substance itself. On the one hand, in all those things that are associated with shape and figure, likeness is considered to be a question of identity of form. On the other hand, all that remains for the nature that is without form and without shape is that it has likeness in the substance itself, and in this case equality is not a question of comparing masses, but rather of identity of power. *Christ is the power of God* [1 Cor 1.24]. It is clear that all the Father's power is contained in him. Hence, whatsoever he should *see the Father doing, these same the Son does likewise* [Jn 5.19].

But he says: "Neither likeness nor comparison nor fellowship in substance allows for any pre-eminence or difference, but

127. Here Basil mocks Eunomius's philosophical understanding, since "size" and "mass" refer to the same aspect of a corporeal entity.
128. This is not an exact quotation, but a paraphrase.
129. That is, being without quantity and without form.

rather they clearly bring about equality." How does this allow for no difference? Not even the difference that exists between causes and their effects? Then he adds: "But who is so stupid or so defiant of piety as to say that the Son is equal to the Father?" So, then, let us state a response to him using the words of the prophet: *You've acquired the face of a whore; you have no shame before anyone* [Jer 3.3]. The ill repute of these women besmirches those who have lived honorably, and Eunomius stigmatizes as stupid and defiant of piety those who desire to exalt the glory of the Only-Begotten, showing harshness toward them for the same reasons that also provoked the Jews when they said: *He makes himself equal to God* [Jn 5.18b].

[1.24] And yet—and let no one think what I am saying here is paradoxical—these people[130] somehow or other seem to perceive the logical consequence of what Jesus said. For they were angry that *he called God his father* [Jn 5.18a]. They inferred what follows from this on their own, namely, that *he makes himself equal to God* [Jn 5.18b]. For "he has God as his father" necessarily entails that "he is equal to him." Eunomius agrees with the first and denies the second, adducing for us the voice of the Lord, who says: *The Father who sent me is greater than I* [Jn 14.24 and 28]. But hasn't he heard the Apostle, who said: *He did not count being equal to God a thing to be grasped* [Phil 2.6]?[131] According to your account, if unbegottenness were the substance and the Lord had wanted to indicate pre-eminence according to substance, he would have said: "The Unbegotten is greater than I." But in your account, the designation 'Father' signifies activity and not substance. So, then, when you say that the Father is greater than the Son, you allege that the activity is greater than the product. There can be no doubt that every activity corresponds proportionally to what is produced from it: from a great activity come great products, and from a small activity smaller products. So in their account, when these people confess that the Father is greater than the Son, it means nothing other than that they posit that the activity is disproportional to the product

130. That is, the Jews.
131. Sesboüé punctuates this sentence as indicative (SC 299.256), but it seems better to take it as interrogative.

and allege in vain that God has moved in proportion to the magnitude of his activity without being able to make the end-result be equal to his activity. Hence one of the two following alternatives is necessarily mistaken. (1) 'Father'[132] does not indicate an activity but rather a substance. If this is the case, their contrived account of the likeness is destroyed. For it posits that the Son is like the Father, that is, like his activity. It claims that the Father did whatever he wanted.[133] That's why they also named the Son the image of his will.[134] (2) But when they stick to this position,[135] they cannot also declare that the Father is greater. For every activity, provided that nothing external opposes it, is proportional to its own end-results. So, then, let these things be said to refute the contradiction in their teachings.

[1.25] Is there anyone in the world to whom it is not clear that *greater than* [Jn 14.28] is said either according to the account of cause, or according to excess of power, or according to preeminence of dignity, or according to superabundance of mass? So, then, Eunomius himself has already said that *greater than* is not to be understood according to mass. Now this is reasonable, since *greater than* is a question of magnitudes to the same extent that both 'lesser than' and 'even more so' are. Who would compare with one another things uncircumscribed by magnitude, or rather things without magnitude and completely without quantity? In what way would superiority be detected in things whose comparison is impossible?

Saying that Christ *the power of God* [1 Cor 1.24] is deficient in power characterizes those who are altogether infantile and have not heard the voice of the Lord, who said: *I and the Father are one* [Jn 10.30]. The Lord takes this *one* as equality in power, as we

132. Gr. τὸν Πατέρα. But Basil seems to be using 'Father' as a term, i.e., τὸ Πατέρα.

133. A paraphrase of Eunomius, *Apol.* 23.22.

134. Designating the Son as "the image of the will of the Father" goes back to the earliest stages of the fourth-century Trinitarian debates. It was a teaching of Asterius; see Fragment 10 (Markus Vinzent, *Asterius von Kappadokien: Die theologischen Fragmente* [Leiden: Brill, 1993], 86). It is also affirmed in the Second Creed of the Dedication Council held at Antioch in 341 (preserved in Athanasius, *Syn.* 23.3).

135. That is, that 'Father' indicates activity.

will show from the very words of the gospel. For after he said concerning believers: *No one will snatch them from my hand* [Jn 10.28] and: *The Father who gave them to me is greater than all, and no one is able to snatch them from the hand of my Father* [Jn 10.29], he added: *I and the Father are one* [Jn 10.30]. Clearly, he takes this *one* as equality and identity in power. Furthermore, if the 'throne of God' is a name of dignity (as we ourselves believe it to be),[136] what else does this seat reserved for the Son at the right hand of the Father signify if not the equal honor of their rank? The Lord also promised that he would come *in the glory of the Father* [Mt 16.27].

All that remains, then, is that *greater than* is said here according to the account of cause. Since the Son's principle comes from the Father, it is in this sense that the Father is greater, as cause and principle. For this reason too the Lord said the following: *The Father is greater than I* [Jn 14.28], clearly meaning insofar as he is Father. But what else does 'Father' signify, other than that he is the cause and the principle of the one begotten from him? Generally speaking, a substance is not said to be greater or lesser than a substance, even according to your wisdom.[137] Hence, according to them[138] and truth itself, there is no way in which the present account of *greater than* can indicate pre-eminence according to substance.[139] In addition, Eunomius himself would not claim that the Father is greater according to mass, since he has declared that one must not suppose magnitude in connection with God.[140] So, then, all that remains is the way of being *greater than* that we have stated, I mean that of principle and of cause.[141] So, then, such is how he attempted to blaspheme against *greater than*.

[1.26] It is worthy of astonishment that in such a short time he has come around to saying things that are as contradicto-

136. See Mt 5.34, 23.22; Heb 12.2; and Rv 7.15, 22.1, 22.3.
137. See Aristotle, *Cat.* 5 (3b33–4a9): οὐσία does not admit of a more and a less.
138. That is, Greek philosophers.
139. That is, there is no way the account of *greater than* according to the account of cause can indicate pre-eminence according to substance.
140. See Eunomius, *Apol.* 11.1–3, discussed in *Eun.* 1.22–23.
141. Cf. Athanasius, *Ar.* 1.58.

ry as possible, as if he had been struck in the eyes of his soul with a certain blindness and was unable to perceive the conflict among his statements. Thus he appears to be so utterly foreign to the peace of God—which peace our Lord left with those who genuinely and sincerely believe in him, when he said: *Peace I leave with you; my peace I give to you* [Jn 14.27]—that he contends not only with others, but even with himself! For after he said that the God and Father is *greater than* the only-begotten Son and accused of being mad those who claim that he is equal, as if he had incontrovertible proofs of this, look at what sort of things he writes a little further on:

But even though many points have been left in abeyance, I believe that what I have already said is sufficient for demonstrating that the one God of all things is unbegotten and incomparable.[142]

Now let this question be put to him: if God is incomparable, on what grounds can one comprehend his superiority? For that which is *greater than* is considered to be so by comparison with things that are inferior. So, then, how can the same one be both *greater than* and incomparable? On the one hand, to demonstrate that the substance of God differs from that of the Son, he accepts that *greater than* is said as a comparison between different substances. On the other hand, to bring the Only-Begotten once again down to equal honor with the creation, he lays it down as a law that the Father is incomparable, fabricating a novel and truly incomparable road to blasphemy! Indeed, on the pretense of elevating the God and Father and making him unique, he belittles the glory of the only-begotten Son and God, even though the Lord testifies against this, saying: *The one who does not honor the Son does not honor the Father* [Jn 5.23], and: *The one who denies me does not deny me but rather the one who sent me* [Lk 10.16].

But the enemy of truth, who causes them to say and write such things, has seen that if he can blind them with respect to their understanding of the glory of the Only-Begotten, he will also remove along with it the knowledge of the God and Father himself. Hence, even if they seem to attribute certain superiorities to the God and Father, it is of no benefit to those who

142. Eunomius, *Apol.* 11.15–17 (EW 46).

remove the knowledge of the way which leads to him.[143] For the Jews also think they glorify God, and anyone can listen to Greeks who wish to say something great about God. Nevertheless, no one can say that they *magnify* God [Lk 1.46] without faith in Christ, through whom there is access to knowledge.

[1.27] So, then, he says that God is incomparable in order to indicate that the Son is equal to creation, in that he falls short of the glory of the Father to a similar degree. For things that are inferior by an equal measure are necessarily equal to one another.[144] In the account of Eunomius, the only-begotten Son is inferior to the God and Father to the same extent that all other things are inferior to the God and Father. That which is incomparable is such that it is unapproachable and unattainable by all to a similar degree. But if the Son falls short of the Father to an extent equal to other things, then he is equal to those things along with which he falls short. What, then, could the Jews say that would be worse than this blasphemy? Could we hear anything worse from the Greeks? These men[145] do not even blush when they make a pretense of honoring the Word of God while expounding teachings that Jews and Greeks would find agreeable and acceptable! If the Son cannot be compared with the Father, just as the angels cannot, nor the heavens, nor the sun, nor the earth, nor any of the animals or plants on it, how will he be different from creatures with which he has affinity? Then again, on what basis will he have affinity with the one who has begotten him? He says: *I and the Father are one* [Jn 10.30].

Let's think about this text once more. Tell me this: aren't these the words of someone comparing himself? What do I mean by "someone comparing himself"? I mean that he is making himself one (so to speak) with the Father and by these words expressing their indistinguishability of nature. But Eunomius declares that God is incomparable. Now the goodness of our God and Savior Jesus Christ leads human beings (insofar as we are capable of it) to likeness to the God of the universe through

143. See Jn 14.6.

144. Basil here draws on the mathematical principle that two things equal to some third thing are equal to each other: if A=C and B=C, then A=B.

145. That is, Eunomius and his associates.

practice and training in good works—when he was among us he said: *Be perfect as your heavenly Father is perfect* [Mt 5.8]. But Eunomius deprives (insofar as he is able to do so) the Only-Begotten of the affinity that he has by nature with the one who has begotten him. And yet even on this point his account will come around to a contradiction. For if the Father is incomparable, where will he find a basis to advance proofs for the unlikeness of the Son? If he says that he has found the unlikeness by comparing the substances with one another, then how is such a one incomparable? And if he is utterly incomparable, then how was he able to recognize the difference? Thus it seems that evil is opposed not only to the good but also to itself.

BOOK TWO

N OW THAT HE HAS secretly prepared his blasphemies against the Son of God in his arguments about the God of the universe (at least to the extent that he was able to do so), it remains for Eunomius to unleash his tongue against the only-begotten God. What does he say, then?

The Son is also one, for he is the Only-Begotten. Now it would be possible to get rid of all concern and trouble associated with this subject simply by quoting the sayings of the saints in which they declare that the Son is both something begotten and something made, thereby making the difference in substance clear by the distinctions in the names. Yet because of those who assume that this begetting is corporeal and stumble over homonymies,[1] it is perhaps necessary to speak briefly about these matters too.[2]

That's what Eunomius says. But as I see it, if it is necessary to think about his entire discussion as a fictitious exercise such as those assigned to boys in schools of vanity for practice in making a lie plausible—for Eunomius acts quite similarly to these people, and everything he does resembles shadowboxing: he picks a fight against accusers who do not exist, makes an apology against an accusation which has never been made, and delivers a discourse for judges who are nowhere to be found—now if it is necessary to take his words in this way, for my part

1. Gr. ταῖς ὁμωνυμίαις. According to Aristotle, "those things are said to be homonyms that have only their name in common, and have a different account of the substance corresponding to the name" (*Cat.* 1, 1a1–2; trans. Strange 40). Eunomius does not make a distinction between homonyms and homonymy as some Neoplatonist commentators do; see Porphyry, *in. Cat.* 61, 1–2 Busse.

2. Eunomius, *Apol.* 12.1–6 (EW 46–48).

I choose to forgo the investigation and advise everyone to pay no attention to what he has said. But if he is promising to do something more than this and many have come to suspect that he has some concern for the truth, then it is altogether necessary to correct each of his statements as best we can. What kind of investigation, then, would be more just than a comparison of his arguments with the teachings that the Spirit gave us? We will accept whatever we find that agrees with them, but give no credence to what is contrary to them and flee from such things as from an enemy.

[2.2] First of all, then, he needs to show us the following: Which of the saints called Christ 'something begotten' and 'something made'?[3] What scriptural passages demonstrate this? If he bases his claims on the statement of blessed Peter recorded in the Acts of the Apostles, where he says: *Let all the house of Israel know that God has made him Lord and Christ, this Jesus whom you crucified* [Acts 2.36], first of all this testimony has no connection to the issue at hand. For though he promised to show that the saints called the Son 'something made,' he furnishes testimony about the God and Father, that *he has made* [Acts 2.36]. After all, not even Eunomius would claim that it is legitimate for him, in discussions of such great importance, to dream up any derivations and transformations of terms.[4] If we will suffer chastisement *on the day of judgment* even for an *idle word* [Mt 12.36], there can be no doubt that we will have to render an account for innovation in matters of such great importance.

Perhaps the divine word has taught us that something is said fittingly in the case of the God and Father, but the same is not applicable to the Only-Begotten—a fact which the Holy Spirit indicates by his silence. So, then, when he alters the form of the phrase *he has made* [Acts 2.36] so as to call the Maker of the universe 'something made,' how is this not fraught with dan-

---

3. Gr. γέννημα καὶ ποίημα. We have chosen to translate these terms in this way in order to make Basil's grammatical argument clearer. They could also be translated, respectively, 'offspring' and 'product/work.'

4. Gr. παραγωγάς τινας καὶ παρασχηματισμούς. Basil here uses technical grammatical vocabulary. "Derivation" (παραγωγή) is the formation of one word from another by altering its ending through the appendage of component. "Transformation" (παρασχηματισμός) is the change of a word's grammatical form.

ger?[5] If such a designation had been suitable for him, the Spirit would not have passed over it in silence. When scripture refers to creation, we do find the designation 'something made' derived from 'he made,' but when referring to the Son of God, we no longer find it. *In the beginning God made the heaven and the earth* [Gn 1.1]. And again: *I meditated on the things made by your hands* [Ps 142.5]. And: *From the creation of the world his invisible things have been clearly perceived, understood by the things that have been made* [Rom 1.20]. Thus scripture employs the term in those cases in which it is useful; in the case of our Lord and Savior Jesus Christ it is passed over in silence as unsuitable for the splendor of his glory. Now scripture is not ashamed to designate *the Lord of glory* [1 Cor 2.8] as *axe* [Mt 3.10] and *cornerstone* [Eph 2.20] and *a stone that will make men stumble and a rock that will make them fall* [1 Pt 2.8; Is 8.14] and other such things which do not seem be very reverential when apprehension of the signification of the names is lacking. But nowhere at all does scripture call him 'something made.' Eunomius, however, says that he took this word from the saints themselves, in order to implicate through his chicanery not only the saints from his own time but also those from long ago.

[2.3] The danger of such ventures is not the only reason he should not change the form of the names of the Lord on his own authority. There is another: it was not the intention of the Apostle to communicate to us the subsistence[6] of the Only-Begotten before the ages, which is the subject at hand. Clearly, he is not talking about the very substance of God the Word, who *was in the beginning with God* [Jn 1.2], but about the one who *emptied himself in the form of a slave* [Phil 2.7], became *similar in form to the body of our lowliness* [Phil 3.21], and *was crucified through weakness* [2 Cor 13.4]. Everyone who has paid even marginal attention to the intent of the Apostle's text recognizes that he does not teach us in the mode of theology, but hints at the reasons of the economy.[7] He says: *God has made him Lord*

---

5. Basil claims that Eunomius has derived the word *poiêma* ("something made") from *epoiêse* ("he has made").

6. Gr. ὑπόστασιν.

7. To engage in theology, for Basil, is to think of Christ's eternal divine be-

and Christ, this Jesus whom you crucified [Acts 2.36]. By using the demonstrative pronoun[8] he makes a clear reference to his humanity and to what all saw. But Eunomius transfers the expression 'he made' to the original begetting of the Only-Begotten. In addition, it causes him no shame that the term 'Lord' does not name a substance but rather is a name of authority. Hence, he who said: *God made him Lord and Christ* [Acts 2.36] is speaking of his rule and power over all, which the Father entrusted to him. He is not describing his arrival at being. We will demonstrate these points a little later when we refute him for adducing testimonies drawn from the scripture in a way contrary to the intention of the Spirit.[9]

Let's now proceed to the next point in his treatise. So, then, why is this name of interest to him? Why in the world does he attempt to designate the Maker of the universe as 'something made'? Self-deceived by his dishonest sophism, he thinks that "the difference in substance is made clear by the distinctions in the names."[10] [2.4] But what sane person would agree with this logic that there must be a difference of substances for those things whose names are distinct? For the designations of Peter and Paul and of all people in general are different, but there is a single substance for all of them. For this reason, in most respects we are the same as one another, but it is only due to the distinguishing marks[11] considered in connection with each one of us that we are different, each from the other. Hence the designations do not signify the substances, but rather the distinctive features[12] that characterize the individual. So whenever we hear 'Peter,' the name does not cause us to think of his substance—now by 'substance' I mean the material substrate which the name itself cannot ever signify[13]—but rather the notion of

---

ing in abstraction from his works. He distinguishes this from thinking of the economy of Christ's saving actions. On this distinction, see *Eun.* 2.15 and Introduction, pp. 51–53.

8. That is, *this* Jesus.   9. See *Eun.* 2.14–15.

10. Eunomius, *Apol.* 12.3–4 (EW 48).   11. Gr. τοῖς ἰδιώμασι.

12. Gr. τῶν ἰδιοτήτων.

13. There are textual problems with this parenthetical phrase. When Gregory of Nyssa quoted it in his own *Against Eunomius,* he inserted an *ou,* making the phrase negative: "now by 'substance' I do *not* mean the material substrate

the distinguishing marks[14] that are considered in connection with him is impressed upon our mind. For as soon as we hear the sound of this designation, we immediately think of the son of Jonah,[15] the man from Bethsaida,[16] the brother of Andrew,[17] the one summoned from the fishermen to the ministry of the apostolate,[18] the one who because of the superiority of his faith was charged with the building up of the church.[19] None of these is his substance, understood as subsistence. Hence the name determines for us the character of Peter. It cannot ever communicate the substance itself. Likewise, when we hear 'Paul,' we think of a concurrence of other distinguishing marks:[20] the man from Tarsus,[21] the Hebrew,[22] as to the law a Pharisee,[23] the disciple of Gamaliel,[24] the zealous persecutor of the churches of God,[25] the man who was brought to knowledge by a terrifying vision,[26] the Apostle to the Gentiles.[27] All these things are encompassed by the single term 'Paul.'

Moreover, if it were true that the substances of things whose

---

which no name can ever signify" (*Eun.* III/5.22 [GNO 2: 168.2–3]). One family of manuscripts for Basil's *Eun.* makes the same "learned" correction of this passage, though this family is generally less reliable. Furthermore, one ms. of Gregory's *Eun.* omits the *ou.* The textual problem is not without doctrinal import: some scholars have taken Gregory's emendation to reflect a general difference between Basil and Gregory in how they understand the term *ousia,* with Basil's view being more Stoic and Gregory's more Platonist. This interpretation of the philosophical background to Basil and Gregory on substance is, according to us, mistaken. For discussion, see Reinhard Hübner, "Gregor von Nyssa als Vorfasser der Sog. Ep. 38 des Basilius: Zum unterschiedlichen Verständnis der οὐσία bei den kappadozischen Brüdern," in Jacques Fontaine and Charles Kannengiesser, eds., *Epektasis: Mélanges Patristiques Offertes au Cardinal Jean Daniélou* (Paris: Beauschesne, 1972), 463–90; David G. Robertson, "Stoic and Aristotelian Notions of Substance in Basil of Caesarea," *Vigiliae Christianae* 52 (1998): 393–417. At p. 415, Robertson comments on *Eun.* 2.4 that "if this is Stoic conceptuality, then it is either confused or heavily adapted." Note that in his early letter to Apollinarius (assuming authenticity), Basil explicitly rules out a material substrate in the case of God: *Ep.* 361.17.

14. Gr. τῶν ἰδιωμάτων.   15. See Mt 16.17.
16. See Jn 1.44.   17. See Mt 4.18.
18. See Mt 4.18–19.   19. See Mt 16.16–18.
20. Gr. ἑτέρων ἰδιωμάτων.   21. See Acts 22.3.
22. See Phil 3.5.   23. See ibid.
24. See Acts 22.3.   25. See Gal 1.3.
26. See Acts 9.3–4; 22.6–8; 26.12–19.   27. See Rom 11.13.

names differ are opposed, then Paul and Peter and all people
in general must be different in substance²⁸ from one another.
But there is no one so stupid and so inattentive to the common nature that he would be led to say this—after all, the passage: *You have been formed from clay, as also have I* [Jb 33.6] sig-
nals nothing other than that all human beings are of the same
substance.²⁹ This being the case, whoever evasively argues that
difference in substance follows upon difference in names is a
liar. For the nature of realities is not consequent to their names,
but names are found posterior to realities.³⁰ If the former were
true, where designations are the same, the substance would also
have to be one and the same. Accordingly, since those perfect
in virtue have been counted worthy of the designation 'god,'³¹
human beings would be of the same substance with the God of
the universe.³² But just as saying this is sheer madness, so too is
his logic here equally crazy.

[2.5] So, then, what I have said makes it clear that in the case
of both 'Father' and 'Son' the names do not communicate substance but instead are revelatory of the distinguishing marks.³³
Hence there is no place for an account that introduces opposition of substances based on diversity of names. If this were the
case, he would refute himself in the presence of all. For if 'something made' and 'something begotten' are different, the substances of the Only-Begotten will be different in consequence of
the difference in names. But if only the deranged say this, only
those who are out of their minds would accept the premise.

Eunomius alleges that he has innumerable proofs that the
saints called the Son 'something made.' But as if hastening onto
other more important matters (I guess), he defers mentioning
them for the moment. This is all part of his scheming captiousness: when he is at a loss for arguments, he prefers silence. If

28. Gr. ἑτερουσίους.
29. Gr. τὸ ὁμοούσιον πάντων ἀνθρώπων.
30. Cf. Athanasius, *Ar.* 2.3.2.
31. See Jn 10.35.
32. Gr. ὁμοούσιοι ἂν εἶεν τῷ Θεῷ τῶν ὅλων οἱ ἄνθρωποι. Here Basil accuses Eunomius of failing to account for homonymy, something which Eunomius himself had claimed to be keenly aware of.
33. Gr. τῶν ἰδιωμάτων.

he had had even a sliver of evidence that they called the Only-Begotten 'something made,' wouldn't he have already deafened our ears with his verbiage?

He says next that "because of those who assume that this begetting" of the Lord "is corporeal and stumble over homonymies, it is necessary" for him "to speak briefly about these matters too."[34] But what prevented him from confirming his argument by testimonies drawn from scripture, by which he could go on to correct the weaker and assuage the damage caused by homonymy, if something like this ever has happened or will happen to anyone? Who is so utterly fleshly in his thinking and so ignorant of divine words that when he hears about the divine begetting, he is brought down to the level of corporeal impressions? At this level there is sexual intercourse of a male with a female, then conception in the womb, then construction, then formation, and then at the right time passage to the outside world.[35] Who is such a brute that when he hears that God the Word came forth from God,[36] when he hears that Wisdom was begotten from God,[37] he sinks down in his thoughts to the level of the body's passions?

34. Eunomius, *Apol.* 12.4–6 (EW 48).

35. Gr. συμπλοκὴ μὲν ἄρρενος πρὸς τὸ θῆλυ, κύησις δὲ ἐν μήτρᾳ, καὶ διάπλασις, καὶ μόρφωσις, καὶ τοῖς καθήκουσι χρόνοις πρόοδος εἰς τὸ ἔξω. "Construction" (διάπλασις) refers to the seed's development into the embryo, and "formation" (μόρφωσις) to the articulation of the embryo into a recognizably human fetus. Basil's description and vocabulary of gestation have much in common with that of a mid-fourth century Christian commentator on the biblical book of Job known as Julian the Arian, probably due to similarities in their secular education: "the beginning [of the process of one living creature coming from another] is the sowing of the seed (τὴν καταβολὴν τοῦ σπέρματος), and next the coagulation of the seed (τὴν τούτου πῆξιν), then the successive construction (τὴν κατὰ μέρος διάπλασιν) of skin, flesh, bones, and sinews, third the formation itself (μόρφωσιν αὐτήν), and finally the animation by God (τὴν παρὰ θεοῦ ψύχωσιν). . . . After the construction (τὸ πλασθῆναι) and the formation (τὸ ἐξεικονισθῆναι) of the embryo, the soul is received from God. . . . Sexual intercourse (μίξις) is first, then conception (σύλληψις), and third construction (διάπλασις), then after this, formation (μόρφωσις), and lastly animation (ψύχωσις)" (Julian the Arian, *Commentary on Job* 10.10–12; Dieter Hagedorn, ed., *Der Hiobkommentar des Arianers Julian*, Patristische Texte und Studien 14 [Berlin: De Gruyter, 1973], 79, 15–18, and 80, 3–4 and 8–9). Also see Galen, *On the Construction (διάπλασις) of the Embryo* 652–702 Kühn; and Soranus, *Gynecology* 17.

36. See Jn 8.42.   37. See Prv 8.25.

[2.6] He concocts this specious form of argumentation along with the others so that he appears to be compassionately taking on the burden of instructing the brothers who lack understanding. Even though he "corrects" (so to speak) the corporeal suppositions that arise because of this designation,[38] he does not seek to make amends for the damages that stem from calling the Lord 'something made.' Indeed, whoever imagines that begetting is corporeal can also devolve to material ways of understanding making. For isn't it true that when a weak-minded person hears the term 'to beget,' he thinks of a certain division and a change and an effluence coming from the begetter's substance? Will he not be led to suppose that material is introduced from an external source in order to bring what you call 'something made' from nothing into existence? So, then, why does Eunomius heal only half of the diseased thoughts of the brothers? Why does he care only about those who suppose that the begetting is corporeal but disregard those who stumble over the designation 'something made'? It's because he knows that 'to have been begotten' is hostile to his own teachings. For the one who has been begotten must have complete and indistinguishable affinity with the begetter. But 'to have been made' is amenable to and allied with his own suppositions because it communicates the notion that something made is alien and foreign to its maker, and altogether lacking in affinity with him.

Then he adds to this by saying:

Therefore, we say that the Son is 'something begotten' in accordance with the teaching of the scriptures. We do not conceive of his substance as one thing and what his name signifies as something else alongside of it. Rather, it is the subsistence that his name signifies, since the designation truly applies to the substance.[39]

And so, with these words he openly fights against the truth. Nevertheless, he says things consistent with his own purpose. Just as he determined in his earlier arguments that 'unbegotten' in the case of the God of the universe signifies his substance, so too here he says that 'something begotten' signifies the substance of the Son. He does this to indicate by the opposition of

38. That is, 'begetting.'
39. Eunomius, *Apol.* 12.6–10 (EW 48).

'something begotten' to 'unbegotten' that the Only-Begotten is contrary to the Father with respect to substance itself. For these reasons he legislates the use of terms which are external to the usage of the divine Spirit, calling the Son 'something begotten.' Where does he get this from? On what sort of teaching is it based? Which prophet's? Which of the apostles applied this name to him? For my part I have not found this term used in this way anywhere in scripture.

[2.7] Eunomius pretends that he has taken these designations from no other source than from the teaching of the Spirit. It is *a trifling matter* for him *to pick a fight with people* [Is 7.13] when he can insolently attack the Spirit himself! Now from many passages we have learned that the Father has begotten, but never to this day have we heard that the Son is something begotten. *For a child is begotten to us, and a son is given to us. And his name is called*—not 'something begotten'—but *the angel of great counsel* [Is 9.5]. If 'something begotten' did signify substance, the Spirit would not have taught us a name different from one which would clearly indicate his substance. Furthermore, Peter, who was deemed worthy of those blessings because of his knowledge of the truth,[40] did not say: "you are something begotten," but rather: *You are the Christ, the Son of the living God* [Mt 16.16]. And no passage can be found in which Paul, who filled all his writings with the designation 'Son,' mentions 'something begotten'—the very term which Eunomius proposes with great boldness, as if he took it from the divine instruction.

Nor should we concede the point to him that he can change and alter the form of the phrase 'he has begotten,' which is used with reference to the Father, in order to designate the Son of God as 'something begotten.'[41] For it is inappropriate for him to be quick to clutch at what may be hinted at by the natural sequence of the words, as anyone trained in the fear of God knows. Instead, one should be content with abiding by the names employed in scripture and use them to glorify God appropriately. The translators who first rendered Hebrew into

40. See Mt 16.17. Eunomius refers to this same verse in *Apol.* 26 in defense of his appeal to Acts 2.36.

41. The change is from ἐγέννησε (*egennēse*) to γέννημα (*gennēma*).

Greek did not audaciously attempt to interpret certain names, but simply transliterated the Hebrew pronunciation into Greek, such as 'Sabaoth' and 'Adonai' and 'Eloi' and other words like these. If they showed such respect not only to the divine names but also to many others, then how much fear should we have with regard to the names of the Lord? When did these translators trust themselves to form one of the names on their own authority? After all, they did not even have the confidence to translate some of these names, lest they water down the clarity of the term's force by introducing meanings that did not fit them.

[2.8] "But if God has begotten," he says, "how is it inappropriate to designate the one who was begotten as 'something begotten'?"[42] Because it is a dreadful thing for us to address him by one of our own names when *God has bestowed on him the name which is above every name* [Phil 2.9]. He says: *For you are my Son, today I have begotten you* [Ps 2.7]. Designating him here as 'something begotten' because he was begotten and not 'Son' would have been more consistent with their reasoning. But that's not what has been said. Therefore, whoever keeps before his eyes the tribunal of Christ and sees how dangerous it is to subtract from or add anything to what the Spirit handed down should not endeavor to innovate on his own, but acquiesce to what the saints announced beforehand.[43]

How is it not sheer madness to venture upon what neither common usage[44] nor scriptural usage exhibits? What father or mother kindly and gently disposed to his or her offspring would neglect to designate him 'my son' or 'my child' and address him instead as 'my something begotten'? For it says: *My child, go to the vineyard* [Mt 21.28]. And: *God will provide himself the lamb for a burnt offering, my child* [Gn 22.8]. And again Isaac: *Who are you, my child?* [Gn 27.18] And: *My son, do not think lightly of the training of the Lord* [Prv 3.11]. And: *A wise son makes his father glad* [Prv 10.1]. There are more passages like these. But there

---

42. This is not a citation of Eunomius; rather, Basil is imagining what Eunomius's response might be.

43. See Rv 22.18–19.

44. See *Eun.* 1.6.

is no indication anywhere that someone addresses his offspring as 'something begotten.' The reason is clear: 'son' and 'child' are the names of living beings, but 'something begotten' is not necessarily such a name. For that which is expelled in miscarriages that occur before full formation can be called 'something begotten,' and such a thing is assuredly not even worthy of the designation 'child.' The fruits of the earth are also 'things begotten,' but they are not 'children.' It says: *I will not drink from what is begotten of this vine* [Mk 14.25].[45] On rare occasions, however, we do find that this designation is adopted and used for living beings. But wherever it is used, one can see that it is a question of an offensive animal employed as an image of wickedness: *You serpents! You things begotten of vipers!* [Mt 23.33][46] I think it is for this reason that common usage disdains this designation and the divine scripture manifestly avoids it, especially in the case of the only-begotten Son of God. But scripture does not even admit the designation 'child'[47] since it has something too human about it. The Apostle makes this clear when over and over again he calls the Lord 'Son' and praises him with various other designations, 'first-born'[48] and 'image'[49] and 'radiance,'[50] but avoids the designation 'something begotten.' If he does use this term, let Eunomius or some other advocate of his doctrine show us, and we will let them strike our entire objection from the record. But he will not be able to do this, unless he imitates the impious Marcion, removing some texts from the divine oracles while interpolating others.[51] So, then, in this way the term 'something begotten' has been exposed as foreign to both common usage and scriptural usage.

---

45. Basil's text of Mk 14.25 reads γεννήματος ("thing begotten") in place of the γενήματος ("thing produced, fruit") found in most mss. and modern critical editions.

46. The traditional English translation is of course: "brood of vipers."

47. Gr. τέκνον.   48. See Col 1.15, 18.

49. See Col 1.15; 2 Cor 4.4.   50. See Heb 1.3.

51. Marcion, born in Sinope in the province of Pontus in Asia Minor, came to Rome around 140, from whose church he was soon excommunicated for his teachings. Marcion accorded scriptural status only to expurgated versions of the Gospel of Luke and select letters of Paul. Basil also mentions Marcion in *Eun.* 2.34; see p. 183 n. 144 below.

[2.9] Now, then, let's see if this name can be applied to the very substance of the Son. Eunomius says that it is impossible to "conceive of his substance as one thing and what his name signifies as something else alongside of it. Rather, it is the subsistence that his name signifies, since the designation truly applies to the substance."[52] Your doctrines here are truly worthy of the judges that you have invented! As if dreaming that you're in a forum or addressing an assembly of drunkards, where no one can hear or understand what is being said, you legislate on the basis of your full indemnity, thinking that it is sufficient to say, "I have spoken,"[53] instead of providing a full demonstration.

Who does not know that some names are expressed absolutely and in respect of themselves, signifying the things which are their referents, but other names are said relative to others, expressing only the relation to the other names relative to which they are said? For example, 'human being' and 'horse' and 'ox' each communicate the very thing that is named. But 'son' and 'slave' and 'friend' reveal only the connection with the associated name. So when anyone hears 'something begotten,' he is not brought in his mind to a certain substance, but rather he understands that it is connected with another. For that which is something begotten is said to be 'something begotten' *of* someone else. So, how is it not the peak of insanity to decree that that which does not introduce a notion of any subsistence, but only signifies the relation to another, is the substance? In addition, we indicated a little before that, even if absolute names seem most of all to reveal some referent, they too do not communicate the substance itself, but delineate certain distinguishing marks[54] in connection with it.[55]

[2.10] But this wisest of men, having devoted his entire life to futile scheming, is not ashamed to say that 'something begotten' signifies the very substance of the Only-Begotten. Look

---

52. Eunomius, *Apol.* 12.7–10 (EW 48).

53. A mocking reference to the Pythagoreans, who habitually cited Pythagoras, whose authority did not need to be demonstrated, with the words: Αὐτὸς ἔφα, "The Master has spoken."

54. Gr. ἰδιώματα.

55. Cf. *Eun.* 2.4.

how absurd this is! For if the substance is something begotten, and vice versa, if anything that is begotten is substance, then all things that are begotten are of the same substance with one another. What results from this line of reasoning? The Creator of the universe appears to have the same substance as all those who participate in begetting! Surely, he will not claim that 'something begotten' signifies substance only when it is used for the Son, but that when it is used for the other things that participate in begetting, it no longer preserves the same notion. So let him give us a clear and incontrovertible explanation why the same designation does not mean the same thing in every case similarly. But he won't be able to do so. For whatever the formula of 'something begotten' he dreams up, Eunomius should apply it similarly to all things that are begotten.

The truth of our account finds its greatest proof in how each of those who hear the word understands it. Let each one ask himself what notion is impressed upon him when he hears that "such-and-such is 'something begotten' of such-and-such." Is it that the one who was begotten is the substance of the begetter? That's ridiculous! Is it that the one has been brought into being by the other through begetting? That's the truth of the matter. So, then, it is appropriate that this term be said similarly of the Only-Begotten and of any of those who have been begotten. Let no one suppose that being in relation, which is common in both cases, diminishes the glory of the Only-Begotten in any way. For the difference between the Son and other things does not reside in being related to something.[56] Rather, the superiority of God with respect to mortals is seen in the distinctiveness[57] of his substance.

Look how their account brings them to such absurdity! If that which is begotten is said to be 'something begotten' *of* an-

---

56. Gr. πρός τί πως ἔχειν. The phrase is Aristotelian in origin: see *Cat.* 8a32, b1–3, and *APr.* 41a4. For him it just means "being related to something." While the Stoics did adopt it to name their fourth "category," the "relatively disposed," it was commonplace in late ancient philosophy and grammatical theory. It should not be taken as evidence of Stoic influence in late ancient texts, for the reasons given by Jonathan Barnes, *Porphyry: Introduction* (Oxford: Clarendon Press, 2003), 52 n. 9, and 312–13.

57. Gr. ἰδιότης.

other, as is established by common usage and denied by no one, but if according to their account this same word also signifies substance, then it would be the substance *of* the one *of* whom it is said to be 'something begotten.'[58] The consequence of this will be that the designation 'something begotten' no longer signifies the substance of the Only-Begotten—which is what these men contend—but rather that of the God of the universe. For if it is impossible to "conceive of his substance as one thing" and something begotten "as something else alongside of it,"[59] then saying 'substance' or 'something begotten' means the same thing. Now the Son is something begotten *of* God. So he would be the substance *of* God, if in fact 'something begotten' reveals substance. And thus it would appear that according to the account of Eunomius 'something begotten' is the substance of the unbegotten! But if this conclusion is ridiculous, let him who proposes the premises inherit the shame. For it seems that once his reasoning diverges from the truth in any way, his error has a logical consequence that results in many dangerous absurdities.

[2.11] So, then, while this serves as a kind of opening act and prologue for his blasphemy, it is in what follows that he introduces the chief point of his evil when he says:

The substance of the Son was begotten but did not exist before its own constitution, yet it exists after it was begotten before all things by the will of the Father.[60]

He still depends on the same scheming tricks. He discusses the substance of the Son with us as if claiming that the Son is something different alongside of it, and in this way he prepares our ears for his blasphemy. He does not openly say that the Son has been begotten from nothing, but rather that his substance "was begotten but did not exist." Did not exist before what? Tell me!

---

58. The argument of this sentence is almost impossible to capture in English. It relies on the use of the Greek genitive, which we have rendered with an italicized *of*. The argument runs as follows: to say "X is begotten" implies "X is begotten *of* some Y." But, on Eunomius's hypothesis, "begotten" is equivalent to "substance." Therefore, by substitution, we can say "X is the substance *of* some Y." But this is absurd: no begotten entity can be the substance of its begetter.

59. Eunomius, *Apol.* 12.7–8 (EW 48).

60. Eunomius, *Apol.* 12.10–12 (EW 48).

Do you see his sophism? He judges the Son's substance with respect to itself so that his statements have the appearance of being tolerable to everybody, saying neither that it did not exist before the ages nor that it simply did not exist, but that it "did not exist before its own constitution." Tell me, are you claiming that the substance of the Father is older than its own constitution? If he does not subject the substance of the Son to temporality, nor conceptualize priority in this sense, his argument is vain and idle, and for this reason unworthy of a reply. Moreover, if one wishes, it is no less possible to transpose this foolishness to the God of the universe. For saying that God does not exist "before his own constitution" and saying that he exists before himself is characteristic of the same stupidity. But if Eunomius takes priority in the case of the substance of the Son as temporal and claims that the Son's substance has been begotten from nothing, or rather that the Son himself has been—for saying it the one way or the other makes no difference in the meaning—he posits first of all that the Son is posterior to time, and (if he so wishes) also posterior to the ages, even though he is the Maker of the ages.[61] But if he then pushes his blasphemies to their logical conclusions, he will claim that even the Father has not been the Father from the beginning, but only later became such.

[2.12] If being Father is good and fitting to the blessedness of God, how is that which is fitting for him not present in him from the beginning?[62] For the lack will certainly be considered either a matter of ignorance of what is better or a matter of inability. As a matter of ignorance, if he discovered what is better only later; as a matter of inability, if while knowing and understanding it he failed to attain what is best. But if—now saying this is irreligious—being Father is not good for him, why did he change, choosing what is worse? May this blasphemy return to its originators! The God of the universe is Father from infinity; he did not at some point begin to be Father. For a deficiency in power did not prevent him from fulfilling his will, nor did he wait for the passage of a certain number of ages to arrive at what

61. See Heb 1.2.
62. Basil's argument in this section draws upon Origen, *Princ.* 1.2.9–10.

he wanted, as is the case for human beings and other living creatures who each attain the power to beget after reaching maturity. Only the insane would think and utter such things! On the contrary, he has a Fatherhood (if I may give it such a name) that is coextensive with his own eternity. Therefore, it is also the case that the Son, who exists before the age and always, did not at some point begin to exist. From whatever point the Father exists, the Son also exists, and the notion of the Son immediately enters along with the notion of Father. For it is clear that the Father is a father *of* a son. So, then, though the Father has no origin, the Son's origin is the Father; there is no intermediary between them.[63] So, then, how could that which is from the beginning not exist—for this is what is meant by their sophism, "before his own constitution"—when he has nothing that can be conceptualized prior to himself except the one from whom he has being, who is not beyond him due to an interval but is ranked prior to him in terms of causality? So the communion of the Son with the God and Father is revealed as eternal, seeing that our understanding advances from the Son to the Father without passing through a void and connects the Son with the Father without any interval between them. For no intermediary separates the Son from the Father. This being the case, what opening still remains for the wicked blasphemy of those who say that he is brought into being from nothing?

[2.13] Our astonishment at their foolishness is justified. For they fail to realize that when they say that the Son is from nothing, they not only proclaim that he is posterior to the Father, but also that he is posterior to that by which they separate the Only-Begotten from the Father. If there is anything between the Father and the Son, this must be prior to the existence[64] of the Son. So, then, what could this be? What else could this be besides an age or a time? If someone thinks that the life of the Father surpasses that of the Only-Begotten, by what interval would he claim to have discovered the superiority other than that of an age or a time? But if this is true, scripture is clearly lying when it says that

63. "Origin" here translates ἀρχή; in the next sentence (and in the first sentence of *Eun.* 2.12) the same word is translated as "beginning."
64. Gr. ὑπάρξις.

through him the ages came into existence [Heb 1.2] and teaches that *all things came into existence through him* [Jn 1.3]. For it is clear that the ages are included among the *all things*. If they claim that they do not deny that the Son came to be before the ages, they should not forget that in reality they are denying that to which they are verbally agreeing.

In fact, let us pose a question to those who make the substance of the Only-Begotten come from nothing: What was the interval "when he was not," as you say? What designation will you dream up for it?[65] Common usage classifies every interval under either time or age, for that which is time among the sensory realities corresponds to the nature of age among the supercosmic realities. So let these people tell me if they can imagine a third kind of interval based on the resources of their own wisdom. As long as they keep silent, they should not forget that they have placed the substance of the Only-Begotten posterior to ages. For if there were any interval prior to the Son that is coextensive with the life of the Father, it would clearly have to be one of these two. But there isn't. Nor can there ever be a notion prior to the subsistence of the Only-Begotten. For one will find that the existence of God the Word who was *in the beginning with God* [Jn 1.2] is beyond everything that could conceivably be called primordial.[66] Even if the mind, by deceiving itself through innumerable fantasies and devoting itself to nonexistent fabrications, has contrived things that do not exist, it will not discover any means at all by which it could extend itself beyond the beginning of the Only-Begotten, leave behind the life of Life Itself as lower than its own movement, transcend the beginning of God the Word by its own rational word, and contemplate ages that are deprived of the God of the ages.

[2.14] After denying the Only-Begotten the glory he is due, notice what sort of words Eunomius uses to extol him: the substance of the Son, he says, "was begotten before all things by the will of the God and Father."[67] He attributes this great thing to the Son, that he is prior to creation and pre-exists the things

---

65. Basil asks a similar question in *Eun.* 1.21.
66. Gr. εἰς ἀρχαιότητος λόγον.
67. Eunomius, *Apol.* 12.11–12 (EW 48).

he himself has made. He supposes that it suffices for the glory of the Creator of the universe that he is ranked prior to the things he himself has created. After he alienates (insofar as he is able to do so) the Son from communion with the God and Father, Eunomius testifies to his glory by honoring him above creatures. Then, spouting his blasphemy to the point of impudence, he hems us in on all sides with arguments so forceful that no one can escape them—or so he thinks.

For God has begotten the Son either when [the Son] existed or when he did not exist. But if it occurred when he did not exist, no one should accuse me of audacity. But if it occurred when he did exist, this reasoning is not only the pinnacle of absurdity *and* blasphemy, but also utter silliness. For that which exists has *no* need of begetting.[68]

So, then, here is that notorious sophism which others discovered long ago but which these people have now brought to perfection on their shameless and impudent tongues.[69] First of all, let us remind the pupils of Eunomius that he feels compelled to make these arguments on account of the ignorance of the many who understand the begetting of the Son in a human way. He is the one who brings unschooled souls from corporeal notions up to spiritual contemplation. Since begotten animals did not exist before they were begotten and the one begotten today did not exist yesterday, he transfers this notion to the subsistence of the Only-Begotten. "And since he has been begotten," he says, "he did not exist before his begetting."[70]

How noble he is for providing us with this theology of the begetting of the Only-Begotten! Through such arguments he heals the infirmities of our brothers, though he is worthy, if anyone is, of hearing the proverb: *Physician, heal yourself!* [Lk 4.23] Still, what remedy can we offer for this absurd sickness that has infected his arguments, if not what the Holy Spirit said to us through the blessed John: *In the beginning was the Word, and the Word was*

68. The words in italics are actually a paraphrase of Eunomius—and a faithful one at that; see *Apol.* 13.1–7 (EW 48).

69. Here Basil is probably accusing Eunomius of reformulating the notorious statement of Arius: "He was not before he came to be" (οὐκ ἦν πρὶν γένηται); see Athanasius, *Ar.* 1.5. This statement was anathematized at the Council of Nicaea.

70. This is a paraphrase of Eunomius, not a citation.

with God, and God was the Word [Jn 1.1].[71] It is impossible to conceptualize something prior to a beginning. After all, a beginning
would not still be a beginning if it were to have something anterior to it. Nor is it possible for them to use reason to go beyond '*was*' to 'when he was not.' For the conceptualization 'that
he was not' is the denial of '*was*.' If 'beginning' is one of those
things said relative to another, such as is the case for *the beginning
of wisdom* [Sir 1.14] and *the beginning of a good way* [Prv 16.7]
and *in the beginning God made* [Gn 1.1],[72] then it would perhaps
be possible to use reflection to go beyond the begetting of what
subsists from this kind of beginning. But since the meaning of
'beginning' here, being absolute and non-relative, reveals the
supreme nature, how isn't it utterly ridiculous when he contrives
things anterior to this beginning or attempts to use reasoning to
go beyond it?

Furthermore, '*was*' is coextensive with the insurpassibility of
this beginning. For '*was*' does not suggest temporal existence,
as is the case for: *There was a man in the land of Uz* [Jb 1.1], and:
There was a man from Armathaim [1 Sm 1.1], and: *The earth was invisible* [Gn 1.2]. In another book the evangelist himself showed
us the meaning of '*was*' in this sense when he said: *I am the one
who is and who was, the Almighty* [Rv 1.8]. The one *who was* is just
like the one *who is*: both are eternal and non-temporal alike.
Saying that the one who *was in the beginning* [Jn 1.1] was not
does not preserve the notion of beginning and does not connect the existence of the Only-Begotten to it. For something
prior to the beginning is inconceivable, and the being of God
the Word is inseparable from this beginning. Hence as far back
as you wish to run by the busy curiosity of your mind, you are
unable to transcend '*was*' and use reasoning to go beyond it.

[2.15] Let us now pose him a question: was God the Word
with God in the beginning [Jn 1.1] or did he supervene later? If
he was, then *keep your tongue from evil* [Ps 33.14], that is, from

---

71. Basil's use of Jn 1.1 to argue for the eternity of the Word draws upon
Origen, *Jo.* 2.8–11. Basil developed this argument more fully in *Hom.* 16.

72. Presumably Basil understands Gn 1.1 to mean: "in the beginning *of the
world* God made. . . ." Otherwise, it is difficult to see how "beginning" here is
said relatively.

the blasphemy of saying 'he was not.' But if . . . (for saying this is irreligious),[73] then I will use your own words against you in a more fitting manner: this account of yours is the pinnacle not only of blasphemy but also of insanity.[74] Here we have human beings demanding an account of the words of the Spirit, claiming to be disciples of the very same gospels against which they rise up in rebellion.

Look how exactly and clearly the divine sayings testify to the Son's begetting[75] before the ages. Matthew explained the Son's begetting[76] according to the flesh, as he himself said: *The book of the generation of Jesus Christ, the son of David* [Mt 1.1]. And Mark made the preaching of John the beginning of the gospel, saying: *The beginning of the gospel of Jesus Christ, as is written in Isaiah the prophet: a voice of one crying out* [Mk 1.1]. Luke for his part also approached the theology[77] by going through the corporeal origins. The evangelist John was the last to write. Because of what the others did, he needed to raise his mind above every sensory thing and time (which is concomitant to such things). Or rather he had to be lifted up in the power of the Spirit and be brought near the one who is beyond all things, all but bearing witness that *even if we have known Christ according to the flesh, but now we know him thus no longer* [2 Cor 5.16]. Since he apprehended the beginning itself and left behind all corporeal and temporal notions as lower than his theology, he surpasses the preaching of the preceding evangelists on account of the nobility of his knowledge.[78] According to him, the beginning was not from Mary, nor from the times mentioned above. What, then,

73. As in *Eun.* 1.17, Basil refrains from expressing what he considers a terrible blasphemy.

74. See Eunomius, *Apol.* 13.6–7.

75. At *Eun.* 2.15, 11 (SC 305.58), we read γεννήσει instead of γενέσει. The change to γενέσει is likely a harmonization with the following citation of Mt 1.1. Also this is not Basil's normal use of the term γενέσει.

76. At *Eun.* 2.15, 12 (SC 305.58), we read γεννήσεως instead of γενέσεως, for the same reasons mentioned in the previous footnote.

77. On "theology," see p. 133 n. 7 above.

78. Basil's esteem for John as a theologian more profound than the other three evangelists and his discussion of the first lines of the gospels to prove this point echo Origen, *Jo.* 1.21–22.

was it? *In the beginning was the Word, and the Word was with God, and the Word was God* [Jn 1.1]. The Son's existence from eternity. His begetting without passion. His connaturality with the Father. The majesty of his nature. All these points he covers in a few words.[79] By including *was*, he guides us back to the beginning. It is as if he is putting a muzzle on the mouths of the blasphemers who say that 'he was not,' and circumventing in advance any chinks whereby such sophisms may enter.

Then, after sketching by his theology a kind of outline, a clear one, of the nature of the Only-Begotten,[80] he alludes to this with the following phrase as if speaking to those who already know: *He was in the beginning with God* [Jn 1.2]. Here once again by including the phrase '*was*' he connects the begetting of the Only-Begotten to the eternity of the Father. There's more: *He was life, and the life was the light of humanity* [Jn 1.4]. And: *he was the true light* [Jn 1.9]. Despite the fact that all these passages that include phrases indicative of eternity thereby confirm this account, Eunomius has rejected all the testimonies of the Spirit and does not seem to have heard the one crying out to us over and over again that he *was*. For he says: "He was begotten when he was not. When he was not, he was adventitiously begotten later on."[81] But if, as you claim, this begetting was not in the beginning, could there be a more conspicuous fight against the sayings of the gospels in which we believe?

[2.16] What sensible person would not agree that, just as an eye that passes out of clearly illuminated places must stop its activity because of the absence of light, so too the mind that is forced outside of true being by imaginations, as if the truth lacked a kind of light, becomes confused and stupid and desists from thinking? So, then, an eye is not able to use its power of sight when there is no light, and a soul led away from the notion of the Only-Begotten is not able to have use of its thinking. For falling away from the Truth makes the mind unable to see and blind. When the mind is empty and demented, it lacks true understanding and thinks that it comprehends things prior to

79. That is, in Jn 1.1.
80. That is, in Jn 1.1.
81. This is a paraphrase of Eunomius, not a citation.

the Only-Begotten. It is as if someone testifies that an eye staring at dark objects can see them clearly. For it says: *in your light we shall see light* [Ps 35.10]. But when Eunomius asserts that he has come to comprehend a point when the light did not yet exist, he resembles the delirious who imagine that they see what is not present. For one cannot conceive anything beyond the Son, since what perceptible light is to the eye, God the Word is to the soul. For it says: *The true light that enlightens every human being was coming into the world* [Jn 1.9]. Hence the unenlightened soul is incapable of thinking. So, then, how could one comprehend that which is above the generation of light?

I think anyone with even a slight concern for the truth would dismiss corporeal comparisons, avoid sullying the notions about God with material imaginations, and follow the theological teachings transmitted to us by the Holy Spirit. Instead of posing these questions, which have no lack of conundrums, in which either of the options contains a risk, they should, on the one hand, conceive of a begetting that is worthy of God, one without passion, partition, division, and temporality, being led to the divine begetting in a way consistent with the radiance that shines forth from light. They should, on the other hand, conceive of *the image of the invisible God* [Col 1.15], not as that which is produced later than the archetype like those images produced by human skill, but as that which is co-existent with and subsists alongside the one who brought him into subsistence. For the image exists by virtue of the fact that the archetype exists.[82] The image is not formed through imitation, since the whole nature of the Father is manifest in the Son as in a seal. It may help you if we say that it is like a teacher inculcating the full reality of an art in his disciples: the teacher loses nothing, and the disciples attain the fullness of the art. But this example surely does not exhibit an exact resemblance because of the temporal interval. It is more suitable to say that it is like the nature of concepts that co-exist non-temporally with motions of the mind.

---

82. Gr. ἀλλὰ συνυπάρχουσαν καὶ παρυφεστηκυῖαν τῷ ὑποστήσαντι, τῷ εἶναι τὸ ἀρχέτυπον οὖσαν. At *Eun.* 2.16, 36 (SC 305.64), we have excised the καὶ before τῷ εἶναι since there is no support for this reading in any extant Greek ms. (the addition is based on the Syriac translation).

[2.17] No one should quibble over our account here, if none of the examples harmonize completely with the matter at hand. For trivial and insignificant things cannot be adapted exactly to divine and eternal realties. They are used only insofar as they refute the false pretenses of those who cannot apprehend begetting with their mind in a way that does not involve passion. Now the Son is said to be and is the begotten *image* [Col 1.15; 2 Cor 4.4], *the radiance of the glory of God* [Heb 1.3], and God's *wisdom, power* [1 Cor 1.24], and *righteousness* [1 Cor 1.30], though not as a possession,[83] nor as a faculty. On the contrary, he is a living and active substance and *the radiance of the glory of God* [Heb 1.3]. For this reason, in himself he reveals the Father in his entirety, as he is *the radiance of his glory* in its entirety. So isn't it utterly absurd to claim that the glory of God is without its radiance? That at some point the wisdom of God was not with God? "But if he was," says Eunomius, "then he has not been begotten."[84] So let us answer that it is because he was begotten that he was. He does not have unbegotten being, but he always is and co-exists with the Father, from whom he has the cause of his existence. So, then, when was he brought into being by the Father? From whatever point the Father exists.[85] Eunomius says that the Father is from eternity. So the Son is also from eternity, being connected in a begotten way to the unbegottenness of the Father.

To prove to them that we are not responsible for this argument, we will cite the very words of the Holy Spirit. So, then, let us take the line from the gospel: *In the beginning was the Word* [Jn 1.1], and the line from the Psalm spoken in the person of the Father: *From the womb before the daybreak I have begotten you* [Ps 109.3]. When we combine both of these, we can say both that he was and that he has been begotten. The phrase *I have begotten* signifies the cause from which he has the origin of his being.

83. Gr. ἕξις.
84. This is a paraphrase of Eunomius, not a citation.
85. Basil says much the same in *Eun.* 2.12; see also Gregory of Nazianzus, *Or.* 29.3. Though both Garnier (PG 29b.605c) and Sesboüé (SC 305.66) punctuate this sentence as interrogative, the argument Basil is making seems to require that his sentence be the premise for the conclusion drawn in the final line of the paragraph. Therefore, we punctuate the sentence as indicative.

The phrase *he was* signifies his non-temporal existence even before the ages.

Striving to promote his own deceit, Eunomius thinks he has reduced this argument to absurdity when he says: "For if the Son was before his own begetting, he was unbegotten."[86] As for that which is "before his begetting," you poor fool, there are two options. Either (1) it is something utterly non-existent and a mental fabrication without any foundation. If this is the case, what need is there to respond to such stupidity? For it would be just as if we were fighting against someone whom delirium has deprived of reason. Or (2), if Eunomius is thinking of something that exists, he will be led to the notion of the ages. But if all ages are understood to be below (as it were) the begetting of the Only-Begotten, being, as they are, things that he himself made,[87] then the one who looks for things prior to the subsistence of the Son is a fool. His question is no less inappropriate than if he were to inquire whether the Father existed "before his own constitution" or not. For just as in this case it is stupid to seek something beyond the one who is without beginning and unbegotten, so also in the case of the one who is with the Father from eternity and has no intermediary between himself and his begetter, it is truly of equal insanity to ask about priority in a temporal sense. Seeking what exists "before the begetting" of the eternal one resembles asking what will exist after the end of the immortal one.

Since the Father's being without beginning is called 'eternal,' these men declare that 'eternal' is the same as 'without beginning.' Since the Son is not unbegotten, they do not confess that he is eternal. But the notional difference between these two terms is great. For 'unbegotten' is said of that which has no beginning and no cause of its own being, while 'eternal' is said of that which is prior in being to every time and age. Therefore, the Son is eternal but not unbegotten. Now some people have previously judged even the ages worthy of the designation 'eternal' since they derive the term 'age' (*aiôn*) from the fact

86. Eunomius, *Apol.* 13.15 (EW 50).
87. See Heb 1.2.

that it always exists (*aei einai*).[88] But we consider it a mark of the same insanity to ascribe eternity to creation and yet refuse to acknowledge eternity in the case of the Master of creation.

[2.18] What does Eunomius say upon bringing his argument to this point of impudence?

For our part, clinging to that which has been demonstrated by the saints of old and even now by us, since the substance of God does not admit begetting and since there is no other substance existing which serves as the substrate for the begetting of the Son, we assert that the Son was begotten when he did not exist.[89]

Who is eager for distinction in piety in this way? Who has made as great a show of being a lover of Christ as these men have, even though they boast of their arrogant and dishonorable words that go so far as to destroy the glory of the Only-Begotten? You godless man! Please stop saying that he does not exist when he is the one who truly exists, the one who is the source of life, and the one who produces being for all that exists. Didn't he find a designation well-suited for himself and fitting for his own eternity when he named himself *He Who Is* in his oracle to Moses his servant? He said: *I am He Who Is* [Ex 3.14]. No one will object when I say that these words were spoken in the person of the Lord, at least no one who does not have *the veil* of the Jews upon his heart *when he reads Moses* [2 Cor 3.15]. It is written that the angel of the Lord appeared to Moses in the bush burning with fire.[90] Af-

---

88. An example of classical etymology, found in Aristotle (αἰών . . . ἀπὸ τοῦ αἰεὶ εἶναι τὴν ἐπωνυμίαν εἰληφώς; *Cael.* 1.9 [279a27–28]) and Plotinus (αἰὼν γὰρ ἀπὸ τοῦ ἀεὶ ὄντος; *En.* 3.7 [45].4, 43; cf. *En.* 3.7 [45].6, 32–33) and often repeated by Aristotelian and Neoplatonist commentators. While Aristotle says that the term *aiôn* is derived from the *fact that* it always exists (*aiei einai*), Plotinus says that the term *aiôn* is derived from the *term* "always existing" (*aei ôn*). Here Basil follows Aristotle.

89. Eunomius, *Apol.* 15.3–7 (EW 50–52). The citation has omissions. The full text reads: "For our part, clinging to that which has been demonstrated by the saints of old and even now by us, since the substance of God does not admit begetting (as it is unbegotten), nor separation or partition (as it is incorruptible), and since there is no other substance existing which serves as the substrate for the begetting of the Son, we assert that the Son was begotten when he did not exist."

90. See Ex 3.2; Acts 7.30.

ter mentioning the angel at the outset of the narrative, scripture introduces the voice of God when it says that he said to Moses: *I am the God of your father Abraham* [Ex 3.6]. A little further on, the same one said: *I am He Who Is* [Ex 3.14]. So, then, who is this one who is both angel and God alike? Isn't it he whom we have learned is called by the name *the angel of great counsel* [Is 9.5]?

For my part, I don't think that this needs much demonstration; just mentioning it suffices for the lovers of Christ. But the incorrigible are not going to derive any benefit from a flurry of words. Even though *the angel of great counsel* comes later, it remains true that previously he did not disdain the designation 'angel.'[91] You see, it is not only in this passage that we find the scriptures naming our Lord both 'angel' and 'God.' For when Jacob narrated an appearance to his wives, he said: *And the angel of God said to me* [Gn 31.11]. And a little further on, it was said: *I am the God who appeared to you in the place where you anointed a pillar to me* [Gn 31.13]. In addition, it was said to Jacob as he stood before the pillar: *I am the Lord, the God of Abraham your father and the God of Isaac* [Gn 28.13]. The one who is called 'angel' in the former passage [Gn 31.11] is the same as the one who said in the latter passage [Gn 31.13] that he appeared to Jacob. So, then, it is clear to all that, where the same one is designated both 'angel' and 'God,' it is the Only-Begotten who is revealed, manifesting himself to human beings from generation to generation and announcing the will of the Father to his saints. Consequently, when he named himself *He Who Is* before Moses, he is understood to be none other than God the Word, who *was in the beginning with God* [Jn 1.2].

[2.19] But these men *who speak what is wrong from on high* [Ps 72.8] have not shrunk from saying that the Son does not exist. Though *the fool has said in his heart: there is no God* [Ps 13.1], these men not only *scoff* but also *speak with malice* [Ps 72.8], showing no restraint when they pass on to all posterity in writ-

---

91. Here Basil seems to be countering the argument that, if the Lord has only been called 'the angel of great counsel' in Isaiah, who lived after Moses, then there is no basis for arguing that the God of the burning bush is the Lord. In what follows Basil demonstrates that the Lord was called 'angel' even before Moses.

ing that they dare to call God "he who does not exist." I suppose that it's because they realize that not even the demons themselves deny that God exists[92] that, when they return to the point later in the treatise, they give free rein to their own impious desire. There they blaspheme by saying that at some point the Son does not exist, on the grounds that he does not exist by his own nature but has been brought into being by God through grace.

Here is what Paul said about the idols: *You served the gods who by nature do not exist* [Gal 4.8]. And there's Jeremiah: *And they swore by the gods who do not exist* [Jer 5.7]. There's also the most wise Esther: *O Lord, do not relinquish your scepter to those who do not exist* [Est c.22 LXX = 14.1 RSV]. When these men[93] apply the same phrase to the true God, how can they still be justified in claiming the designation 'Christian'? Somewhere in another letter of this same Apostle, speaking in the Spirit of God, he calls the nations "that which does not exist" because they have been deprived of the knowledge of God: *God chose that which does not exist* [1 Cor 1.28]. Given the fact that God is both Truth and Life, I think it is to be expected that those who were not united by faith to the God who exists, but affiliated themselves with non-existent falsehoods through the error of idolatry, are designated as 'not existing.' For they have been deprived of the Truth and have alienated themselves from Life. Furthermore, when he was writing to the Ephesians, whom he treated as people genuinely united through knowledge to *He Who Is*, he gave them a peculiar name, "those who exist," when he said: *to the saints who exist and are faithful in Christ Jesus* [Eph 1.1]. For this is how our ancestors have transmitted the verse to us and how we ourselves have found it in the oldest copies.[94] But Eunomius

92. See Jas 2.19.

93. Eunomius and his associates.

94. Basil witnesses to a textual variant of Eph 1.1 found in several important mss. that lacks the words "in Ephesus" after "to the saints who exist" or "who are." See Bruce M. Metzger, *A Textual Commentary on the Greek New Testament*, 2d ed. (New York: United Bible Societies, 1994), 532. Basil's interpretation of the lacunate version ultimately stems from Origen, *Fragments from the Commentary on the Epistle to the Ephesians* 2, 1–6: "In the case of Ephesians alone we find the phrase *to the saints who exist*. We ask what the phrase *who exist* can mean, if it is not redundant when added *to the saints*. Consider, then, if not as in Exodus he

could not even bring himself to judge our God worthy of the
designation in which the servants of Christ participate. On the
contrary, he calls the one who brings creation into being from
nothing 'non-existing.'

His contempt is all the more perceptible from how he pretends to glorify the Lord:

We do not construe the Only-Begotten as having a substance in common with those which have come to be from nothing. For that which
is nothing is surely not a substance. Rather, we allot him as much superiority as the maker necessarily has over the things he himself has
made.[95]

After much groundwork to bring his account to this point, with
these words he shows his love for humanity, saying that he does
"not construe the Only-Begotten as having a substance in common with those which have come to be from nothing." But if
the God of the universe, because he is unbegotten, is of necessity distinct from those which have been begotten, and if all those
who have been begotten have it in common that they subsist
from nothing, how is it that the latter are not necessarily joined
in nature? For just as in the former case God's inaccessibility[96]
distinguishes the natures, so too in the latter case their equality
in honor joins them to one another as identical in this respect.
Though they say that the Son and those which he has brought
into being are from nothing, and construe them[97] as having a
nature in common in this respect, they deny that they attribute
to him a substance that is like those who are from nothing.

There's something else: as if he himself were Lord, Eunomius
provides as much dignity as he wants to the Only-Begotten, writing as follows: "We allot him as much superiority as the maker

who utters the words *He Who Is* to Moses speaks his own name [Ex 3.14], so
those who participate in *He Who Is* become those *who exist,* called, as it were,
from non-existence into existence" (J.A.F.Gregg, "Documents: The Commentary of Origen upon the Epistle to the Ephesians," *JTS* 3 [1902]: 234–44, 398–
420, and 554–76; trans. [modified] Ronald E.Heine, *The Commentaries of Origen
and Jerome on St Paul's Epistle to the Ephesians* [Oxford: Oxford University Press,
2002], 80).

95. Eunomius, *Apol.* 15.7–11 (EW 52).
96. See 1 Tm 6.16.
97. That is, the Son and those he has brought into being.

necessarily has over the things he himself has made." He did not say "we comprehend" or "we are of the opinion" as would have been suitable when speaking about God, but rather "we allot" as if he himself were responsible for the measure of the distribution. How much superiority does he give him? "As much as the maker necessarily has over the things he himself has made." This falls short of providing evidence for a difference in substance. Though human beings are superior to their own products by virtue of their artistic skill, they are nevertheless of the same substance with them. Examples include the potter and his clay, and the shipbuilder and his lumber.[98] Both[99] are similarly bodies. Both are similarly perceptible by the senses and made of earth.[100]

[2.20] After admitting only this much difference between the Son and creation, he immediately also does damage to the notion of the Only-Begotten:

> For this reason he is the Only-Begotten, since he was begotten and created by the power of the unbegotten, as only one from only one, thereby becoming his most perfect minister.[101]

I don't know with which of these statements I should be more enraged. On the one hand, he cunningly damages the name 'Only-Begotten' in order to use it in a sense contrary to both the customary usage of people and the pious tradition of the scriptures. For in common usage 'only-begotten' does not designate the one who comes from only one person, but the one who is the only one begotten. On the other hand, there's the blasphemous term 'creature.' He has maliciously linked this term with "was begotten" so that he might indicate that the Lord participates in the designation 'has been begotten' no differently than creatures do. He thinks that the Lord has been named 'Son' in the same way as in the passages: *he has begotten sons and raised*

---

98. By "clay" and "lumber" Basil must mean the clay that the potter has formed into an object and the lumber fitted together to construct a ship, not the raw materials before they are shaped into a product. The artisan transcends the product as cause to the effect.

99. That is, the artisan and his products.

100. That is, the element earth, not the planet.

101. Eunomius, *Apol.* 15.14–15 (EW 52). Note that "from only one" is an addition.

them [Is 1.2] and *Israel is my firstborn son* [Ex 4.22], and that he does not have *the name which is above every name* [Phil 2.9], but has been deemed as equally worthy of the designation as the others.

These men have recourse to the text of Solomon, and from it, as if from a base of military operations, they launch an assault on the faith. On the basis of that passage said in the person of Wisdom: *the Lord created me* [Prv 8.22], they have supposed that it is permissible for them to call the Lord a 'creature.' But for my part, I have many things to say about this line.[102] First of all, this is said only once in all the scriptures. Second, in this book a great deal of the meaning is hidden and on the whole it proceeds by means of proverbs, parables, dark sayings, and enigmas,[103] such that no one may take anything from it that is either indisputable or crystal-clear. I'll refrain from saying more lest I prolong this treatise by making lengthy digressions. Elsewhere in the proper place we will conduct the examination, deferred for now, of what they have understood in an evil way; in that place, if God grants it, the correct understanding of this verse will be found. At any rate, I think that, whatever is said with God's help, the sense will be much more consistent with the text in question and will bring no danger when it is clarified by the investigation.[104] But in the meantime let us be sure not to let the following point go unnoticed: that other translators, who have hit upon the meaning of the Hebrew words in a more appropriate way, render it as "he acquired me" instead of *he created me*.[105] This is going to be a great obstacle for them against their blasphemous term 'creature.' For the one who said: *I have*

102. For a discussion of Basil's comments on Prv 8.22 in this section, see Mark DelCogliano, "Basil of Caesarea on Proverbs 8.22 and the Sources of Pro-Nicene Theology," *JTS* n.s. 59 (2008): 183–90.

103. See Prv 1.6.

104. Basil never returns to the exegesis of Prv 8.22, either in *Eun.* or elsewhere in his corpus.

105. Here Basil summarizes Eusebius, *E. th.* 3.2.15 and 20. Eusebius cites the three alternative renditions of Prv 8.22 on the part of the three post-Septuagint translators of the Hebrew scriptures into Greek, Aquila, Symmachus, and Theodotion, all of whom translate "he acquired me" (ἐκτήσατό με) instead of the LXX's "he created me" (ἔκτισέν με).

acquired a man through God [Gn 4.1] clearly used this term, not because he had created Cain, but rather because he had begotten him.[106]

[2.21] Let's return to the beginning of the passage. "For this reason," says Eunomius, "he is the Only-Begotten, since he was begotten and created as from only one, thereby becoming his most perfect minister."[107] So if he is called 'only-begotten' not because he is the only one begotten, but because he is begotten from only one, and if in your view being created is the same thing as being begotten, why didn't you also name him the 'only-created'? For there is no thought that you don't have a knack for expressing! At any rate, according to your account it seems that no human being is only-begotten since everyone is begotten as the result of sexual intercourse. Not even Sarah, in your view, was the mother of an only-begotten child, for she did not produce him by herself, but together with Abraham.[108] If your opinions were to prevail, it would be necessary for the entire world to re-learn this term, that the name 'only-begotten' does not indicate a lack of siblings but the absence of a pair of procreators.

Furthermore, creation is already inferior in dignity to God the Word because he is its cause. For creation falls short of being only-begotten insofar as the Son joins the Father in creating it.[109] But these men would still not concede this point. For they name him "his most perfect minister." So, then, how in your

---

106. Basil attributes this verse to a masculine speaker, presumably Adam, even though in Gn 4.1 it is Eve who speaks this line. Basil makes the same error in *Spir.* 5.12. Once again, Basil is summarizing Eusebius, who explicitly attributes the verse to Adam; see *E. th.* 3.2.21–23.

107. Eunomius, *Apol.* 15.14–15 (EW 52). Note that Basil omits "only one" and adds "from only one" (as before).

108. See Gn 21.2.

109. According to Basil, Eunomius thinks that what comes from more than one source cannot be only-begotten, but that the world comes from two sources, the Father and the Son. It is for this reason, then, that Eunomius thinks the world cannot be only-begotten. In what follows, Basil counters Eunomius by pointing out that Eunomius does not believe that the world comes from two sources, since the Son is merely an instrument of the Father. Therefore, according to Basil, Eunomius does not adequately distinguish the created order and the Son.

view has creation not come to be from only one when you give
God the Word to the Father as a kind of lifeless instrument?
This will be the case unless someone is going to deny that only
the shipbuilder has made the ship because he has used instruments to construct it. As a consequence of your view, creation
and its parts are only-begotten: not only the invisible powers,
but also perceptible bodies, even the most worthless of these,
wood-boring insects, locusts, and frogs. For *God commanded
and they came to be* [Ps 148.5]. After all, what ministering could
have been needed by the one who creates by will alone, seeing
that creation came into existence simultaneously with his willing it? What, then? How do *we* say that all things come to be
through the Son? In this way: the divine will, taking its origin
from the Primal Cause as from a kind of spring, proceeds to activity through his own image, God the Word. But Eunomius has
designated the only-begotten Son as a minister, attributing to
him this great thing: that he is well-suited for administering the
things that have been assigned to him. But if he possesses glory
not in virtue of being perfect God, but in virtue of being a reliable minister, how will he be different from *the ministering spirits*
[Heb 1.14] who blamelessly accomplish their task of administering? He has linked "was created" with "was begotten" so that
on this basis he might show that there is no difference between
the Son and a creature.

[2.22] The exhortation he gives also deserves a hearing:

> When one attends to the designation 'Father and Son,' one must not
> think of his begetting as human, and one must not start from genera-
> tion among human beings and subject God to the names and passions
> of partnership.[110]

His exhortation amounts to this: one must not think of any
likeness of substance between the Son and Father. For this is
his intent when he forbids the term 'partnership,' as if the sub-

---

110. Eunomius, *Apol.* 16.1–3 (EW 52). The term "partnership" (μετουσία)
referred to any kind of fellowship or union. Eunomius used it in the sense of
the sexual "partnership" of a man and a woman. But this term also had a technical meaning of "participation" or "the sharing of substance." It is this sense that
Basil exploits, understanding the term as referring to the ontological fellowship
or union (i.e., the sharing of substance) between a father and a son.

stance of the Father has no communion with that of the Only-Begotten. This is why he pompously makes distinctions between names. We have not bothered with such things. For it is not the case that whenever the form of a word is the same, the meaning is the same, such that he can deny, for instance, that God is the Father of the Son because of those named 'fathers' upon the earth.

As I see it, while there is much that distinguishes Christianity from Greek error and Jewish ignorance, I think there is no doctrine in the gospel of our salvation more important than faith in the Father and the Son. For even schismatics, whatever their error might be, agree that God is the Founder and the Creator.[111] Now in which group should we put Eunomius? He declares that 'Father' is a pseudonym and that 'Son' only goes so far as a mere designation.[112] He thinks that it makes no difference whether one confesses 'Father' or 'founder,' and whether one says 'Son' or 'something made.' So in what party should we count him? Among the Greeks or the Jews? For whoever denies the power of piety and the distinctive character (so to speak) of our worship will not affiliate himself with Christians. For we have not put our faith in the Creator and something made. Rather, we have been sealed in the Father and the Son through the grace received in baptism. Hence when he dares to deny these terms, he simultaneously takes exception to the whole power of the gospels, proclaiming a Father who has not begotten and a Son who was not begotten.

"But I say these things," says Eunomius, "in order to avoid the notion of passion that term 'Father' introduces."[113] He who knows for certain how to live a pious life repudiates whatever is incongruous in how we understand these words[114] (if there even is such a thing in them). He understands that he should not

---

111. Gr. κτίστην καὶ δημιουργόν. Only here and in the next sentence does Basil speak of God as the κτίστης ('Founder'). Elsewhere he employs the terms δημιουργός and ποιητής ('Creator' and 'Maker').

112. Gr. μέχρι προσηγορίας ψιλῆς. Cf. Aetius, *Synt.* 8: ἕως ψιλῆς προσηγορίας.

113. This is not a citation of Eunomius, but a résumé of his thought in *Apol.* 16 and 17.

114. That is, the words 'Father' and 'Son.'

reject the entire term once and for all because, if he does so on the pretext of inappropriateness, he may also discard whatever is useful in it. He knows that when it is a question of doctrines about God he should purify words of lowly and fleshly concepts and think of the begetting that is suitable for the holiness and impassibility of God. On the one hand, he must lay aside as ineffable and incomprehensible the manner in which God has begotten. On the other hand, he must be mentally conveyed from the designation 'begetting' to likeness in substance. Indeed, it is clear to anyone who examines these names, I mean 'Father' and 'Son,' that they do not in their proper and primary sense naturally give rise to the notion of corporeal passions. On the contrary, when they are said by themselves they indicate only their relation to one another.[115] The Father is he who provides to another the beginning of being in a nature similar to his own, whereas the Son is he who has the beginning of his being from another in a begotten way.

[2.23] So, then, when we hear that a man is a father, at that time the notion of passion occurs to us as well. But when we hear that God is Father, we reason our way back to the cause that is without passion. Since Eunomius has become accustomed to using this designation for the nature that is subject to passion, he denies what is beyond the comprehension of his own reasoning as an impossibility. It is inappropriate to refuse to believe in the impassibility of God because of attention to the passion of corruptible beings. And it is inappropriate to compare the immutable and inalterable substance with the transient nature that is subject to countless changes. The following thought is also not to be entertained: since mortal animals beget through passion, God too begets in this way. On the contrary, the following consideration must be our guide to the truth: since corruptible beings beget in this way, the incorruptible one does so in the opposite way.

115. In other words, 'Father' and 'Son' are by their very nature relative terms. Cf. *Eun.* 2.9. This distinguishes them from terms which are not relative in themselves, but which can be used relatively. For example, 'God' can be used on its own, but it can also be used relatively, such as: 'the God of Israel.' A term like 'father' is by nature relative because it always indicates the existence of a child, whether explicitly stated, as in 'father of a son,' or not.

Furthermore, it should not be said that we attribute these names to God in an improper sense[116] on the grounds that they are used in the proper and primary sense for human beings. For our Lord Jesus Christ leads us back to the principle of all things and the true cause of beings when he says: *Call no man your father on earth, for you have one Father, who is in heaven* [Mt 23.9]. So, then, how can Eunomius believe that we ought to reject these terms because they principally indicate the passions of the flesh, when the Lord transfers them from human beings to God as fitting for his impassibility? Even if he is also called the Father of creatures, this still does not conflict with our account. For according to the saying of Job, *he who gave birth to the drops of the dew* [Jb 38.28] did not give birth to the drops and the Son in a similar way. Nonetheless, if they dare to make this claim, such that they call the substance of the dew a 'son' who is equal in rank, then it is no longer incumbent upon us to provide any argument against them. For in this case they would have brought their blasphemy to the point of the most obvious shamelessness.

When God is called the 'Father of us all,' he is not our Father and the Father of the Only-Begotten in the same way. If their impiety is based on the fact that the Lord is designated *the first-born of all creation* [Col 1.15] and *the firstborn among many brothers* [Rom 8.29], they should learn from the gospel that the Lord gives the designation 'his own mother and brothers' to those who come into affinity with him by the works of virtue. For he says: *Who is my mother, and who are my brothers,* other than those who *do the will of my Father in heaven?* [Mt 12.48–50] Hence God is named our Father not in an improper sense, nor metaphorically, but in the proper, primary, and true sense. For he brings us into being from nothing through corporeal parents and into affinity with him by caring for us. If God has been truly called our Father since he had judged us worthy of adoption as sons by grace, what argument will deny that he is not unfittingly designated the Father of the one who is his Son by nature and has proceeded from his substance?

On account of "the designation of Father and Son," says Eu-

---

116. Using words καταχρηστικῶς, "in an improper sense," is the opposite of using them κυρίως, "in the proper sense."

nomius, "one must not think of the begetting of the Lord as human."[117] Even I would say this. But what prevents the pious from believing in a begetting that is divine and without passion? I think he uses these words not in order to show that God has begotten him without passion, but to show that God has not begotten at all. So, then, how was it that you declared in your words above, O noblest of men, that the substance of the Only-Begotten is something begotten? For if he has not been begotten, on what basis does 'something begotten' belong to him in your account? Because of the opposition between 'begotten' and 'unbegotten,' he strives to show that the substance is something begotten. Then again, when he sees how affinity of substance is signified by this term, he deprives the one who is something begotten of being begotten.[118]

Furthermore, if he refuses to use this term on the grounds that it indicates passion, what prevents him from not admitting for the same reasons that God is the Creator? For a certain fatigue always accompanies all corporeal activities, which is of greater or lesser intensity in proportion to the power of the maker and the various magnitudes of its tasks. Saying that the divine and blessed nature is constrained by weariness is no less impious than subjecting it to dishonorable passions. So if he creates without passion, you should also admit that the begetting is without passion.

[2.24] So, then, there has been sufficient discussion of the fact that God is called Father in the proper and suitable sense, and that this is not a name of passion but of affinity, affinity either by grace as in the case of human beings, or by nature as in the case of the Only-Begotten. Now let us grant that even this term, like so many others, is figurative and is said metaphorically. But when we hear that God becomes angry, falls asleep, and flies,[119] and other descriptions like these which produce meanings that are not suitable when taken in their obvious sense, we neither strike out the words of the Spirit nor take what has been

---

117. Eunomius, *Apol.* 16.1–2 (EW 52). Basil adds "of the Lord."

118. At *Eun.* 2.23, 62 (SC 305.96), we read γεγεννῆσθαι instead of γη-γεννῆσθαι, presumably a misprint.

119. Such language is frequent in the Psalms.

said in a bodily manner. Why shouldn't we also inquire into the notions of this term, so often employed by the Spirit, that are appropriate for God? Or shall we expunge only this term from the scripture, denouncing it on the basis of how humans use it? Let's examine the issue in this way. According to customary usage here below, the designation 'to beget' signifies two things: the passion of the begetter and the affinity to the one begotten. This being the case, when the Father says to the Only-Begotten: *From the womb before daybreak I have begotten you* [Ps 109.3] and: *You are my Son; today I have begotten you* [Ps 2.7], which of these two do we say is communicated by means of this word? That begetters are subject to passion? Or that there is an affinity of nature between begetter and the one begotten? For my part, I claim the latter. I can't imagine that these men would ever contradict me, unless they have been reduced to manifest delirium. And so, if the term is proper to God, why do you dishonor it as if it were foreign? Since it has been transferred from human affairs, latch onto its sound sense and put aside the meanings that are less good. When it is a question of a polyvalent expression, it is surely possible to be guided by the word to its correct notion and thereby go beyond its lowly and dishonorable meanings.

Do not say to me: "What is the begetting? What kind of thing is it? How could it happen?" Even now we are not going to repudiate the solid foundation of our faith in the Father and the Son because the manner of the begetting is ineffable and utterly inconceivable. If we are going to measure all things by comprehension and suppose that that which is incomprehensible to our reasoning does not exist at all, the reward of faith will be gone, the reward of hope will be gone. How could we still be worthy of the blessings stored up for faith in invisible realities, if we trust only in that which is evident to our reasoning? Why did the nations *become futile and their senseless heart darkened* [Rom 1.21]? Wasn't it because they followed only what was apparent to their reasoning and refused to believe the proclamation of the Spirit? Whom does Isaiah mourn for as lost? *Woe to those who are wise in their own eyes and smart in their own sight!* [Is 5.21] How can it not be men such as these?[120]

120. That is, Eunomius and his associates.

I will pass by many things Eunomius says in the meantime—
everything he openly puts forth about the Son not being begotten and everything he says by way of pretense about how
the Only-Begotten admits of being a creature and something
made—because I want to get to the most important part of his
impiety. I will indicate only the following about what we are
leaving out: wishing to conceal with his words the blasphemy
he prepared earlier in the treatise and to soften the shamelessness of his account, he said that he does not construe the Only-
Begotten as something in common with creation.[121] But he has
forgotten his own doctrines which he expounded above with
naked and undisguised expressions. Because of them he once
again falls into a shameless contradiction that is as obvious as
can be. So, then, this is what he writes:

Let no one be disturbed when he hears that the Son is something
made, as if a common substance were construed for them by the commonality of the names.[122]

So, then, O wisest of men, if diversity of substance necessarily
follows upon difference in names—for you surely recall that he
uttered these words in his earlier arguments[123]—how is it not
true even in this case that commonality of substance follows
upon the commonality of names? For he clearly did not make
this statement just once or incidentally. As soon as he says that
the commonality of names does not mean there is a substance
in common, a little further on, as if regretting what he just said,
he adds the following to attack his opponents:

If in fact these people had any concern for the truth, they should confess that when names are different, the substances are also different.[124]

How could anyone use language more carelessly? In short measure, he switches between contrary positions: now he says that a
difference in names necessarily intimates diversity in substance,
now he says that commonality of names does not mean that
there is a substance in common. But here I think we are behav-

121. See Eunomius, *Apol.* 15.7–11 (EW 52); cf. *Eun.* 2.19.
122. Eunomius, *Apol.* 17.8–9 (EW 54).
123. See Eunomius, *Apol.* 12.3–4 (EW 48), discussed in *Eun.* 2.4.
124. Eunomius, *Apol.* 18.13–14 (EW 56).

ing very similarly to those who accuse a murderer of an insult or a punch or some such misdemeanor.

[2.25] So, then, let's pass on to his capital offense. Eunomius saw that there is a common preconception that exists similarly in all Christians—at least in those who are truly worthy of this designation. It concerns the fact that the Son is the begotten light who has shone forth from the unbegotten light, that he is life itself and goodness itself that has proceeded from the lifegiving source and the paternal goodness. Then he noticed that, unless he threw these notions of ours into confusion, there would be nothing left of his sophisms. For the one who confesses that the Father is light and that the Son is light will spontaneously be led, because the notion of light is one and the same, to the confession of their affinity in substance. According to the very definition of light, there is neither a verbal nor a notional difference between a light and a light. So, then, in order to take this away from us, Eunomius casts the nets of his scheming tricks around the account of faith. He teaches that these lights are absolutely incomparable and have nothing at all in common with one another, saying that the opposition between the unbegotten and the begotten is the same as that between light and light. If we deny his claim, he says that we are obligated to confess that God is composite.

But let's hear it from his very text:

Does light, when said of the unbegotten, signify something different from the unbegotten, or does each[125] signify the same thing? On the one hand, if one thing and another, then it is perfectly clear that that which is compounded from one thing and another is itself composite, and that which is composite is not unbegotten. But on the other hand, if the same thing, then, as much as the begotten differs from the unbegotten, so much must the light differ from the light, and the life from the life, and the power from the power.[126]

Behold and grasp the horrible blasphemy! "As much as the begotten differs from the unbegotten," he says, "so much will the light differ from the light, and the life from the life, and the power from the power." So let's put a question to him: How far

125. That is, 'light' and 'unbegotten.'
126. Eunomius, *Apol.* 19.9–15 (EW 56–58).

apart is the begotten from the unbegotten? Is it just a little bit, and just enough so that they will sometimes be able to come together at the same point? Or is this utterly unfeasible and even more impossible than the same person being alive and dead at the same instant, being healthy and sick at the same time, and being simultaneously awake and asleep? These sorts of states are set against one another in such an extreme opposition that when one is present the other is necessarily absent, being by nature absolutely incapable of coexisting and coinciding.[127]

[2.26] So, then, given that the opposition between the begotten and the unbegotten is like this, consider the one who names the Father 'light' and the Son 'light' and says that the one light differs from the other light as much as the begotten differs from the unbegotten. Isn't it clear that, even if he makes a verbal show of his concern for humanity when he pretends to name the Son 'light,' he is on the contrary leading the notion of light to its opposite by the force of his words? See for yourself. What is opposed to the unbegotten? Is it another unbegotten or the begotten? Clearly, it is the begotten. But what is opposed to the light? Another light, or darkness? Surely, it is the darkness. So, "if as much as the begotten differs from the unbegotten, so much must the light differ from the light," then who in the world can fail to see his impiety? He introduces that which is opposite to light when he designates him as 'light' and thereby suggests that the substance of the Only-Begotten is contrary to the nature of the light.

Let him show us a light that is opposed to light and has the measure of opposition that exists between the begotten and the unbegotten. If this light does not exist and Eunomius himself cannot conceptualize it, no one should remain unaware of the scheme he uses in secret to construct his blasphemy. Since he

127. Eunomius said that the light predicated of the unbegotten differs from the light predicated of the begotten by as much as the unbegotten differs from the begotten. Basil interprets the difference between the begotten and unbegotten as that between two items that are not only contradictory of one another, such that if one exists, the other cannot exist, but are actually contraries. Whereas Eunomius envisioned a difference of degree between the two, Basil understands it to be a qualitative difference.

thinks that the begotten is opposed to the unbegotten by way of contrariety, he holds that the same opposition obtains between light and light in order to show in every way that the substance of the Father is antagonistic and hostile to that of the Only-Begotten. Such is the reason for this novel legislation of doctrines: "as much as the begotten differs from the unbegotten, so much must the light differ from the light." On the one hand, there is a certain opposition, as they themselves affirm, between the unbegotten and the begotten according to the imposition of the words, even if not according to the nature of the realities. On the other hand, between light and light no one can conceptualize either a verbal or a notional opposition.

So he appears to mislead himself through his deceptive sophisms. For he thinks that things that follow upon contraries have the same conflict with one another that the things that entail them also have, and that whenever a contrary is present to one of a pair of contraries, the contrary of it will in every case follow in the other member of the pair. For example, if light follows upon vision, then darkness must follow upon blindness. If perceiving by the senses follows upon being alive, then not perceiving by the senses must follow upon being dead. But anyone with even a little understanding recognizes that such conclusions are feeble and errant. Just because being alive follows upon being awake, being dead does not in every case follow upon being asleep. Nor is the begotten contrary to the unbegotten. If they are contraries, they are also destructive of one other—may this be on the head of the blasphemers! On the contrary, they are not hostile in nature. Nor will that which follows upon them necessarily have the same interval between them as the things that entail them have been shown to have.

[2.27] So you have two choices: either retract your words or stop denying your impiety. This is what your blasphemy says: "as much as the begotten differs from the unbegotten, so much must the light differ from the light." Therefore, just as the begotten one will never participate in unbegottenness, so too you will never grant him participation in the light. In your view the substance of the Only-Begotten will be equally distant from both being unbegotten and being conceived as and named 'light.'

Even though John cries out to you with the piercing voice of the Spirit, saying: *He was the true light* [Jn 1.9], you do not have the ears to hear or the heart to understand.[128] Instead, with your sophisms you drive the substance of the Only-Begotten over to the nature that is antagonistic to the light and cannot coexist with it. You cannot claim convincingly that you do not deprive the Only-Begotten of the designation 'light.' For piety is not a matter of producing empty noises in the air, but concerns the force of what is signified.

Eunomius did not stop with these claims, but also makes both the life and the power have the same measure of separation when he says: "as much as the begotten differs from the unbegotten, so much must the light differ from the light, and the life from the life, and the power from the power." Therefore, in your view, the Only-Begotten is neither life nor power. Would you edit the Lord himself when he says: *I am the life* [Jn 14.6]? Would you edit Paul when he says: *Christ the power of God* [1 Cor 1.24]? The demonstration above fits the present case as well. For no one would claim that life is opposed to life and that power is opposed to power. It is death and powerlessness which constitute the most complete opposition to them. With respect to these points, Eunomius hides his cunning in the craftiness of his words, secretly and altogether hiddenly preparing his horrible impiety. He removes the nature of the Only-Begotten to that which is contrary to the Father by means of his verbal trickery, retaining only the reverent honor of the names.

So, then, what is our position? When we confess that the Father is unbegotten and the Son is begotten, how can we avoid implying that they are contrary according to being itself? What do we say? We say that he is the good Son of the good Father, the eternal light that has shone forth from the unbegotten light, the lifegiving source that has proceeded from the true life, and the power of God that has appeared from power itself. But darkness and death and weakness are classed with the ruler of this world, with *the world rulers of the darkness* [Eph 6.12], with *the spirits of wickedness* [Eph 6.12], and with every power that is an enemy

128. See Mt 11.15 and 13.15.

of the divine nature. None of these have acquired opposition to the good according to their substance. If so, the blame would redound to the creator. It is by their own freewill that they have fallen away into evil, depriving themselves of what is good. Giving God a tongue-lashing, Eunomius endeavors to bring the nature of the Only-Begotten over to this very class. When he posits that the substance of the Father is light, he certainly cannot say that it is superior in glory and in splendor, supposing that the substance of the Only-Begotten itself is also light but dimmer and, as it were, obscured. Such claims do not belong to a pious way of thinking because they deprive the image of its likeness by making it faint. We are justified in wishing to accuse him of holding these opinions, for it would not require much effort on our part to correct him.

[2.28] As it is, the difference between the unbegotten and the begotten is not in terms of a more and a less, as if between a lesser and a greater light. On the contrary, there is an interval between them as great as that between things which are completely incapable of coexisting with one another. It is unfeasible that the one paired with the other will ever be transformed into the opposite state by changing, such that either the unbegotten becomes begotten or, vice versa, what is begotten is transformed into something unbegotten. So he who once declared: "as much as the begotten differs from the unbegotten, so much must the light differ from the light," cannot even retain this argument as an escape route. On the one hand, the light that is pure is the same in kind as the light that is (so to speak) fading and dimmer, differing only in intensity. On the other hand, the unbegotten is not an intensification of the begotten, and the begotten is surely not a kind of attenuation of the unbegotten. On the contrary, they stand apart from one another (so to speak) in diametrical opposition. So, then, those who posit the begotten and the unbegotten as substances are faced with the following absurd consequences, and even more than these: the contrary will be begotten from the contrary, and instead of a natural affinity, a certain necessary discord between them will be revealed in their very substances. But it is more ignorant than impious to say that the substance is contrary to anything whatsoever, as was acknowledged long ago even by the wise men outside of the faith. Whenever these men[129] could not find support for their blasphemy in them, they paid no attention to their arguments as if they were of no worth. At any rate, it is unfeasible that contrariety exists in the substance.[130]

If anyone wants to accept that which is true, namely, that begotten and unbegotten are distinctive features that enable identification and are observed in the substance,[131] which lead to the clear and unconfused notion of the Father and the Son, then he will escape the danger of impiety and preserve logical coherence in his reasoning. The distinctive features, which are like certain characters and forms observed in the substance, differentiate what is common by means of the distinguishing characters and do not sunder the substance's sameness in nature. For example, the divinity is common, whereas fatherhood and sonship are distinguishing marks: from the combination of both, that is, of the common and the unique, we arrive at comprehension of the truth. Consequently, upon hearing 'unbegotten light' we think of the Father, whereas upon hearing 'begotten light' we receive the notion of the Son. Insofar as they are light and light, no contrariety exists between them, whereas insofar as they are begotten and unbegotten, one observes the opposition between them.[132]

129. That is, Eunomius and his associates.

130. The wise man outside of the faith is Aristotle, *Cat.* 3b24–25. Yet Basil equivocates between Aristotle's point that there is nothing contrary to substance (*ousia*), whether primary or secondary substance, and the mistaken point that the defining characteristics of two substances cannot be contrary to one another. The latter is inconsistent not only with Aristotle, but also with Basil's own account below in *Eun.* 2.28 of contrary differentiating properties like aquatic and terrestrial, rational and irrational, which mark off species within a common generic substance.

131. Gr. γνωριστικὰς ἰδιότητας ἐπιθεωρουμένας τῇ οὐσίᾳ. For similar language, see Porphyry, *Sent.* 38: "And in general they [i.e., the ancients] have made its nature clear [i.e., the nature of Being] through the positing of the most contrary characteristics, assuming both of them simultaneously, in order that we may eliminate from it conceptions fabricated from the corporeal realm, which serve only to obscure the particular features which serve to identify Being (τὰς γνωριστικὰς ἰδιότητας τοῦ ὄντος)" (Luc Brisson, ed., *Porphyre. Sentences* [Paris: J. Vrin, 2005], 360; trans. John Dillon in Brisson 824).

132. Basil's ideas in this paragraph found earlier expression in *Ep.* 361 to

It is the nature of the distinguishing marks to show otherness in the identity of the substance. And as for the distinguishing marks themselves, while they are often contradistinguished from one another such that they are separated to the point of being contraries, they certainly do not rupture the unity of the substance, as with the winged and the footed, the aquatic and the terrestrial, and the rational and the irrational.[133] Since there is one substance that underlies all of them, these distinguishing marks do not make the substance foreign to itself, nor are they persuaded to join each other in a kind of rebellion. They implant the activity of the things they identify as a kind of light in our soul, and guide to an understanding attainable by our minds. But Eunomius, having transferred the opposition of the distinguishing marks to the substance, takes from this the starting-point of his impiety, scaring us with sophisms as if we were children: if the light should indeed be something other than unbegottenness, then we will necessarily demonstrate that God is composite.

[2.29] What do I claim? I say that unless the light is something different from unbegottenness, then one can no longer attribute it to the Son, just as one cannot attribute unbegottenness itself to him. The following teaches us how the meanings of the words differ. God is said to *dwell in light* [1 Tm 6.16] and to be *robed in light* [Ps 103.2], but nowhere does the Word say that he dwells in his own unbegottenness or that unbegottenness surrounds him externally—for such things are ridiculous. Rather, begottenness and unbegottenness are distinctive features that enable identification. If there were nothing that characterized the substance, there would be no way for our understanding to penetrate it. Since the divinity is one, it is impossible to receive a notion of the Father or the Son that distinguishes each, unless

---

Apollinarius (assuming authenticity). For a discussion of Basil's correspondence with Apollinarius, see Drecoll 21–37 and Hildebrand 37–41.

133. The examples Basil gives are standard examples of the differentiae of the genus "animal." They originate with Plato (*Sph.* 220a–222b, *Ti.* 39e–40), are discussed by Aristotle (*Cat.* 1b18–19, 14b38, 15a2–3; *PA* 697b2–3), and are taken up in the late ancient commentaries on Aristotle. See Jaap Mansfeld, *Heresiography in Context: Hippolytus' Elenchos as a Source for Greek Philosophy*, Philosophia Antiqua 56 (Leiden: Brill, 1992), 80–81.

our thinking is nuanced by the addition of the distinguishing marks.

Our response to the objection that God will be revealed as composite unless the light is understood as the same thing as unbegotten goes as follows. If we were to understand unbegottenness as part of the substance, there would be room for the argument which claims that what is compounded from different things is composite. But if we were to posit, on the one hand, the light or the life or the good as the substance of God, claiming that the very thing which God is is life as a whole, light as a whole, and good as a whole, while positing, on the other hand, that the life has unbegottenness as a concomitant, then how is the one who is simple in substance not incomposite? For surely the ways of indicating his distinctive feature will not violate the account of simplicity. Otherwise, all the things said about God will indicate to us that God is composite. And so, it seems that if we are going to preserve the notion of simplicity and partlessness, there are two options. Either we will not claim anything about God except that he is unbegotten, and we will refuse to name him 'invisible,' 'incorruptible,' 'immutable,' 'creator,' 'judge,' and all the names we now use to glorify him. Or, if we do admit these names, what will we make of them? Shall we apply all of them to the substance? If so, we will demonstrate not only that he is composite, but also that he is compounded from unlike parts, because different things are signified by each of these names. Or shall we take them as external to the substance? So, whatever account of attribution they dream up for each of these names, they should apply the designation 'unbegotten' in the same way.

[2.30] At this point, his argument is packed full with empty nonsense. He has disparaged in one fell swoop all those who have ever been devoted to the knowledge of God, as if he has hewed out a new and *novel path* [Heb 10.20] leading to God that none of his predecessors discovered. And so, last of all he introduces the blasphemy against the Son, as if he has been taught by the very substance of God:

The [substance] that transcends kingly power and admits of no generation whatsoever, which gives instruction in these matters to the mind that approaches them with goodwill, exhorts us to thrust aside as far as possible, in virtue of a law of nature, its comparison with another thing.[134]

Does he not clearly indicate that he has been deemed worthy of receiving a revelation of inexpressible realities because he has brought his mind to God with goodwill? For this reason he has thrust aside the Only-Begotten as far as possible from communion with the Father, not counting him worthy of being admitted into comparison. Yet he also says that by a law of nature the substance of the Only-Begotten is separated from that of the Father. Why does he say this? Because the God of the universe, even if he willed it, could not admit the Only-Begotten into affinity of substance. For this connection with him is precluded by a law of nature. And so, it would seem that God is not the lord of himself, but subject to the limits of necessity. After all, things that are compelled by a law of nature are such as to be conducted not by choice towards whatever seems good to the nature. Just as the heat of the fire belongs to it by nature and not by choice, and by necessity does not admit of coldness, being deprived of communion with it by a law of nature, so too Eunomius wants the God and Father to have a substance that is foreign to the Son by a law of nature. But the laws of nature suggest, not a mutual distance between the Son and the Father, but a necessary and unbreakable communion. Now if Eunomius were to say that the God of the universe established by his will that which has no communion with him, not even in this way would the principle of the goodness of God allow Eunomius to be persuasive when he says that no communion in the things that belong to the Father is granted by him to the one who is from him. Nonetheless, the statement would be logically consistent. But the one who has investigated the nature of things perceptible to the senses would not say that there is estrangement by a law of nature; in this nature, each entity naturally produces things which are not foreign or contrary to it, but things that have affinity and kinship with it.

[2.31] So, then, here again he has not perceived that his state-

---

134. Eunomius, *Apol.* 20.11–14 (EW 58–60). On Eunomius's understanding of "goodwill" (εὐνοία), see Vaggione 87–88.

ments are self-contradictory. For a little before this, irritated with those who say that the Only-Begotten is like the Father in substance, he wrote as follows:

To begin with, these men, who dare to compare the substance which is without a master, superior to every cause, and free from all laws, to the begotten substance that submits to the laws of the Father, seem to me either to have completely failed to investigate the nature of the universe or to have failed to make judgments on these matters with a pure mind.[135]

So, then, how does the substance which is without a master and free from all laws now appear to be incomparable, not voluntarily, but because it is predetermined by a law of nature and precludes, not by free choice, the begotten from communion with itself, such that for this reason it turns out to be unapproachable even to the Only-Begotten himself? Such is the great discord between his statements. But how great is his impiety? On the one hand, he designates the substance of the Father as 'without a master' and 'free,' if, that is, the substance that submits to the law of its nature is truly without a master. On the other hand, he declares in contrast that the substance of the Only-Begotten is servile, and on this basis deprives his nature of equality in honor. Now there are two realities, creation and divinity: while creation is assigned to the rank of service and submission, divinity rules and is sovereign. Isn't it clear that the one who deprives the Only-Begotten of the dignity of sovereignty and casts him down into the lowly rank of servitude also by the same token shows that he is co-ordinate with all creation? Indeed, there is nothing noble about him being set at the head of fellow-servants. Rather, unless one confesses that he is king and sovereign, and that he accepts submission not because of the inferiority of his nature but because of the goodness of his free choice, this is objectionable and horrible, and it brings destruction upon those who deny this.

Eunomius adds: "*Since the substance of God follows upon* the laws of nature, *it does not even admit of* comparison with another, *and* it permits *us* to understand that *its* activity is consistent with and

135. Eunomius, *Apol.* 20.1–5 (EW 58).

appropriate to its *own* dignity."[136] While he has said this to demonstrate the Only-Begotten's estrangement from the Father,
it actually confirms our account. For if the substance of God
"permits one to understand that its activity is consistent with
and appropriate to its own dignity," then unbegottenness is a
dignity (as Eunomius thinks). Yet in their view unbegottenness
is also substance, and the Only-Begotten is either an activity
of God or an image of an activity. All this agrees with their account, and they cannot contradict these statements. Otherwise,
I would place a high value on their renunciation of the same
blasphemy.

Since it is they who made these statements, let us draw an inference from their own words: if unbegottenness is a dignity of
God, and the same is also substance, and if the activity of God is
consistent with and appropriate to his dignity, and according to
their supposition Christ is this activity, then he will have affinity
and propriety with the substance of God. None of these premises comes from us: combining their very own statements, we
have made our demonstration on the basis of their claims. The
dignity, says Eunomius, is consistent with the substance of God;
his activity is proportional to the dignity; the Only-Begotten is
an image of the activity. And vice versa, if the Only-Begotten
is an image of the activity, and the activity is an image of the
dignity, and the dignity is an image of the substance, then the
Only-Begotten will be an image of the substance. So in this way
even these men who often produce falsehood, when compelled
by the evidence, testify to the truth, albeit not willingly. The
demons similarly did not perform the work of the evangelists;
rather, unable to look directly at the light of truth, they cried
out: *We know who you are, the Holy One of God* [Mk 1.24].

[2.32] Let's see what follows:

If someone were to base his investigation on the created works, from
them he would be led up to the substances, discovering that the Son
is something made by the Unbegotten, whereas the Paraclete is something made by the Only-Begotten. Convinced on the basis of the su-

---

136. Eunomius, *Apol.* 20.13–15 (EW 60). The words in italics are additions
on the part of Basil—and faithful ones at that.

periority of the Only-Begotten that their activities are different, he accepts their difference in substance as indisputably demonstrated.[137]

First of all, how is it possible to reason back from created works to substance? This is something which I for my part fail to see. For things which have been made are indicative of power and wisdom and skill, but not of the substance itself. Furthermore, they do not even necessarily communicate the entire power of the creator, seeing that the artisan can at times not put his entire strength into his activities; rather, he frequently attenuates his exertions for the products of his art. But if he were to set his whole power into motion for his product, even in this case it would be his strength that could be measured by means of his products, not his substance that could be comprehended, whatever it may be.

If, because of the simplicity and incompositeness of the divine nature, Eunomius were to posit that the substance is concurrent with the power, and if, because of the goodness that belongs to God, he were to say that the whole power of the Father has been set into motion for the begetting of the Son, and the whole power of the Only-Begotten for the constitution[138] of the Holy Spirit, so that one may consider the power of the Only-Begotten simultaneously with his substance on the basis of the Spirit, and comprehend the power of the Father and his substance on the basis of the Only-Begotten, note what the consequence of this is. The very points he uses to try to confirm the unlikeness of the substance actually confirm its likeness! For if the power has nothing in common with the substance, how could he be led from the created works, which are the effects of power, to the comprehension of the substance? But if power and substance are the same thing, then that which characterizes the power will also completely characterize the substance. Hence the created works will not bring one to the unlikeness of substance, as you say, but rather to the exactness of the likeness. So, once again, this attempt confirms our account rather than his.

Either there is no basis on which to demonstrate his claims, or,

137. Eunomius, *Apol.* 20.15–19 (EW 60).
138. Gr. ὑπόστασις.

if he were to draw his images from human affairs, he would discover that it is not from the products of the artisan that we comprehend the artisan's substance, but that it is from that which has been begotten that we come to know the nature of the begetter. After all, it is impossible to comprehend the substance of the housebuilder from the house. But on the basis of that which is begotten it is easy to conceive of the nature of the begetter. Consequently, if the Only-Begotten is a created work, he does not communicate to us the substance of the Father. But if he makes the Father known to us through himself,[139] he is not a created work but rather the true Son, *the image of God* [2 Cor 4.4], and *the character of his subsistence* [Col 1.15]. So much for this subject.

[2.33] Look how much he adds to his blasphemy! After disdaining the warning which the Lord extends in the gospels to those who blaspheme against the Holy Spirit,[140] which is as fearful as could be, Eunomius says that the Spirit is a created work. He barely concedes that he is alive, since this designation for the most part applies to lifeless things. Surely, his inclusion of the Lord in this blasphemy does not justify slackening our irritation one bit. For this does not nullify his impiety but adds to his condemnation. The Lord has allowed the blasphemy against himself on account of his goodness, whereas he has declared that the blasphemy against the Holy Spirit is unforgivable for those who dare to do it. So, of all those who have attacked the truth from the time when the proclamation of piety was announced, Eunomius is the first to dare to utter this term about the Spirit. We have certainly never heard anyone, even unto today, calling the Holy Spirit a created work, nor have we found this designation in the treatises they have bequeathed to us.[141]

---

139. Jn 17.26.

140. Mt 12.31–32; Mk 3.29; Lk 12.10.

141. Basil cannot be claiming that Eunomius is the first to affirm the creaturely status of the Holy Spirit. For example, both Origen (e.g., *Jo.* 2.73–75) and Eusebius of Caesarea (e.g., *E. th.* 3.6.1–2) held that the Holy Spirit was created. Basil must be objecting to Eunomius's explicit use of the term δημιούργημα (and probably ποίημα), translated as "created work" and "something made," to designate the Spirit. Neither Origen nor Eusebius employs these terms for the Holy Spirit; in fact, Origen explicitly denies that scripture permits them (see *Princ.*

Then he says: "If someone should base his investigation on the created works in order to comprehend the substances, he would discover that the Son is something made by the Unbegotten, while the Paraclete is something made by the Only-Begotten."[142] Here is a different kind of impiety, uttering two blasphemies with a single statement! After taking his contempt of the Holy Spirit as granted, he proceeds from this to the demonstration of the inferiority of the Only-Begotten. While *the heavens proclaim the glory of God* [Ps 18.2], it appears that the Holy Spirit announces the inferiority of the glory of the Only-Begotten. When the Lord was speaking about the Paraclete, he said: *He will glorify me* [Jn 16.14], whereas that evil-speaking tongue declares that he prevents the Son from being compared with the Father. For Eunomius says that the Son is the maker of the Spirit—have mercy on us, O Lord, for saying these things! But this adds no nobility to the one who has created him. Therefore, he is not even worthy of being compared with the Father, since the worthlessness of what he has made has deprived him of that dignity of his which is equal to the Father's in honor.

[2.34] Have you ever heard a blasphemy more insidious? Has anyone fallen so conspicuously into the inescapable judgment for having blasphemed against the Holy Spirit? Only Montanus raged to such an extent against the Spirit, insulting him with lowly names and disparaging his nature to such an extent that he said that the Spirit brought ignominy on the one who had made him.[143] Eunomius should have avoided speaking in

---

3.3.3). In *Eun.* 2.2–7 Basil makes a similar argument about applying the terms 'something made' and 'something begotten' to the Son.

142. Eunomius, *Apol.* 20.15–17 (EW 60).

143. Montanus flourished in the last quarter of the second century, in Phrygia in Asia Minor. He gained a reputation for prophecy inspired by the Spirit, and attracted a following. The movement, known by its adherents as the "New Prophecy," quickly spread throughout the Roman world. Perhaps its most famous devotee was Tertullian of Carthage, who came under its influence in the early third century. Montanism can be understood as a protest against the laxity of the ecclesiastical organization. Rather than to ecclesial structures and officials, the Montanists ascribed authority to the Paraclete, who reinforced church discipline and was thought to be the guarantor of correct scriptural interpretation. The New Prophecy was rejected by mainstream Catholics primarily because of its rigorism in ecclesial practice, not doctrinal aberrations. Given the

a lowly manner about the Spirit to keep from deflating his own self-importance. We will speak of this when we have the time.

Isn't it clear to everyone that no activity of the Son is severed from the Father? That none of all the existing things that belong to the Son is foreign to the Father? For he says: *All that is mine is yours, and all that is yours is mine* [Jn 17.10]. So, then, how does Eunomius impute the cause of the Spirit to the Only-Begotten alone and take the creating of the Spirit as an accusation against the Only-Begotten's nature? If he says these things to introduce two principles in conflict with one another, he will be crushed along with Mani and Marcion.[144] But if he makes the beings depend on a single principle, that which is said to come into being from the Son has a relationship with the first cause. Hence, even if we believe that all things have been brought into being through God the Word, we nevertheless do not deny that the God of the universe is the cause of all.

How is it not an unmistakable danger to separate the Spirit from God? On the one hand, the Apostle hands down to us that they are connected, saying now that he is the Spirit of Christ, now that he is the Spirit of God. For he writes: *If anyone does not have the Spirit of Christ, he does not belong to him* [Rom 8.9]. And again: *You have not received the spirit of the world, but the Spirit that comes from God* [1 Cor 2.12]. On the other hand, the Lord says

---

Montanists' high regard for the Paraclete, it is difficult to understand Basil's characterization of their views on the Spirit. But *Ep.* 188.1 provides us with some hints. Here Basil reports that the Montanists had called Montanus and Priscilla (an associate of Montanus) by the name 'Paraclete.' Basil sees this as blasphemous because it either elevates humans to divine status or compares the Holy Spirit to a human being. While this explains what Basil meant when he said that Montanus insulted the Spirit "with lowly names," the basis for the remainder of his charges remains unclear.

144. On Marcion, see p. 141 n. 51 above. Marcion's doctrines were perceived by mainstream Christians as dualistic. He did not identify the Jewish God of the Old Testament with the Christian God of the New Testament, seeing the former as an evil and ignorant creator God and the latter as the true God revealed by Jesus. Mani, who was from southern Mesopotamia and died a martyr in 276 at the hand of Persian authorities, was the founder of a quasi-Christian sect that espoused a radical dualism of light and darkness. The religion particularly flourished within the Roman Empire, the young Augustine being its most famous adherent. By the fourth century, Christian polemicists routinely employed Marcionism and Manichaeism as paradigmatic examples of dualism.

that he is *the Spirit of truth* [Jn 15.26]—since he is himself the Truth[145]—and that *he proceeds from the Father* [Jn 15.26]. But Eunomius, in order to diminish the glory of our Lord Jesus Christ, separates the Spirit from the Father and imputes him exclusively to the Only-Begotten in order to diminish his glory, insulting him (or so he thinks) without any anticipation of the recompense for his wicked words and ideas on the day of retribution.

145. See Jn 14.6.

On the Holy Spirit

BOOK THREE

FTER NEARLY GORGING HIMSELF with blasphemies against the Only-Begotten, Eunomius shifts to the Holy Spirit, making claims about him as well that are consistent with his whole intention. Here's what he writes:

Now if we are satisfied with these arguments about the Only-Begotten, the next logical step would be to speak about the Paraclete, not by following the unquestioning opinions of the multitude, but by guarding the teaching of the saints in all matters. Since we learn from the saints that the Holy Spirit is third in dignity and in rank, we have come to believe that he is third in nature as well.[1]

This statement adequately shows that Eunomius does not think that he must abide by the simple and uncontrived faith of the multitude, but believes instead that he should redirect the truth through scheming and sophistical arguments to that which seems good to him. By dishonoring the opinion by which the multitude glorifies the Holy Spirit,[2] he makes a pretense of guarding the teaching of the saints. Yet even now he keeps silent about who transmitted this teaching to him, just as he did in his arguments about the Only-Begotten (as we have shown).

Eunomius says next that while he has learned on the authority of the saints that the Holy Spirit is third both in rank and in dignity, he has come to believe on his own authority that the Holy Spirit is third in nature as well. Who are the saints that taught this? In what treatises have they expressed it? Has there ever been someone so audacious as to introduce innovations

1. Eunomius, *Apol.* 25.1–5 (EW 66).
2. Here Basil employs an untranslatable pun with "opinion" (δόξαν) and "glorifies" (δοξάζουσι).

about the divine doctrines? If the Spirit is third in dignity and in rank, is there some necessity that he be third in nature as well? Perhaps the word of piety[3] transmits that he is second to the Son in dignity.[4] But we have not learned from the holy scriptures that a third nature is necessary. Nor do the preceding claims make it possible to infer such a conclusion.

The Son is second to the Father in rank because he is from him. He is second to the Father in dignity because the Father is the principle and cause by virtue of which[5] he is the Son's Father and because we approach and access the God and Father through the Son.[6] Even so, the Son is not second in nature, since there is one divinity in both of them. Likewise, it is clear that, even if the Holy Spirit is below the Son in both rank and dignity—something with which we too are in total agreement—it is still not likely that he is of a foreign nature. What follows will make this conclusion clear.

Just as all the angels share a single designation, so too they share a nature that is absolutely the same. Yet some of them preside over the nations, whereas others accompany each individual believer. An entire nation, however, is more honorable than a single person to the same extent that the dignity of the nation-leading angel is necessarily greater than that of the angel who has been entrusted with the care of a single individual. No one will deny that every believer has an angel that accompanies him, acting like a kind of pedagogue and shepherd and directing his life, if he calls to mind the saying of the Lord: *Do not despise one of these who are least of all, for their angels continually behold the face of my Father in heaven* [Mt 18.10]. And the Psalmist says: *The angel*

3. That is, the scriptures.

4. At this point several mss. add: "having his being from him and receiving from him, announcing to us and entirely dependent upon this cause." This text is not original to Basil. On this controversial addition, see PG 29.655 n. 79; SC 305.146–47 n. 1; M. van Parys, "Quelques remarques à propos d'un texte controversé de saint Basile au Concile de Florence," *Irénikon* 40 (1967): 6–14; G.M. de Durand, "Un passage du IIIe livre contre Eunome de S. Basile dans la tradition manuscrite," *Irénikon* 54 (1981): 36–52; and Anastos, "Basil's Κατὰ Εὐνομίου," 112–13 n. 153.

5. At *Eun.* 3.1, 32 (SC 305.146), we read τῷ with some mss. and Garnier instead of τοῦ.

6. See Eph 2.18.

of the Lord is encamped around those who fear him [Ps 33.8]. And:
The angel who rescued me from my youth [Gn 48.15–16]. There are
other passages similar to these.

In addition, Moses taught us in the song that certain angels
preside over entire nations: *When the Most High divided the nations,
when he scattered the sons of Adam, he fixed the limits of the nations
according to the number of his angels* [Dt 32.8]. In his vision of the
angel, the wise Daniel heard him saying: *The prince of the kingdom
of the Persians has made a stand before me, and behold! Michael, one of
the chief princes, came to help me, and I left him there with the prince of
the kingdom of the Persians* [Dn 10.13]. A little further on, the same
one says: *And the prince of the Greeks was coming* [Dn 10.20]. But
the one who appeared to Joshua the son of Nun at the Jordan
is called *commander of the force of the Lord* [Jos 5.14]. Then again,
some are called legions of angels, as when the Lord said to his
disciples: *Do you think that I cannot ask my Father, and he will provide
me with more than twelve legions of angels?* [Mt 26.53] So it is clear
that the *prince* is the one who is the *commander* of the angels that
are ranked into *legions*.

[3.2] So, then, what is the point of this argument? It is this: if
something is second or third in rank and dignity, it does not in
every case have a different nature. For in the case of angels, one
is a prince, another a servant, and yet all are angels in nature:
while they differ in dignity, there is communion in nature. Indeed, *star differs from star in glory* [1 Cor 15.41], but all the stars
have a single nature. And *there are many places to live in the Father's
house* [Jn 14.2]; that is, there are differences in dignity, whereas
the nature of those who are glorified is similar. Likewise, the
same clearly holds true for the Holy Spirit, even if he is subordi-
nate in dignity and rank, as they claim. "For we have gathered,"
says Eunomius, "that he is numbered third after the Father and
the Son, seeing that the Lord himself taught this order when he
taught the baptism of salvation, saying, *Go, baptize in the name of
the Father, and of the Son, and of the Holy Spirit* [Mt 28.19]."[7] But
we have never learned from anywhere that the Holy Spirit is cast
out into some sort of nature third from the Son and the Father.

It is said that there are two realities: divinity and creation, sov-

---

7. This is not a citation of Eunomius but an imagined objection to Basil.

ereignty and servitude, sanctifying power and sanctified power,
that which has virtue by nature and that which achieves virtue
by freewill. In which class shall we rank the Spirit? Among those
who are sanctified? But he is sanctity itself. Perhaps among those
who come to possess virtue by good deeds? But he is good by
nature. Among those who minister? But *the ministering spirits sent
to minister* [Heb 1.14] are different. So it is unrighteous either
to say that he is our fellow-servant, as he is a leader by nature, or
to number him along with the creatures, as he is counted in the
divine and blessed Trinity. It would make no sense to say that
the principalities and powers and all such creatures, which have
holiness from diligence and attention, are holy by nature. After
all, yearning for the good, they receive a measure of holiness
proportionate to their love for God.

Furthermore, when iron is placed in the middle of fire, while
it does not cease to be iron, it is nonetheless inflamed by the
intense contact with the fire and admits the entire nature of fire
into itself. And so in both outward appearance and activity the
iron is transformed into fire. Likewise, the holy powers, from
their communion with that which is holy by nature, possess a
holiness that pervades their whole subsistence, and they become
connatural with that which is holy by nature. The holy powers
and Holy Spirit differ in this regard: for the latter, holiness is
nature, whereas for the former, being made holy comes from
participation. Those for whom the good is adventitious and introduced from another possess a nature that can change. Indeed, *Lucifer who rises at dawn* would neither *have fallen* nor *been
cut down to the earth* [Is 14.12] if by nature he was not capable of
admitting that which is worse. So, then, how is it pious to rank
the Spirit together with creation, when he is separated from
creation by such a great distance? It is the nature of creation
to have holiness as the prize for its progress and for becoming
well-pleasing to God. By its nature it employs self-determination
and is capable of moving itself toward either direction by choosing the good or the bad. But the Holy Spirit is the source of holiness. Just as the Father is holy by nature and the Son is holy by
nature, so too is the Spirit of truth[8] holy by nature. Hence the

8. See Jn 14.17; 15.26; 16.13.

Spirit has been judged worthy of the designation 'holy,' which is peculiar to him and distinctly identifies him.

[3.3] So, then, if holiness is the Spirit's nature, as it is for the Father and the Son, how does he have a nature that is third and foreign to theirs? I think that Isaiah recorded the Seraphim crying out "Holy!" three times[9] for this reason: because holiness in nature is observed in three subsistences.[10] Not only does the Spirit have the name 'holy' in common with the Father and the Son, but he also has the very designation 'Spirit' in common with them. *God is Spirit, and those who worship him must worship him in spirit and in truth* [Jn 4.24]. The prophet says: *The Spirit before our face, Christ the Lord, of whom we said, "in the shadow of his wings we will live"* [Lam 4.20].[11] The Apostle refers to the Lord with the designation 'Spirit,' saying: *The Lord is the Spirit* [2 Cor 3.17]. These testimonies make it clear to everyone that the communion of the names does not communicate the Spirit's estrangement of nature, but rather his affinity with the Father and the Son. Furthermore, God is said to be and is good.[12] The Holy Spirit is also good, possessing a goodness that is not adventitious, but coexistent with him by nature. Otherwise, it would be possible to say the most irrational thing of all: the one who is holy by nature does not have goodness by nature, but as something supervening and accruing to him from without. When the Lord said: *I will ask my Father, and he will give another Paraclete to you* [Jn 14.16], he indicated that the Spirit is also our Paraclete. Hence the designation 'Paraclete' also contributes no small amount to the demonstration of the glory of the Holy Spirit.

[3.4] Such are the names that indicate the magnificence of the nature of the Holy Spirit. But what are his activities like? *By the Word of the Lord the heavens were made firm, and by the Spirit of his mouth all their power* [Ps 32.6]. So, as God the Word is the cre-

---

9. See Is 6.3.

10. Gk. ἐν τρισὶ ταῖς ὑποστάσεσιν. This is the only time in *Eun.* that Basil speaks of the Father, Son, and Holy Spirit as three *hypostases*.

11. Basil slightly alters the LXX version of Lam 4.20, which reads: "The spirit of our face [*or:* the breath of our nostrils], the Christ of the Lord, was taken by their destruction, of whom we said: 'In his shadow we will live among the nations.'" Basil adds the phrase "of his wings" from Ps 56.2.

12. See Mk 10.18; Lk 18.19.

ator of the heavens, so too the Holy Spirit bestows firmness and steadfastness upon the heavenly powers. Again, when Job said: *The Spirit of the Lord who made me* [Jb 33.4], I do not think he was referring to when he was created, but to when he was perfected in human virtue. In addition, when Isaiah was speaking in the person of the Lord, it was clearly in his human aspect that he said: *The Lord and his Spirit sent me* [Is 48.16]. Furthermore, the psalm communicated that the power of the Spirit pervades the universe: *Where can I go from your Spirit, and where can I flee from your face?* [Ps 138.7]

As for the benefits that proceed from him to us, what are they like? How great are they? Just as the Lord himself *gave to those who received him the power to become children of God* [Jn 1.12], so too the Holy Spirit is *the Spirit of adopted sonship* [Rom 8.15].[13] Just as our Lord is the true teacher according to the following statement: *Call no one your teacher on earth, for one is your teacher, Christ* [Mt 23.9–10],[14] so too the Lord himself testified that the Holy Spirit teaches all those who have come to believe in the name of the Lord, when he said: *The Paraclete, the Holy Spirit, whom the Father will send, will teach you all things* [Jn 14.26]. Just as it is said that the Father distributes the activities to those who are worthy of receiving the activities and that the Son distributes the services by the worth of the service, so too it is testified that the Holy Spirit distributes the spiritual gifts to those who are worthy of receiving the spiritual gifts: *Now there are distributions of gifts, but the same Spirit; and there are distributions of service, but the same Lord; and there are distributions of activity, but it is the same God who works all of them in all people* [1 Cor 12.4–6]. Do you see how here too the activity of the Holy Spirit is ranked with the activity of the Father and the Son? The divine status[15] of the nature

13. Gr. υἱοθεσία. The word literally means "adopting as a son (υἱός)," a nuance that the normal English translation, "adoption," does not capture. For Basil and many other Greek fathers, the title "Spirit of adopted sonship" shows the Spirit's intimate connection with the Father's adoption of sons in Christ.

14. Here Basil has condensed Mt 23.9–10, which in full reads: *Call no one your father on earth, for one is your Father who is in heaven; nor be called teachers, for one is your teacher* (καθηγητής), *Christ*. Basil has replaced *father* with 'teacher' (διδάσκαλος).

15. Gk. τὸ θεῖον. In *Hom.* 24.7 Basil defends calling the Spirit "divine" on the basis of Jb 33.4 and Ex 35.21.

of the Holy Spirit is even better shown by what is added a little further on. Indeed, what does he say? *All these things are worked by the one and the same Spirit, who distributes to each individual as he wills* [1 Cor 12.11]. This testifies that he has nothing other than authoritative and sovereign power.[16]

This is why the prophets in the New Testament cried out: *Thus says the Holy Spirit* [Acts 21.11]. On what basis does it belong to the Spirit to scrutinize the depths of God? *No one knows the things that belong to a human being except the human spirit that is in him; likewise, no one knows the things that belong to God except the Spirit of God* [1 Cor 2.11–12]. No one who is strange or foreign to the soul can examine its internal reasonings; likewise, if the Spirit truly has any of the secret things in common with God, it is clear that he is able to scrutinize the depths of the judgments of God only because he is neither strange nor foreign to God.

Next, God lavishes life upon us through Christ in the Holy Spirit. As Paul says, God gives life: *I charge you before God who gives life to all things* [1 Tm 6.13]. Christ gives life: *My sheep hear my voice,* he says, *and I give them everlasting life* [Jn 10.27–28]. We are given life through the Spirit, as Paul says: *The one who raised Christ Jesus from the dead will also give life to our mortal bodies through his Spirit who dwells in you* [Rom 8.11].

[3.5] Eunomius, who is audacious in every way, does not cower before the impending danger faced by those who have audaciously fired a blasphemous word against the Holy Spirit.[17] He declares that the Spirit has no share of divinity when he writes as follows:

He is third in rank and in nature, since he was brought into existence by the Father's commandment and by the Son's activity. He is honored in third place, as the first and greatest of all, and the only thing of this kind made by the Only-Begotten, bereft of divinity and creative power.[18]

He who says this seems not to believe that the divinity is in us, as John says about God: *From this we know that he is in us, from the Spirit whom he has given us* [1 Jn 3.24]. And the Apostle: *Do you not know that you are a temple of God and that the Spirit of God dwells in*

16. Cf. Athanasius, *Ep. Serap.* 1.30; Didymus, *Spir.* 96–97.
17. See Mt 12.31–32; Mk 3.29; Lk 12.10.
18. Eunomius, *Apol.* 25.22–26 (EW 68).

you? [1 Cor 3.16] And again: *In whom the whole structure is joined together and grows into a holy temple in the Lord, in whom you also are integrated into a habitation of God in the Spirit* [Eph 2.21–22]. So, if God is said to dwell in us through the Spirit, how is it not blatantly impious to say that the Spirit himself has no share in the divinity? And if we call those who are perfect in virtue 'gods,' and this perfection comes through the Spirit, how does he make others gods if he is himself bereft of divinity? Moreover, it is impious to say of the Spirit, as one can say of human beings, that the divinity honored in him comes by participation and does not coexist with him by nature. For the one divinized by grace possesses a nature subject to change and falls away from the better state whenever he is careless.

This claim of Eunomius is clearly opposed to what has been handed down about the saving baptism: *Go, baptize in the name of the Father, and of the Son, and of the Holy Spirit* [Mt 28.19]. Baptism is the seal of faith, and faith is an assent to divinity. For one must first believe, then be sealed with baptism. Our baptism accords with exactly what the Lord handed down: it is in the name of the Father, and of the Son, and of the Holy Spirit. In this formula, no creature or servant is ranked together with the Father and the Son, as if the divinity becomes complete in a Trinity. Everything external to them is a fellow-servant, even if generally some are valued more than others on account of their superior dignity.

[3.6] Once again, the following wisdom is not mine:

If he is not a creature, therefore he is something begotten or unbegotten. But there is one God who is without a beginning and unbegotten. Nor again is he something begotten. So, then, it remains that he is to be named 'creature' and 'something made.'[19]

For my part, if I were to declare that our knowledge can comprehend all things, I would probably be embarrassed to confess ignorance. But the truth of the matter is that there are countless things of which we do not have clear and incontrovertible knowledge—not only those things reserved for us in the age to come and those now hidden in the heavens, but also those things that

---

19. This is not a citation of Eunomius, but a résumé of his thought in *Apol.* 25–26.

belong to our bodily existence. Let's take vision as an example: does apprehension of visible things happen when we receive their images? If so, when we see gigantic objects, such as the immense earth and the boundless sea and even the heaven itself, how are the images contained in the tiny space of our pupil? Or is it the case that perception of visible things happens when we send out from ourselves something that draws near to the visible objects? If so, what is this thing and how great would it have to be, such that when it is spread over earth and sea, there is enough of it to traverse the space between earth and heaven and to come into contact with the heaven itself, moving with such great speed that both the surrounding body and the stars in heaven are perceived at the same time?[20] What need is there to speak of other things? But as for the very movements of the mind,[21] is

20. The two theories Basil mentions appear to be those of Epicurus and Plato, respectively. For Epicurus, vision results from images that emanate from objects to our eyes. These images share the color and shape of the object from which they come, but are of such a size as to fit our visual capacities (a point that Basil's summary ignores). See Epicurus, *Ep. Her.* 46–53 (Diogenes Laertius 10.46–53). The first theory may be Stoic, however, since the Stoics also believed vision occurred through impressions upon the soul from external reality. By contrast, for Plato, vision occurs when the internal fire passes out through the eyes and meets with the object of vision, or perhaps with rays of light emanating from these objects. *Ti.* 45b–d, 67c–68d. Aristotle reports that Empedocles held both theories at different times: *Sens.* 2, 437b25–438a4. Basil employs the same argument in *Hom.* 24.7.

21. By "the very movements of the mind" (αὐτὰ τὰ τοῦ νοῦ κινήματα) Basil seems to mean "deliberations" or "choices." In *Ep.* 233.1 Basil describes the mind (ὁ νοῦς) as ever-moving (ἀεικίνητος) such that it variously imagines non-existent things and attains the truth. Then Basil claims that there are three activities of the mind, each of which corresponds to one of the three states of life: the virtuous, the indifferent, and the wicked. In describing the latter he says: "For it is either the case that our practices are wicked and so the motions of our mind (τὰ τοῦ νοῦ κινήματα) are clearly wicked, for example: instances of adultery, theft, idolatry, extortion, quarreling, wrath, selfishness, arrogance, and all such things that the apostle Paul numbered among the works of the flesh" (Courtonne 3.39–40). Here Basil appears to root our outward activities or "practices" (τὰ ἐπιτηδεύματα) in our interior choices, or "movements of the mind." A similar idea can be found in Evagrius of Pontus, whom Basil ordained a lector. He calls both a "choice" (προαίρεσις) and a "deliberation" (βουλή) "a kind of movement of the mind" (ποιὰ νοῦ κίνησίς ἐστιν); cf. Scholia 10 on Ecclesiastes (Paul Géhin, ed., *Évagre le Pontique. Scholies à l'Ecclésiaste*, SC 397 [Paris:

it the nature of the soul to create or beget them?[22] Who can say
with precision?

So, then, why is it shocking that we are not ashamed to confess our ignorance even in the case of the Holy Spirit, but we
still render him the glorification for which there is undeniable
testimony? The teaching transmitted by the scripture sufficiently communicates to us that he is beyond creation. For it is impossible for the one who sanctifies and those who are sanctified
to be of the same nature. The same holds true for the one who
teaches and those who are taught, and the one who reveals and
those who are in need of revelation. No one is so completely
out of his mind as to dare to designate anything other than the
God of the universe as 'unbegotten.' The same goes for 'Son'
since the Only-Begotten is unique. So, then, what should we call
him? Holy Spirit,[23] Spirit of God,[24] Spirit of truth sent from God
and bestowed through the Son,[25] not a servant,[26] but a holy,[27]
good,[28] and guiding[29] Spirit that gives life,[30] Spirit of adopted
sonship,[31] the one who knows all that is God's.[32] Indeed, the account of singleness will be preserved in the Trinity in this way,
by confessing one Father and one Son and one Holy Spirit.

[3.7] They cite two proofs that the Holy Spirit should be
called a creature. The first is from the prophet, when he says:
the one who gives strength to thunder and who creates spirit [Am 4.13].
The second is from the gospel: *All things came to be through him*
[Jn 1.3].[33] As for ourselves, we have been convinced that the

---

Cerf, 1993], 74) and Scholia 23 on Proverbs (Paul Géhin, ed., *Évagre le Pon-*
tique. Scholies aux Proverbes, SC 340 [Paris: Cerf, 1987], 116).

22. Basil seems to have made up his mind later. In *Hom.* 16.3 Basil speaks
of the human word as "something begotten of the intellect" (PG 31.477d). In
Ep. 140.2 he speaks of human ideas as "things begotten of the mind" (Courtonne
2.61).

23. E.g., Jn 14.26.   24. E.g., Rom 8.9.
25. See Jn 15.26.   26. See Rom 8.15.
27. See Ps 50.13.   28. See Ps 142.10.
29. See Ps 50.14; 142.10; Jn 16.13.   30. See Jn 6.63.
31. See Rom 8.15.   32. See 1 Cor 2.10–11.

33. On Basil's interpretation of these two verses here, see Mark DelCogliano, "Basil of Caesarea, Didymus the Blind, and the Anti-Pneumatomachian Exegesis of Amos 4:13 and John 1:3," *JTS* n.s. 61 (2010): 644–58.

prophet's text does not refer to the Holy Spirit, but rather to ordinary wind, which is to say the current of air.[34] This is clear from the following: he did not say, "the one who has created spirit," but rather, *the one who creates spirit* [Am 4.13]. For thunder is not created once for all as a particular corporeal entity, but its nature is to be continually actualized and dissipated, effected by the will of God to scare human beings, and this holds true for spirit as well. At one time it comes into being as a flowing river of air; at another time it stops and the air that was earlier moving now comes to rest. All this happens according to the will of the one who administers all things for the well-being and maintenance of the universe. Hence thunder, winds, and the rest of the created works announce the Creator throughout all creation. Thus, after saying, *The one who gives strength to thunder and who creates spirit*, he says, *and who proclaims his Christ to humanity* [Am 4.13]. For just as *the heavens proclaim the glory of God* [Ps 18.2] for those who can reason back from them to the skill of the Creator, so too do the claps of thunder and the movements of the winds proclaim their Creator.

Perhaps this text is even a prophecy that refers to the incarnation of the Lord. The voice that came from heaven, thought to be thunder by those who heard it,[35] was sent by God the Father to *proclaim Christ to humanity* through it. There are also the spirits that moved and stirred up the sea and then abated at the commandment of the Lord.[36] Clearly, they too *proclaimed his Christ to humanity*.

As for, *All things came to be through him* [Jn 1.3], this text in no way communicates to us that the Holy Spirit is created, as if the Spirit were numbered among *all things*. For if there is only one Holy Spirit, how can that which has the singular nature[37] be included among *all things*? Furthermore, no one should think that denying that the Spirit is a creature nullifies his subsistence. For it is a mark of a pious mind to beware of attributing to the Holy

---

34. The Greek text of Am 4.13 reads: κτίζων πνεῦμα. In Greek the word πνεῦμα can mean either "spirit" or "wind."

35. See Jn 12.28–29.

36. See Mt 8.26–27; Mk 4.39–41; Lk 8.24–25.

37. Gk. τῆς μοναδικῆς φύσεως.

Spirit those things that the holy scriptures omit in silence,[38] and
to be convinced that experience and exact comprehension of
him is reserved for us in the subsequent age, when, passing beyond the vision of the truth that comes *dimly in a mirror,* we will
be deemed worthy of contemplating *face to face* [1 Cor 13.12].

---

38. The point here is that we should not say that the Spirit is a creature because the scriptures never call the Spirit a creature (κτίσμα).

INDICES

GENERAL INDEX

Acacius of Caesarea, 22, 31, 32,
85n19, 85n20
Aetius the Syrian, 10n29, 11, 19,
29–32, 34, 35, 44, 48, 49, 61, 82,
83n14, 85n18, 86n23, 89n33,
94n43, 163n112
Aëtius (philosopher), 74n300
Alcinous, 74
Alexander of Alexandria, 20–22, 24,
26, 61, 88
Alexander of Aphrodisias, 69
Alexandria, 11, 16, 17, 19–22, 24, 31,
37, 58, 60, 65
Amand de Mendieta, E., 67n275
Amphilochius of Iconium, 14, 16,
108n77
Anastos, M. V., 41n151, 186n4
Anatolios, K., 25n88
Ancyra, Synod of (358), 29–30
Annisa, 6, 7n10, 9, 12, 13, 33
Antioch, Council of (341). *See* Dedi-
cation Council of Antioch (341)
Antioch, 11, 12n37, 16–17, 26, 29,
58, 85n22
Apollinarius of Laodicea, 15, 16, 18,
37, 134n13, 174n132
Arcadius, 38
Ariminum, Council of (359), 30, 32
Aristotelians, 69, 70n282, 71–74,
75n302, 114n94, 134n13, 143n56,
155n88
Aristotle, 50, 60, 67, 71, 72n290, 74,
75n302, 93, 95n46, 103, 110n85,
114n94, 127n137, 131n1, 143n56,
155n88, 174n130, 175n133,
193n20

Arius, 19–22, 25–27, 35, 61, 88,
148n69
Arles, Council of (353), 28
Armenia, 14, 15
asceticism, 6, 8–10, 13, 33, 44, 57, 67
Asia Minor, 6, 17, 141n51, 182n143
Asterius the Sophist, 11n34, 22–23,
25–28, 39, 126n134
Athanasius of Alexandria, 11n34,
15, 17, 19–22, 24–28, 30, 34, 60,
63–66, 94n40, 126n134, 127n141,
136n30, 148n69, 191n16
Athanasius of Anazarbus, 21
Athens, 7, 8
Ayres, L., ix, 4, 15–18, 20–23, 25,
28n93, 30–32, 51, 52n190,
63n260, 65n263, 73n297, 99n55

Barnes, J., 69n280, 71n287, 77,
143n56
Barnes, M., 11n32, 44n165
Barnes, T. D., 17n53, 24n84
Basil of Ancyra, 10n29, 11n34,
28–32, 60, 64, 65, 85n22
Basil of Caesarea, *Fid.*, 67n275, 81n1;
Hex., 55n205, 56, 81n1, 109n82;
Hom. 16, 56n218, 57n220, 149n71,
194n22; *Homily against Sabellians,
Arius, and the Anomoians* (*Hom.* 24),
35, 190n15, 193n20; *Homilies on
the Psalms* (*Ps.*), 55n205, 56n211,
56n212, 67n272; *Spir.*, 5, 15–16,
51, 56n211, 63n259, 112n89,
112n90, 161n106
Basil the elder, 7
Beeley, C., x, 7n14, 52n190

199

INDEX OF HOLY SCRIPTURE